Growing Great
VEGETABLES
in the
HEARTLAND

Growing Great
VEGETABLES
in the
HEARTLAND

Andrea Ray Chandler

Taylor Trade Publishing
DALLAS, TEXAS

Copyright © 2001 by Andrea Ray Chandler

Published by Taylor Publishing Company
1550 West Mockingbird Lane
Dallas, Texas 75235

Designed by Barbara Werden

Library of Congress Cataloging-in-Publication Data

Chandler, Andrea Ray.
    Growing great vegetables in the heartland / Andrea Ray Chandler.
        p. cm.
    Includes bibliographical references.
    ISBN 0-87833-258-8 (pbk.)
    1. Vegetable gardening—Middle West. 2. Organic gardening—
Middle West. I. Title.

SB352.34.M6285 C48 2001
635'.0977—dc21   00-049756

2 4 6 8 10 9 7 5 3 1

Printed in the United States of America

For my growing sprouts: tomato connoisseur
Anna, who helped proofread; and Quin, who
insists that I grow sweet corn every year.
And to my dear hubby Andy, who
provided technical support.

Special thanks to the Kansas State University
Master Gardener program and to
the staff of the Olathe Public Library.

Eat your vegetables!

Contents

What Makes the Heartland So Special

WHY HEARTLAND GARDENERS NEED THEIR OWN BOOK

The Heartland comprises over one-fifth of the United States, including South Dakota, Nebraska, Kansas, Iowa, Missouri, most of Wisconsin, Illinois, Michigan, Indiana, Kentucky, and Ohio. Parts of Minnesota and Oklahoma are also included in our zones of 4, 5, and 6. Although these same zone numbers snake all around the country, the soil and weather patterns change so much that a zone 5 gardener in Maine or Oregon is going to find many different circumstances than we do. (In Chapter Two, see "USDA Zones: What They Do and Don't Mean.")

Alas, few of the fine books out there mention the many problems Heartland vegetable gardeners run into:

- "What do I **do** about this awful clay? I can't do a lot of heavy lifting."
- "How do you know when you need to water? It just rained, but everything's still droopy."
- "Look, is CCA wood a problem or not? People keep telling me different things."
- "What do all those funny abbreviations in seed catalogs mean?"
- "How do I cope with our winter-spring-winter-summer-winter-spring weather? It's driving me crazy!"
- "I grew this big sage plant; now what do I do with it?"
- "There's all this neat stuff, but what tools do I really need?"
- "How can anyone garden with floods and droughts?"
- "What do I need to do each month?"

As you can tell by these questions, most of what's missing is advice about coping with the weather. The other questions refer to various topics that are rarely mentioned in books and magazine articles. They need to be in this book too, so they are.

If you're a beginner, you're probably like the students in my gardening classes. They have lots of questions about material left out of how-to books, or about the seeming contradictions that appear in the books. Sometimes the problem is that you don't know what the gaps are in your knowledge until you run into them (*boink!*).

If you're a "seasoned" gardener, in this

book you'll find lots of useful information not included elsewhere, and plenty of reference sources—such as graphs and charts—to aid you. There's also lots of information at the back of this book about catalogs, an extended glossary (that was made for gardeners, not botanists!), tables of measures, and more good information.

Since most gardeners limit themselves to the same standard salad-and-squash crops every year, I've broadened the food base to make room for unusual things. Recipes are included that have been tested on various veggie-haters. When half a dozen avowed squash-haters rave about the soup, or my husband takes seconds on cauliflower, you know it's gotta be good. So welcome to vegetable growing in the Heartland! Grab yourself a cuppa and pull up a chair.

Garden Gleanings: Throughout this book, the quotes you'll see in this typeface are observations about the art of gardening:

Neither wisdom nor riches nor fame are necessary to garden.

TRUE CONFESSIONS

I have a confession to make: The first garden I ever planted was a dismal failure. The tomato and pepper transplants limped along, hardly fruiting. Most of the seeds didn't even sprout. A more adventurous acorn squash vine limped through the summer and finally produced a single squash, which I had no idea when to pick. My response, come the retrospection of winter, was to check out some books and find out *why*.

WHY GARDENING BOOKS SEEM TO DISAGREE

If you've ever read any gardening books, the following scenario may be familiar. Here's what my research yielded:

In one well-worn tome, I read about traditional row gardening—the wartime "Victory garden" method previous generations of gardeners had been taught. Row gardening is tilling up half the back yard to loosen the soil, planting an entire package of seed in straight rows; ripping out most of the extra seedlings to make room for the ones you need; hoeing earnestly and frequently to keep weeds out of the paths and rows; and then having everything ripen at once for canning up.

The next two books were on the newer intensive/raised-bed method, which involves improving the soil by adding materials to create a growing bed higher than ground level, planting seeds or transplants in blocks arranged in space-efficient checkerboards or honeycombs, and then having everything ripen at once for selling at the farmer's market or canning up.

I was confused. These books seemed to disagree! Which was the "right" way to do it? The raised-bed method involved less weeding, but out in the suburbs I didn't have access to manure for giant compost piles. And all the seed packets I'd bought assumed I was going to grow using the row method, and gave spacing information to that end. But either way, I didn't need quite *that much* food!

THE COMMON FACTORS

Actually, gardening books don't disagree as much as they might seem to. The spacing for loose-leaf lettuce is the same whether you grow them in rows or blocks: 6 inches. There are basic principles to growing no matter what approach you take: Improve the soil; protect from forces of nature like weather, insects, and diseases; and be able to think like a plant. Soil improvement and seasonal protection are important topics, and they are addressed in Chapters One and Four.

Thinking like a plant isn't usually discussed. It sounds a bit odd, but it simply means being able to empathize with the plant's needs and figure out how to fulfill them. But to do this, you have to know what a plant's needs *are*. Plants suffer the terrible problem of being immobile: Everything out there in the environment is going to help them or hinder them. Except for tumbleweeds, plants can't pack their bags and move elsewhere, away from annoying neighbors, rambunctious children, or inadequate housing.

Since that first year, my acquired knowledge and skills have earned me magnificent crops. I've become a master gardener and given talks to garden groups. I write articles for garden magazines. I do variety testing for *Organic Gardening* magazine. But all this took more than the simple instructions on the back of a seed packet!

WEATHER WEIRDNESS IN THE HEARTLAND

Some gardeners think that soil is their biggest challenge; "You should see this clay!" they complain. But for all their well-deserved kvetching, I disagree. This isn't your *biggest* problem. Soil, whether clay, rocky or sandy, can be improved. It can even be improved easily, in a year's time (in Chapter 1, see "Barrow Composting"). Beyond anyone's control is (ominous drumroll) . . . The Weather.

Every year the gardeners and storm junkies go around muttering, "Boy, is **this** a weird year!" After doing that for several years, you begin to realize that all the years are weird. There is no "normal";

IS IT WORTHWHILE TO GROW YOUR OWN?

I'm frequently asked, is it really cost-effective to grow your own stuff? You can buy a large bag of potatoes for very little money!

My answer is that when you have a garden, you can go out and pick *gourmet, organically grown*, exceedingly fresh vegetables with no nutrient loss from endless days of shipping and storage. You can have enough to put up your own recipe sauces instead of relying on generic store-bought stuff. Your table will be set with food that's seasonally appropriate, perhaps grown from seeds that were handed down from family members and friends. Children in your life will learn what real food tastes like, and where it comes from.

Perhaps the biggest benefit (other than fresh food) is the exercise program that accompanies gardening. If you remember to stretch first, and limit yourself to a productive half hour a few days a week (rather than trying to catch up in an exhausting weekend marathon), you'll get real exercise and have something to show for it besides sweaty leotards. Shoot, I exercise and do weights during the winter to keep myself in shape for gardening!

there are only statistical averages. That's important to remember, so I'll repeat it: *There is no "normal"; there are only statistical averages.*

This means that your great spot for a plum tree during drought years will be a sodden, death-dealing spot for a plum tree during flood years.

This means that my neighbor's magnolia tree will bloom well every third year. Our last frost date will be anywhere from mid-April through mid-May. And that winter-spring-winter-summer-winter-spring weather complaint was no exaggeration; it's an annual event. We go through these struggles every March and April.

Just when you thought you'd seen it all: thundersnows one day, eighty degrees the next.

Gardeners who live around the Great Lakes enjoy some temporizing influences, but also receive great amounts of precipitation. (Michiganders get winter sports; Kansans must drive hundreds of miles west or northeast for their snow skiing.)

But all of us must cope with the unabashed hot and cold fronts that clash overhead. Our fronts here have names like "Alberta Clipper" and "Siberian Express," to give you some understanding of how speedily the weather can change. Seasoned veterans only grin when someone complains about the weather. They just wave off the complainers, saying, "If you don't like the weather, just wait a day!"

Resist the temptation to claim boredom of the weather, for it will spite you.

Unseasonable highs in February and March delight the pent-up gardener who wants to go out and prune fruit trees, or tidy the yard. (We call these "unseason-able" not because they don't happen every year, which they do in my part of the Heartland, but because they ought not happen.)

However, these rapid and temporary fifty-degree changes make mulching flowerbeds and wrapping fruit trees imperative. Mulch and wraps are not to keep the plants cozy and warm; they're to keep the plants cold and asleep! (See the section on mulching in Chapter Four.) Without them, the plants would start waking up too early, and would then be crippled by frost.

Weather can even be completely different just a few miles down the road. Hail is a good example of this, as are rain and snow. Temperature fluctuations of even fifty or sixty degrees in a single day pose challenges. (See Chapter Four for information about frost protection devices.) Zigzagging temperatures from day to day in the spring months of March, April, and May make the gardener feel like Mother Nature is being maliciously whimsical with her convulsions. "What *is* this nonsense?" the gardener asks.

A glance at my composite data journal shows the following temperature ranges for Olathe, Kansas (zone 5B), years 1987 through 2000:

> January from 10s–40s.
> February from 10s–40s.
> March 20s–60s, with rainy season beginning.
> April zigzags from 20s–70s.
> May zigzags from 40s–80s, with late frosts possible.
> June from 50s–90s.
> July from 60s–100s, with dry season beginning.
> August from 60s–100s.
> September temperatures zigzag from 40s (late month) to 100s (early month), with frosts possible.

October zigzags from 40s–80s.
November zigzags from 30s–70s.
December zigzags from single digits to
60s.

One afternoon in mid-January of
1996, the temperature peaked at sixty-six
degrees; I call this our "Siberian Summer." The next day it was blizzarding
with 4 inches of snow predicted, temperatures were around -10 °F, and strong
winds gave a windchill factor of -45 °F.
The averages just got changed!
Please realize that these are our local

averages; your patterns will probably be
different.
We can't change the weather, but we
can do our best to ameliorate its effects
on our gardens. But before you go out
and order all kinds of goodies through
your favorite garden tool catalog, you can
do the most good by choosing the best
possible location for your vegetable garden. (Yes, dedicated gardeners scope out
the yards more than they do the interiors
of new homes they're shopping for, although large garages will rank highly.)

The secret to happiness: Always have something to look forward to. In the depth of winter come the catalogs; in the early days before spring warms, start your seedlings.

Growing Great
VEGETABLES
in the
HEARTLAND

CHAPTER ONE

Your Garden Ground

SITE SELECTION CONSIDERATIONS

Why did my first garden fail so miserably? Simply put, it was location, location, location; weeds, weeds, weeds; and soil, soil, soil.

- The location was too dark, the location was in competition with tree roots, and the location was too far for the hose.
- Weeds stole the limited sunlight, weeds sucked up the limited rainwater, and weeds stole the few nutrients.
- The soil was compacted, the soil was clay mixed with gravel, and the soil was unimproved by compost.

It was, in sum, a wretched site for growing vegetables.

For an ideal vegetable and herb garden site, you will need:

- **At least eight hours of full sunshine.** This includes the second half of the summer, when tree shadows have moved.
- **Accessibility to running water.**

- **No interference from tree roots.** Black walnut trees give off a toxin called juglone that inhibits the growth of most other plants, so are especially to be avoided.
- **No interference from gas lines or power lines.** Call your local utility companies. They'll be glad to find the lines for you, rather than risk interrupting service. In some areas there is a single phone number you can call for the "flag and tag" crew to come by; check the beginning of the phone book.
- **Decent soil conditions.** Yes, you may have clay. I mean the darker topsoil, rather than builder's fill of funny-colored subsoil and gravel.
- **Close to the house.** There's no requirement that you put your garden out in the "back forty" of your backyard. When it's close to the kitchen, it's easier to keep an eye on, harvest, do pest control, and water. A raised-bed garden is attractive.
- **There should be good drainage.** This is admittedly hard to determine during drought years. Wait until there's a 1-inch rainfall or greater. If water is

Fog settles into valleys and low spots, as does frost.

still standing half a day after the rain's quit, the drainage is poor.

- **Not too windy.** We once lived in a new subdivision with a bad case of "arboreal tokenism": one little baby tree in each front yard. Forty-mph gusts were common. They dried out my garden beds and knocked over my toddler.
- **Not in a valley, where fog and frost will collect.** However, the top of a hill is rather windy.

Note that I said *ideal,* not *real.* Ideal gardens exist only in magazine pages. You will have to do, as Teddy Roosevelt used to say, "the best you can, with what you have, where you are."

THE DIRT ON SOIL

Soil is what the plants grow in. Dirt is what gets on you, your clothes, and the kitchen floor. Plenty of fine gardeners say they grow plants in dirt though, so let's agree not to get picky about these terms.

Soil is not an inert mineral base with stray nutrients and water molecules (which hydroponics growers seem to believe). Rather, it is a complex living environment: a subecology of fine rock particles, partially decomposed organic matter, roots, water, air, minuscule soil animals, microorganisms that are mostly benign—some beneficial—and a few pathogens (plant germs).

Dedicated growers say that they're growing soil, not plants. Why is this? It's because they're constantly improving their soil. Whether you're starting out with glacial grit in northern Michigan, sand in the Mississippi River basin, or clay in Kansas, you need to fix up your soil. The improvement and regeneration of soil is the goal of all gardeners.

IN THE BEGINNING: THE HISTORY OF YOUR SOIL

If you're not gardening on farmland that was tilled from native fields, you're probably gardening in a yard. And yards, being part of housing developments, have their own inherent problems.

The topsoil may have been removed, sometimes permanently, and sold to give extra money to the developer. It may have been graded under the subsoil when they were digging the basement. It may have been mixed with the construction trash and gravel, especially around the foundation. If a field nearby has dark brown soil, and your yard has reddish soil, you are probably lacking your topsoil! (In some areas, *all* of the soil is red. This simply means that there's lots of iron in the soil, and it's "rusty.")

If you're having a house built, it can help to write soil-saving and grading particulars in the contract. A landscape architect can help determine proper grading, drainage, and landscaping details. Then keep an eye on those workers!

Grading equipment, tractors, trucks, playing children, and heavy pedestrian traffic all can compact the soil, pounding it down into a hard, nearly lifeless lump.

Land that has been chemically farmed or gardened may have low levels of natural beneficial organisms. Pesticides are harmful to the 99 percent of beneficial and benign microbes as well as the 1 percent of harmful ones. Adding compost and other organic matter will help boost these organisms and add them back into the ecology. Be sure to add inoculants—beneficial bacteria that helps the roots secure nitrogen from the soil—when planting peas, beans, clover, and other nitrogen-fixing crops.

Chemical fertilizers are harmful to worms. The worms leave when the resultant salts build up in the soil. They will also return with the increase in organic matter. Once you begin the regeneration process, you'll find that your soil will be literally livelier.

Want to find out what your soil was like before it was developed into something else? Get a copy of your county's soil survey. The U.S. Department of Agriculture Soil Conservation Service puts these together. They'll tell you about the long-term history of your soil, where it came from, and what it's good for and what it's not good for (including your house foundation that's giving you fits).

THE COMPOSITION OF YOUR SOIL

There are three kinds of materials comprising soil: sand, silt, and clay. These names refer to how big the particles are.

Sand particles are between 2.0 and 0.05 millimeters in size. They're so large that water is not retained well. These are the Papa Bear size of soil grains.

Silt is middle-sized soil particles, between 0.05 and 0.002 millimeters. These are the Mama Bear size of soil grains.

Clay particles are of such minute size (less than 0.002 millimeters) that they can pack together tightly, causing drainage and aeration problems. However, clay soils are usually rich in nutrients. These are the Baby Bear size of soil grains.

The ideal "loamy soil" that garden writers wax rhapsodic about is a balance of 40 percent sand, 40 percent silt, and 20 percent clay.

So what's the problem with having sandy soil? Well, there's the fact that it's getting tracked in all the time. Sand particles are so large that they can't hold onto

HOW TO DETERMINE YOUR SOIL TEXTURE

There are two ways to do this.

WITH AN EYE-AND-HAND TEST

Clay looks hard-baked and crusty when dried out. You can't see the individual particles. Clay soil feels harsh and rock-hard when dried out; it's sticky, rubbery, or possibly greasy when wet; it makes a ball when you squeeze it. Clay soils warm up slowly in spring, dry out slowly, and turn into stubborn lumps when wet. Fortunately, clay soils are generally high in nutrients.

Sandy soil looks loose, porous, and full of big pieces of minerals and sand. It feels grainy, gritty; it crumbles when you try to make a ball. Sandy soils are easy to work and dig in; they warm up quickly in spring and dry out quickly. Sandy soils are generally low in nutrients.

Loamy soil looks full of various-sized crumbs and porous. It feels spongy, making a ball when squeezed; but it crumbles easily, is powdery when dry and plastic-like when wet. Loamy soils are nearly perfect in texture.

WITH A SIMPLE HOME TEST

This is a test for soil *structure*, not nutrients ("Fun Science Tricks You Can Do!"). Get a one-quart jar with a lid, such as a canning or food jar, and a small box of Calgon bath beads. Mix it today, and learn the results tomorrow.

1. Dig up one cup of your natural soil, from several locations in the vegetable garden.

2. Put the soil in the jar, then add water until it's nearly full (about an inch from the top).

3. Pour in one tablespoon of Calgon bath beads (this breaks up the adhesion between the particles so they'll separate into layers). Save the rest of the bath beads to share with other gardeners,

water very well. Imagine that sandy soil is like a house of cards: all framework and air spaces, with no filler.

Clay soil also has problems. It sticks abominably to your shoes, your gloves, and your tools. It's gumbo in the spring and adobe in the summer. Clay particles are so small that they pile up with hardly any room between them for air and water. Imagine that clay soil is like a pile of cards, all tumbled flat atop each other with hardly any room for air and water.

How do you find out what your soil nutrients are? Get a soil test from your local cooperative extension office to determine your soil fertility and pH (and to

inquire about the presence of heavy metals if that's a concern). You can find the office in the phone book Blue Pages under "County Government."

HOW TO TAKE A SOIL SAMPLE

Is your neighbor a chemist? Only a soil test will tell you what is really needed. Before you start giving your plants fertilizer, it's wise to know how much, if any, extra nutrition they need. A soil sample, taken at the beginning of your gardening expedition and then again every few years, does this for you. You really don't need one every year.

or to use yourself after a big day of digging.

4. Put the lid on really tight and shake-shake-shake for 5 minutes (yes, 5 whole minutes; this is more fun with music).

5. Put the jar someplace safe and let it sit for 24 hours.

Next day:

6. Get a pencil, paper, and ruler. Measure and write down how many inches of total soil are in the jar, height-wise.

7. Shake-shake-shake for another 5 minutes. Let it stand for just 45 seconds. Measure the stuff that's settled; that's the amount of sand you have. Write down how many inches of sand you have. Divide the amount of sand by the total soil amount, then multiply by 100. That's your sand percentage.

8. *Do not* shake any more (whew!). Set a timer for 2 hours. Then measure the amount of settled stuff again. That's your new total soil inches.

9. Subtract your sand inches from your new total soil inches; that's how much silt you have. Divide the amount of silt by the new total soil amount, and then multiply by 100. That's your silt percentage.

10. The last step is to subtract the sand and silt percentages from 100; this gives you your clay percentage. (Your sand, silt, and clay percentages should all add up to 100 percent.)

You will probably end up with clay, clay loam, silty clay, sandy loam, or any number of other combinations. Now that you know what you have, you will know how to cope with it during wet and dry seasons. But the answer for improving the texture is always the same: Add compost!

In addition to nutrient levels, a soil sample also gives you the pH level of the soil, telling you how acidic or basic it is. Some plants, such as azaleas and blueberries, prefer slightly acidic soil, while most plants prefer a balanced pH. The proper pH helps plants draw the nutrients from the soil.

Any time of year except the dead freeze of winter is fine for taking a soil sample. Several soil-sampling kits are available for you to use at home, with varying levels of accuracy; for a small fee, you can get one done by the county extension office.

If you want a soil test for your lawn,

your azaleas, and your vegetables, you will need three different soil tests. This is because you need information about three completely different kinds of plant requirements.

You want your sample to be representative of all the soil in the growing area. So, you want to take a bit of soil from five or six spots.

Remove the surface debris of your flower or veggie bed (or pull away the sod if you're taking a lawn sample). Don't take your samples from odd contaminated places such as around walls, fences, stone piles, and compost bins, or near spilled fertilizer or other chemicals.

With your clean trowel, dig 6 inches deep (or just 2 inches deep for a lawn soil test), and pull out an evenly sized slice from top to bottom of the hole.

Mix this sample thoroughly together in a clean bucket. Remove any sticks, gravel, worms, bugs, and so on. Keep your hands out of the soil.

Then pour the cup or so required into the bag provided by the extension office. The bag will have spaces for your name and address, and for indicating what you are trying to grow. Your answers can be general in some instances, such as "flowers" or "vegetables." In other cases, such as testing an area devoted wholly to potatoes, blueberries, or fescue, you should be specific.

BETTER THAN READING TEA LEAVES

The test results will be back in a few weeks. You will then know the levels of phosphorous, potassium, and the pH level of your soil, with recommendations for additions. (The nitrogen may not be listed because it is a volatile nutrient; it can change from day to day.) It's the recommendations for additions that make this type of test more useful than an off-the-shelf color indicator kit.

So, what is a good pH? Good pH is a range, rather than an absolute figure. If your pH is between 5.5 and 7.0, you can grow crops successfully. Different vegetables have preferred pH ranges, though, as shown in the table on page 7.

THE ABCs OF NPK

When you go shopping for fertilizer, you will see three numbers marked on the bag or box, sometimes with the letters "NPK." *NPK* stands for *nitrogen, phosphorus*, and *potassium*, the "big three" of plant nutrients. Both organic and chemical fertilizers will have a number printed on the bag telling you what percentage of NPK the package contains. The higher the numbers, the more concentrated it is. Lawn fertilizers have a higher nitrogen number, because nitrogen provides greening and growth.

Garden fertilizers should have a balanced NPK listing, since all three major nutrients are necessary for different functions. Sometimes garden fertilizers have a higher "P" rating, because phosphorus helps develop flowers and fruits. Plants also require many lesser nutrients, which chemical fertilizers often do not provide. Organic fertilizers frequently provide micronutrients, and won't add chemical salts to the soil like chemical fertilizers do. I use organic materials in my garden. Different organic fertilizers are discussed after composting, in the section "Other Soil Amendments."

For the happiest gardening, you will need to fix up the soil. It doesn't matter if you're growing in clay, silt, or sand—your vegetable garden will require additional nutrients. Add as much compost as you can get your hands on; you can't add too much.

If your soil is heavy clay, add 30–50 percent as much sand (sharp sand) to the depth you're digging loose. (Sharp sand is also called builder's sand. Its granules are coarse and sharp, unlike round river-sand granules, and they compact less easily.) This may seem like a lot of sand, but that's only a few bucketsful for six cubic feet of soil. Why so much? Because a little sand added to clay soil tends to

Optimum Range of pH for Common Garden Crops

	5.0	5.5	6.0	6.5	7.0	7.5	8.0
Asparagus			x	x	x	x	x
Beets			x	x	x	x	x
Cabbage			x	x	x	x	x
Muskmelons			x	x	x	x	x
Peas			x	x	x	x	
Spinach			x	x	x	x	
Summer squash			x	x	x	x	
Celeriac			x	x	x		
Chives			x	x	x		
Endive			x	x	x		
Rhubarb			x	x	x		
Horseradish			x	x	x		
Lettuce			x	x	x		
Onions			x	x	x		
Radishes			x	x	x		
Cauliflower			x	x	x		
Corn		x	x	x	x	x	
Pumpkins		x	x	x	x	x	
Tomatoes		x	x	x	x	x	
Beans		x	x	x	x		
Carrots		x	x	x	x		
Cucumbers		x	x	x	x		
Parsnips		x	x	x	x		
Peppers		x	x	x	x		
Rutabagas		x	x	x	x		
Winter squash		x	x	x	x		
Eggplant		x	x	x			
Watermelons		x	x	x			
Potatoes	x	x	x	x			

make (thud, thud) something like concrete.

The worse thing that can happen to soil is compaction. Don't work, dig, or rototill the soil when it's really wet. In fact, excessive rototilling—especially if you're not adding organic materials—can ruin the soil texture.

HOW TO SPIN STRAW INTO GOLD: COMPOSTING

"I don't have lots of time!"
"Do I need one of those expensive bins?"
"My compost just sits there!"
"I can't do a lot of heavy lifting."
"Will it attract flies and rats?"

These are the questions people commonly ask about composting. It seems like a strange, alchemical process in which you must add precisely the right ingredients, perform the necessary rituals, and if you are so blessed, you will end up with compost.

Actually, composting has been around as long as there has been plant life on Earth, because in its simplest form, compost is just decayed plant material (humus), which recycles nutrients into usable forms for new plant growth. Compost happens naturally in woods and fields. Because there's little plant matter in deserts, there's little compost, and hence little soil (it's a vicious circle). All plant life on Earth has evolved by relying on the Sun, the rain, decayed plant matter, and trace minerals for growing.

People have been adding compost to their crops for thousands of years. The Mesopotamians had a word for compost; so did the Greeks and Romans, and the material is mentioned in the Talmud. The Chinese have been able to farm the same ground for thousands of years because they have been adding compost all that time. All this without the use of chemical fertilizers!

Sir Albert Howard, a British government agronomist working in Indore, India, in the early part of this century, invented the modern composting method as we know it. Howard realized the need for improvement in the Indian soils, and eventually developed the Indore method of making compost by layering different materials together like a great Dagwood sandwich. The materials were then turned by hand or mixed by industrious earthworms.

But why bother making compost when you can just get the nitrogen, phosphorus, and potassium out of chemical fertilizers? For partly the same reason that you and I cannot simply live on vitamin pills and energy bars: We need fiber and dozens of micronutrients.

Compost adds more to the soil than the mere NPK that chemical fertilizers do. Compost improves the physical texture of the soil. It makes sandy soils hold more water. It makes clayey soils drain better. Thus, it helps protect plants from drought. It also provides trace minerals and nutrients to plants, and releases the NPK minerals in gentler doses, over a longer period of time.

Compost also feeds the beneficial microorganisms and the earthworms and red wrigglers in the soil. Worms are nature's little rototillers; they're good for your garden. Every autumn I put two to three feet of shredded leaves on top of my garden beds. By springtime, the material has settled down and rotted into humus, and I am able to turn it in. Every time I pull out my shovel, it drips worms. Now that is wonderful!

Compost also helps aerate the soil. Aerated soil is loose enough for plants to get their roots into. It's also easier for you to dig in.

Compost gives body to the soil and helps prevent erosion. This is especially important in sandy soils.

Compost helps control the pH of the soil. If you're trying to correct a pH problem because your soil is too acidic or basic, adding lots of compost will provide this benefit as well.

Compost is also excellent mulch, especially for plants that root along their stems, such as corn, tomatoes, and squash. You may know that these plants are also heavy feeders. The compost provides nutrients as well as weed-smothering, cooling mulch.

It's really not that difficult. Most compost problems break down into two categories: (a) not enough stuff and (b) the wrong proportions of brown stuff and green stuff.

What if your compost "just sits there"? Then there isn't a minimum of a cubic yard of stuff, the chunks are too large to decompose quickly (it helps to chop up stems and stalks), or you don't have 25 percent green stuff (see "Ten Rules for Making Compost" later in this chapter).

You can reassure your neighbors that properly constructed compost heaps do *not* attract flies and rats. Leave out meats, fats, and dairy products. They decompose slowly and are the only attractants to these pests. If you're adding kitchen waste to the pile, tuck it under a bit of garden stuff. Some things (banana peels and cabbage cores come to mind) decompose slowly because they're so dense and tough. A simple trick is to toss these into the blender with some water and *bzzzt!* You can just pour the slop into the compost heap and they'll disappear very quickly. Worms love it, too.

Manure is a great addition, but it's not necessary. Be sure to use only the manure of herbivores (plant-eating critters). Cat and dog manures can contain harmful pathogens (which is why pregnant women are advised not to change kitty litter). Rabbit pellets are excellent; use a biodegradable litter such as corncob pellets. Horse manure must be thoroughly composted under hot conditions and aged; otherwise you'll have tons of weed seeds coming back to haunt you, because of the horse's less-efficient digestion system.

Thankfully, most newspapers have switched to soy-based, lead-free inks (call and ask if you're not sure). Newspaper is a high-carbon material, and when shredded it makes a good replacement for straw, hay, or leaves. You can buy a home/office paper shredder that fits atop a plastic waste bin and shred all of your non-glossy waste paper for the compost heap. It'll be a good balance to all those kitchen trimmings and grass clippings.

Many municipalities are refusing to pick up yard waste like grass clippings and leaves, or are charging extra for this service. Suddenly composting has become very popular, with all kinds of products out on the market to aid confused homeowners. Some of those products are fancy bins.

A BEVY OF BINS

Should you make or buy a bin, or just make a heap somewhere? Neither is best; composting works either way. I have a compost mound, which sometimes exceeds the volume of a standard wire bin. For lots of lazy compost production, I build long compost piles, which I call "barrows," right atop the garden bed itself (more on that soon).

Although bins are not necessary, they certainly make the garden tidier (an important consideration in neatnik neighborhoods). You can, if you're so motivated, build a bin out of most anything: chicken or hog wire nailed to a framework, snow fence, boards, cinder blocks, used shipping pallets, or whatever else you can scrounge or buy. You want the bin to be at least a cubic yard (or a cubic meter) in volume, or even larger. This doesn't mean the bin has to be square or rectangular. The simplest bin is a circle of wire or snow fence. Just make sure that you can easily open one side to turn the compost or dig out the finished goody from the bottom.

Jointed panels are handy in compost bins; you can add extra panels to enlarge the bin. I've also seen bins made in a cloverleaf pattern: three 3-sided bins, all opening toward a common center. This design allows the gardener to turn compost by shoveling or pitching it into the next bin.

Do those "compost starters" work? Or do you need "compost accelerator" if the material is decomposing slowly? Well, yes, they work somewhat; but no, you don't need them. Building a pile with a good ratio of brown and green stuff will do the trick. If you're really concerned,

The next spring, after the barrows have settled down.

then add a few shallow layers of garden soil to introduce extra microorganisms.

BARROW COMPOSTING: THE PAINLESS WAY TO ENRICH YOUR GARDEN

The problem with traditional composting, of course, is the amount of work involved. First you build the frame, then you haul the raw materials out to the bin, then you go through that laborious stirring or shoveling every other day or every other week, and then you haul the finished compost back over to the garden. (Tired yet?) Golly, I needed a wheelbarrow to do all that. But I didn't have one. It always seemed low priority on the budget, below car batteries and children's shoes—silly things like those.

One day I stopped dead in my tracks, a four-gallon bucket filled with compost in each hand. Why, I wondered, am I *moving* this stuff? Why is my compost pile over here, in the corner of the orchard, and my new herb bed over *there*, in the opposite corner of my big backyard?

Why aren't the compost piles where we need them, *right on the garden?* Is it some hangover from the Victorian era, when people had squadrons of estate gardeners to truck things from the private working area into the public viewing area? Probably. Maybe it's that prudish idea that compost making is somehow a nasty procedure, or a holdover from when organic gardeners had to hide their workings from nosy neighbors and municipal code enforcers. Those days are over, blessed be! But composting is still seen as a separate activity from the garden plot itself.

Let's get real. To combat these problems, I developed a new method, barrow composting. It has the following benefits:

- Less hauling of raw materials and no more turning of compost piles.
- Adding a foot of compost to the entire garden in one season with very little work.
- No tillers, hoes, compost bins, or wheelbarrows needed.

Sound good? Here's how it works.

In the autumn, on established beds or virgin ones that have been stripped of their sod and loosened, I make what I call compost barrows. They aren't really compost piles; the word *pile* implies something tidier than a heap, but still a round or square lump.

Barrow is an old Middle English word with a diversity of meanings, ranging from the box on a wheelbarrow to the contents thereof, and to the hillocks that cover ancient graves. The latter gives the right picture: a long mound of earth covering something. (In fact, after my barrows had settled, I had the impish urge to upholster them in sod and plant stone gnomons about the yard for that true Old English effect.)

But a compost barrow is no different to build than a compost heap. You'll need to build up the material at least 3 feet deep and 3 feet wide, and as long as your wide-row beds are themselves. With all that mass, the barrows heat up quickly.

If you garden in a large generic plot, you may still want to build long barrows anyway, leaving a 2-foot-wide aisle between each for walkways or to plant your rows of early crops.

Of course, this means that you still have to bring the materials into your garden. But you're moving the stuff only once to set it there, not out to the compost works and back into the garden. And you don't have to turn it, stir it, or move it from one bin to another! Isn't that swell?

If you want compost in only two or three weeks, yes, you will have to stir it. But if you build your barrows in the autumn when are the leaves are available, then there is all of the winter for the organic processes to work.

So where do you get all the stuff to make the compost? You know all those leaves that pile up in the autumn? That's what they're there for.

I've also found a neighbor with a humongous yard who religiously uses his lawn mower to pick up the leaves every weekend. The mower shreds them quite nicely, and often throws in a little grass as well, all mixed together. Perfect!

One neighbor's trash is another neighbor's compost.

I just drive around in my van on trash day, picking up 12–20 bags of leaves along the block. The nice thing about leaves is that unlike N-rich grass clippings, they don't get obnoxiously smelly from anaerobic decomposition if you leave them in the bags for a few days, and virtually no one puts chemicals on their shedding trees!

If the leaves you pick up aren't in small pieces, you'll probably want to run them through a shredder. A friend of mine dumps them on the ground and runs his power mower over the leaves to do this. There are also leaf-shredding machines like the Leaf-Eater, which is like a cross between a large blender (or funnel) and a weed whip. Of course, you don't have to use leaves. But most gardeners find this material in abundance, and in many cases it's already neatly bagged for the taking. It took about twenty-five bags of already-shredded leaves to cover a 4-foot-by-32-foot vegetable bed. That may sound like a lot until you realize you have two whole months to cover your veggie beds a yard deep with composting material.

If all the leaves in your neighborhood are acidic (oak leaves or pine needles), sprinkle a little lime in with them when you build your autumn barrows. Having just some oak leaves mixed in with the other leaves does not present a problem.

Worms are knights in slimy armor.

Building this kind of compost pile is child's play. Literally. When my daughter Anna was three, she could drag a bag of leaves from the car and empty it on her four-by-four-foot patch of the garden. Being able to move such a large bag of stuff was very satisfying for a small kid, and all kids love to dump things!

I frequently don't bother to turn these piles on my established beds, so that's the end of the story until next spring. The material will then have composted and settled to a depth of 12 to 15 inches. I'll go into detail about how to grow vegetables in Chapters Four and Five. The following examples are to show you how much the barrow method simplifies Heartland gardening.

The first crop I planted using the new method was an experimental square of potatoes. I figured, why bother to plant something and then have to dig it up? I just stuck the potato pieces in a few inches deep. When the plants got a foot tall, I added more mulch so none of the spuds would get green from the sun and threaten to make us ill. When it was time to harvest, Anna grabbed the stems and pulled up the potatoes. It was also a ridiculously easy way to find new potatoes without bothering the plants overmuch.

The second crop I planted was an autumn set of Sugar Ann peas. I sprinkled in some inoculant [beneficial bacterial that helps the roots secure nitrogen from the soil], and just threw the peas on the patch. Because the area was full of crumbly leaves, the seeds all found places to hide and sprout out of sight from the birds. The mulched compost retained moisture well and couldn't bake hard. Even though the August heat ranged from 88 to 100 °F, I simply kept the seeds moist, and the peas were happily up in two weeks! I could not have had results like this in our normal clay soil.

If you're planting corn, this system is perfect. Just reach down to plant the seeds atop your baseline of soil, cover with an inch of compost, and then leave room above for them to sprout. The compost around them will help keep the seeds moist and hide them from birds. As the young plants grow, allow the compost to settle back around them, and your plants are automatically fed and mulched. Corn is a shallow-rooted plant as well as a heavy feeder, and it loves this kind of coddling. You'll be well rewarded.

Another added benefit is that in one year you will have raised beds. I had to dig the compost into the soil on one spot of my garden where the graders had dumped a load of subsoil clay. But you'll still end up with a raised bed, and can astound your soil-testing office with a suddenly higher organic content.

Turning the finished compost under.

Garden beds like this are a haven for worms. Out of curiosity, I did a head count of red wrigglers present in two cubic feet of compost: there were thirty-eight. After finding that many, I quit sifting compost; I knew it was Worm City.

UNDERSTANDING THE BARROW METHOD

If you are using barrow heaps on a new garden, you can rototill the finished compost in, or you can turn it under with a shovel. The outside few inches of leaves don't break down as much since they don't get hot, but I just declare them to be mulch instead of compost, and the vegetables certainly don't know any better. The material eventually gets turned in as I harvest and plant.

Half-finished compost piles are useful for growing squashes, pumpkins, and cucumbers. The mounded soil warms up sooner in the late spring, there are lots of nutrients, and the pile can continue slowly decomposing during the growing season.

Gardeners in areas with lots of clay or sand know that organic matter disappears quickly. You will need to add compost to your garden every year to replenish the nutrients and organic matter. Compost is just organic material that is decayed to a certain point. Alas, the decay process never stops (just like that entropy process that never stops and keeps your house or desk messy).

Time and compost wait for no one; both diminish relentlessly.

With barrow composting you can easily keep your beds at maximum composure. Gardeners in stony areas where glaciers dropped their loads can also profit by finally being able to grow root vegetables without spending hours sifting the soil out from the rocks.

'Nuf said!

OTHER SOIL AMENDMENTS

What about peat as a soil amendment? Peat is a useful material for seed-starting mixes (usually along with perlite and vermiculite). It holds moisture and drains well. But unlike compost, peat does not add nutrients. And when peat dries out completely, it has the ability to repel water! It's like adding fiber to your diet: useful, but not nutritious.

Why do leaves blow all over your yard and collect along the fences and under the shrubs? They are there to mix with your grass clippings for spring.

Never use fresh manures right on your garden; they can contain harmful pathogens. Instead, toss them into the compost pile. Fresh manure contains soluble nitrogen compounds and ammonia, which can "burn" your plants. It's also generally full of undigested weed seeds, and those are the last things you want to add to your garden!

There are quite a few organic fertilizers out there, each with different amounts of NPK. Most of these fertilizers contain either processed natural materials (such as alfalfa meal, coffee grounds, cottonseed meal, blood meal, and bonemeal), or mineral dusts (such as colloidal phosphate, granite meal, gypsum, and dolomitic limestone). The supplying company will include the NPK ratios on the packaging.

Mineral dusts include rock dusts. Rock dusts are simply special kinds of rock ground up *very* fine (it can go through a 200-mesh screen). Other names quarries give for rock dusts include pond silt, pond sand, pond fines, swamp sand, crusher screenings, crusher fines, float, fill sand, or flume sand.

Gypsum is often recommended for "lightening" clay soils. Gypsum is a wonderful rock dust for clay soils. It helps loosen up the structure, and supplies 22 percent calcium and 17 percent sulfur. *Do not* use gypsum if your soil pH is below 5.8. A downside is that gypsum takes a year to really make a difference. Another downside is that the effect is not permanent.

Another common but erroneously recommended soil additive is a calcium-rich material, such as TUMS or eggshells. These are supposedly to prevent blossom-end rot on tomatoes and squashes. Blossom-end rot (BER) looks like a black mushy spot on the bottom of the tomato fruits, but it is rarely caused by calcium deficiency in the soil. (We have tons of limestone in our soils, and I still see BER on occasion.) What happens is that the young plant is growing so fast, the leaves get nutrient priority over the fruits. As the plant growth slows down, the calcium levels normalize. Spraying calcium on the plant won't help either; it isn't absorbed that way. Think of BER as a youth phenomenon, not unlike "tomato zits." They grow out of it. There's no need to go around planting TUMS and eggshells in your garden.

Yet another fertilizer myth is planting matches to make peppers grow better, or produce hotter fruits. However, the sulfur

A "cooking" compost pile can get to 160 degrees hot!

used in making matches is not the right sort to help plants.

How can you tell if you need rock dusts or mineral supplements for your garden? Ask for a mineral analysis on your soil test. You may receive a recommendation for the appropriate supplement. The standard dosage for rock dust is 45 pounds per 100 square feet. There is no standard dosage for mineral supplements because their nutrient values are so variable.

If the leaves on your plants grew really slowly, or are getting a very light green at the tips and on top, you probably have a nitrogen deficiency. Apply thirty pounds of blood meal or fish meal per every 1,000 square feet of garden.

Baby tomato seedlings can develop a purple tinge on the undersides of leaves. This is not generally a problem, but if it happens later on after transplanting, your plants are low in phosphorus. Apply thirty pounds of bonemeal or sixty pounds of colloidal phosphate per 1,000 square feet.

Don't let minor nutritional problems worry you. They're not common, and adding lots of compost usually takes care of most problems. A soil test will alert

you to any major deficiencies. Interestingly, our state soil-testing lab says that sometimes their recommendation to home gardeners is to *quit applying so much fertilizer!*

TEN RULES FOR MAKING COMPOST

1. **Use 75 percent carbon material ("brown stuff") and 25 percent nitrogen material ("green stuff") for optimum mix.** You can use all carbon material (leaves), but it will take longer. If your compost pile gives off an ammonia odor (like a diaper pail), then you have too much green stuff (probably grass clippings). It needs more brown stuff to balance it, or maybe you just need to stir the pile more.

   We used to classify compost materials as being "carbon" materials and "nitrogen" materials, but that tends to confuse people. So now we call them brown stuff and green stuff.

   Brown Stuff (high-carbon materials)
   - Corncobs and stalks
   - Hay

- Straw
- Leaves
- Nutshells and husks
- Shredded white paper or newspaper (no slick, color advertising pages)
- Pine needles
- Sawdust

Green Stuff (high-nitrogen materials)
- Coffee grounds
- Cover crops
- Eggshells
- Feathers
- Fruit materials
- Grass clippings and grains
- Hair
- Manures
- Seaweed
- Veggie materials, weeds without seeds

2. **Stockpile brown [high-carbon] materials.** You may wish to store dry leaves in bags to mix with summer lawn clippings, or mix clippings into an existing shredded leaf compost pile. I stockpile autumn leaves to mix them with spring grass clippings in a regular compost pile, and then it's all ready by midsummer for the next round of planting. To everything there is a season. . . .

3. **The smaller the particles, the faster the decomposition.** I learned more about cooking in my Chemistry class than I did in my Foods class! Here's an explanation: If you want mashed potatoes in half an hour, what do you do? Peel the taters, dump them in boiling water, and cook for 30 minutes. Say you want mashed potatoes in a quarter hour, what do you do? Peel the taters, dice them, dump them in boiling water, and cook for 15 minutes. The smaller the particle, the faster the chemical reaction.

    Leaves decay faster if they're shredded with a mower or Leaf-Eater (See

Chapter Nine, "Tool Selection").

4. **Do not include fats, meats, and dairy products, or weed seeds, rocks, and sticks.** Avoid cat or dog manure. Watch out for Zoysia or Bermuda grass roots or stems (they will come back to haunt you).

5. **Anything else that was once alive can go in.** Include grass clippings, leaves, weeds *without* seeds or weed killer on them, leftover crops and overripe things from your garden, manure, spoiled hay, eggshells, feathers, shredded bark, coffee and tea grounds, apple pomace from cider making, peanut shells, peelings and trimmings from the kitchen, dead houseplants (no bugs), straw, bonemeal, blood meal, shredded corncobs, seaweed, soil, and wood ashes (not grill briquette ashes).

6. **A bin is helpful, but not necessary.** A cubic yard or cubic meter (or more) of material is *required*. Without the necessary mass, the pile won't heat up. Even larger or longer is fine. I have seen compost heaps the size of minivans!

7. **The pile should be damp, like a sponge.** In heavy rains, cover the pile with a tarp.

8. **Turning the pile is not necessary.** But it does speed up decomposition.

9. **Worms are good.** You can add red wrigglers if you want, but you don't have to. Using ground-contact bins lets worms into your system. Here's why I call worms my knights in slimy armor: They are nature's rototillers. They digest dead plant materials and excrete nutrient-rich worm "castings." Just one acre can contain over a million earthworms, eating ten tons of leaves and other plant material, with the result of turning over forty tons of soil! Having lots of worms (both earthworms and red wrigglers) is a

Raised beds save the garden from heavy rains.

sign of a healthy soil.

10. **Keep your pile turned and moist so it will heat up.** A cooking compost pile can reach 160 °F (it will steam on cool mornings), which kills pathogens and weed seeds. Unless you're certain your pile gets this hot *and* is turned frequently for all the material to be heated up, then *don't* put in weed seeds. Just make a habit of not putting seedy or diseased items in your compost pile.

THE BENEFITS OF RAISED BEDS

Raised beds are those in which the soil is amended or increased until it's above ground level. Raised beds are often held in with walls. Walls are handy but not necessary. If you have a disability or an impairment that prevents you from reaching ground level easily, a raised bed will bring the garden up to you. Hard paths can be installed for easy access during all kinds of weather. Some botanic gardens have examples of accessible gardens.

Raised beds are also a good choice because it seems kind of silly to rototill a whole bunch of the backyard to get the soil all loose and crumbly, and then walk around the garden and squash the soil all over again.

Raised beds also drain better during heavy rains, and can keep your garden from being flooded out.

- With a raised bed, your soil stays nice and loose, just the way plants like it.
- You don't have as much ground to weed, since you aren't making walkways in the growing area itself.
- You don't have so much watering to do, because the garden isn't as big.

- You're more able to keep an eye on the good bugs and bad bugs, because you can get close to your plants.

Of course, nothing's perfect. Raised beds have a few problems, too. They can dry out faster (especially if there's not a lot of compost to help retain moisture). If you've invested in a big rototiller, it's hard to use one on a raised bed. But then, why would you need to?

I've read books that recommend you dig up the soil from the pathways to add to your raised beds. The idea of walking in a trench where water can collect doesn't sound like much fun though. Hence the addition of compost to raise the soil level instead.

BREAKING NEW GROUND

First, you need to decide where you want your garden. As mentioned before, pick a place that's in the sunshine all day long, because your plants will need the sun all day to grow well. Your garden should be close to the outdoor faucet for watering. It's also good if your garden is close to the back door, because then you can visit it more easily.

Your garden beds should probably not be any wider than three or four feet, so you can reach the middle without stepping inside. Otherwise, the beds can be any length you want, and any shape you want.

You might need to pull the grass off your future garden. Measure and outline the bed with lime or flour. Pulling up the sod is sometimes hard work. You can shovel it off in pieces if you want, and reuse the sod someplace else in the yard, or you can cut the sod with a sharp gardening knife. (Don't use a good kitchen knife, because the blade will get dull and nicked up.) For large areas, you can rent a sod-cutting machine. Such machines require some "wrassling" (like large ro-

totillers do). But they save you great amounts of time and effort, cutting your homegrown sod into the familiar sheets that you can roll up and reuse.

After you've removed any unwanted sod, you need to loosen up the soil so the plants can grow more easily. People have been walking all over this ground, and the soil is hard. Using a shovel or spading fork (see Chapter Nine, "Tool Selection"), dig as deep as one shovel head, or one spit. (*Spit* is an old-fashioned term meaning the depth of a spade blade, about 11 inches.) Then break up the soil into little pieces.

There are three methods for starting new beds: double digging (a traditional, labor-intensive method), hill culture, and compost barrows.

THE FIRST METHOD: DOUBLE DIGGING

You may want to double-dig your plot. The reasoning for this is to loosen up the subsoil and avoid a hardpan problem. Hardpan means that you have a somewhat shallow layer of loose soil atop a rock-hard one. The plant roots don't want to overwork, and kind of go "boink" when they reach the hardpan. Hardpan also interferes with drainage. Repeated, shallow tilling can create a hardpan problem. Double digging was developed in the United Kingdom, a land of fanatic diggers.

The good news: You only have to do this once! You'll need a freshly sharpened shovel, gloves to prevent blisters, shoes or boots with hard arch supports (not sneakers), and a tarp or wheelbarrow. You'll also need a strong back and a constitution of iron, but don't let that scare you off. A digging partner, a jug of lemonade, and some boogying music also help.

Remember, you don't have to do it all in one day! I would suggest digging up 16 square feet of garden space at a time if you're new to digging. Watch out—it's 36 to 48 hours later that the muscle stiffness sets in.

Use good body mechanics. This is physical therapist jargon for moving heavy things sensibly. Digging up ground is hard work. First, stretch to warm up and loosen your muscles (I'm not kidding).

Think about all those fried-chicken dinners you've enjoyed: Which is the meatier piece? It's not the back; it's the thighs! So use your leg muscles, not your back, for bearing loads. Always bend your knees, not your back, when digging (and picking up heavy things, too). Swivel your body and let the soil fall off your shovel onto the tarp or wheelbarrow.

Before you dig, make sure the ground is moist. Run a sprinkler for several hours the day before if it's not. Mark off the area of your new bed. Gardening books usually recommend doing this with a handy sprinkling of lime. I rarely have lime on hand though, so I use a handy sprinkling of flour, which is always on hand, cheap, and biodegradable.

To bite into the ground (new ground has the potential to be really chewy), hold your shovel near the top, and stamp on it to get the edge in. Gardeners who are small or lightweight (like myself), or who have really tough ground, usually end up jumping on their shovels and then rocking back and forth. Beware of buried rocks! Many a gardener has envied Superman's x-ray vision.

Once you have the blade in about half a spit, pull back to remove a bite of soil. Take more bites off the edge of the hole; after the first cubic foot, the bites are easier because you're just enlarging the hole.

For the double digging, you first dig a foot-wide trench along one side, removing the soil one spit deep, and setting the soil aside, taking it down to the opposite end of your new bed.

Next, loosen the subsoil you've exposed. Wiggle a spading fork in to loosen up the clumps. Sift in some compost.

Dig a second trench next to the first trench. Remove the soil, breaking up clods and adding in compost (and from 30 to 50 percent sand, if the soil is clayey). Put the soil from the second trench atop the subsoil of the first trench.

Next, loosen the subsoil you've exposed in the second trench. Wiggle a spading fork in to loosen up the clumps. Sift in some compost.

Continue "ad exhausteum" until you've reached the last trench. Put the amended topsoil from the first trench atop the loosened subsoil of the last trench. Are we having fun yet?

I've double-dug one garden bed, and probably won't do it again, unless I find some really cruddy subsoil on my property that needs heavy amending or removing.

THE SECOND METHOD: HILL CULTURE

For another method of compost making right on site, you can build a hill. *Hugelkultur* (hill-culture), as it's known in Germany, builds a compost pile right on the bed, but with a different variety of ingredients.

Hills are usually made in long rows, rather than piles. For a 4-foot-wide row, do the following:

1. Dig out your topsoil, one spit (11 inches) deep, and set it aside.
2. Drop in a bottom layer of coarse, woody stuff on the bottom, such as branches.
3. Put down a two-inch layer of one of the following atop the branches: the sod you stripped off, manure, or rough compost.
4. Divide your topsoil in half, and layer on half of it atop the manure.

5. Add a layer of rough, chopped vegetable matter, four to six inches deep.
6. Add a healthy layer of compost, four to six inches deep.
7. Finish with the rest of your topsoil.

THE THIRD AND EASIEST METHOD: BARROW BEDS

Dig up just one spit deep. Remove the topsoil. Mix it in with the topsoil compost, peat, aged or composted manure, and/or builder's sand. Dumping the materials on a tarp (or an old shower curtain) most easily does this. Four cubic

You can wash off the dirt, but not the calluses.

feet of soil at a time is sufficient for mixing. Add sand and compost, each in equal volume to your soil. The resultant mixture resembles potting soil (for a good reason!). Dump the improved topsoil back atop your bed.

After a season of barrow composting, the loose, improved soil will be nearly a foot higher than ground level. The topsoil you've loosened and improved is now the "subsoil" layer (and wonderful subsoil it is), and the compost is the topsoil.

Sometimes your barrow compost is rather chunky, and you may feel funny about trying to sow in small seeds. If I'm transplanting something big, like a tomato seedling, it doesn't matter. But for direct seeding, I usually dig down a shovel's depth past the compost, bring up the soil, let the compost fall into the hole, and dump the soil atop the compost, knocking the lump to shatter it. Smooth out the soil, and now it's ready for seeds.

Since the soil's been loosened at the bed's inception, it now takes only one stomp of a foot on my shovel to bite in that deep! Stomp, lift, flip. Next square, stomp, lift, flip. Quick and easy. Be sure to bend your knees, not your back.

It's a good idea to add walls to your beds, so they don't spread out, and to protect your soil and plants. You can make the walls out of all kinds of things: wooden boards, rocks, cinder blocks, bricks, or whatever else you have.

The easiest way I've found to secure board walls is to use galvanized, predrilled pieces of 90-degree angle iron and connector plates. These are screwed in to connect boards. (In tired desperation, I have hammered screws in. It works pretty well, for this low-stress application, but it's *not* a good idea for "real" structures!) Gardening tool catalogs also sell plastic corners and connectors for fit-

An average rain shower gives about 0.2" of rain; gardens need about 1 inch a week.

ting boards into, if you want to try the "Tinker Toy" approach to building.

If you can't bear to trim along those edges of your garden beds, then "bare to not trim!" That is, rip out the grass in a 2- to 3-inch-wide band around the outside of your bed (walls). Lay down two or three inches of grass clippings on the bare zone to suppress weeds. When you mow, be sure not to suck up your mulch. (See the section on mulching in Chapter Four.)

If I'm starting a new flowerbed, I'll build my compost pile right where the garden goes. After a winter—or a month during growing season—the compost is dug into the soil. As you've probably discovered, soil around the foundations is often full of junk, such as pieces of concrete and tile, bits of wire, chunks of subsoil clay, and so on.

Rock 'n' roll: It's a sad fact of life that rocks migrate. Not all of this movement is due to the actions of lawnmowers and small children. Frost heaving can cause decorative white pebble and lava rock to burrow into the ground. Likewise, a previous gardener's decorative rock will annoyingly keep reappearing if you're trying to get rid of it. (Personally, I find that Hawaiian lava rock in Kansas looks supremely silly.)

To remove the rocks and junk from your soil, or conversely, in stony ground to remove your soil from the rocks, you will need a riddle, a kind of gardening sieve (see Chapter Nine, "Tool Selection").

CCA WOOD AND OTHER THINGS TO AVOID

When you're choosing materials for the walls of your raised beds, you need to be careful about the wood type you choose.

Three kinds of treated wood are commonly sold as rot resistant: CCA-treated lumber (*CCA* stands for *chromate copper*

arsenic). This product is also known as pressure-treated wood. The others are creosote-treated railroad ties, and wood treated with "penta" (pentachlorophenol). These woods contain dangerous substances, which continually leach into the soil. The plants take up these chemicals. Sometimes these woods are erroneously recommended for garden-bed walls. Many research reports from various research labs and government agencies disprove this claim.

What should you use instead? If you want to use wood (instead of rocks, bricks, cinder blocks, and so on), then choose naturally rot-resistant woods like cypress, locust, and cedar. I use cedar in my beds because it's locally available and not terribly expensive.

You can't add too much compost.

In your gardening supply catalogs, you'll also find several raised-bed kits, which are made of recycled plastics. These are more expensive initially, but you know how long plastic lasts! They're also attractive, modular, and extendable.

FIGURING RAINFALL AND YOUR WATERING NEEDS

One of the most important—and inexpensive—gardening tools you need is a rain gauge. It can be the little yellow plastic one from the garden center, or just a can set upright with a ruler standing inside. However you decide to collect your rainwater, you need to be able to measure it.

Why? Because the average garden, whether you're growing veggies, herbs, or flowers (or all three together) needs an inch of rain a week. That's oh, say, 50 to

Drip jug. Bury it halfway down into the ground.

55 inches of rain a year, maybe a bit less during the winter, when only the perennial plants and soil need moisture. It takes about ten inches of snow to equal one inch of rain.

Different areas of the Heartland get varying levels of rain each year, and it's rarely spread out in nice, tidy sums. Here in eastern Kansas, we're in a semiarid zone—we average thirty-five inches of rain a year. This isn't nearly enough for fescue and bluegrass lawns; they go dormant July through September, looking sere and brassy brown. At that time of year, the gardeners are out watering their flowers and veggies every week.

The average rain shower gives you 0.1 to 0.3 inches of rain. That's *not* a week's ration. A whole inch of rain in an hour's time is a real toad-strangling gully-washer. More than five inches of rain in a couple days' time spells flooding trouble, unless you've just come out of a drought. After a drought, the flood chance depends on the amount of time over which the water arrives. Five inches in two hours is a disaster, but over two days' time it'll just disappear into the thirsty ground.

To combat this problem, gardeners turn to several kinds of watering devices: sprinklers, soakers, and reservoirs.

You're probably already familiar with sprinklers that spin or wave back and forth. Sprinklers should not be used if it's windy; you'll mostly be watering the atmosphere. And if you are having difficulties with mildew or other airborne viruses, then *don't* use a sprinkler!

Soaker hoses solve both of these problems neatly. The only problem with soaker hoses is their semi-permanence. Once you arrange them in an efficient layout, there they are. Digging, planting, or tilling means rearranging the hose.

Drip jugs are less commonly used. They were probably devised by gardeners who were too impatient to stand there with a hose, or who realized that hose watering requires more time than it takes to merely wet the top surface of the soil. Empty (clean) gallon plastic jugs work well and are often handy. Simply remove the cap and puncture a few small holes in the bottom of each jug. Set the jugs buried halfway down into the ground, and fill them up. They'll slowly percolate the water into the ground, and you'll spend less time watering. Established, thirsty plants like cucumbers, peppers, tomatoes, melons, and such especially like drip jugs.

CHAPTER TWO

Understanding Catalogs

They're everywhere: catalogs sliding out from under the bed, atop the television, in the bathroom, beside the sofa, even beside the driver's seat in case you're in a long drive-through line or have a dental appointment. A few seed catalogs even arrive with the rest of the Christmas mail, to be set aside for after the holiday ornaments are packed away. (I always give my mail carrier a box of fudge for Christmas, because she is required to deliver us such an incredible poundage of catalogs!)

But at some point, the winter doldrums set in. Football fans are listless after the Super Bowl. But we gardeners turn feverishly to our catalogs, with lust in our hearts. Soon the pages are flagged with sticky-notes or yellow highlighting pen, and lists are being made. Then the calculator is turned on (yikes!)—and then the lists are made again.

BEYOND THE "HYPER-KODACHROME": DECODING CATALOG-SPEAK

If your gardening experience is expanding beyond buying a few six-packs of tomatoes and petunias at the grocery or garden center, the upcoming slew of catalogs are sure to please you. Every year there is something new! Starting plants from seed is cost-effective, and the selection of different cultivars (a hybrid word, meaning "CULT-ivated VAR-ieties"), colors, heights, and varieties in catalogs is even greater than in most garden centers.

But if you're new to catalog reading, it can be confusing. The copywriters assume that you already know all about gardening, including what all those abbreviations mean.

Hyperbole produces catalogs; sweat produces gardens.

For instance, did you know that the phrase "85 days to maturity" in a tomato description does *not* mean that you'll be picking ripe 'maters eighty-five days after planting that seed?

On a plant that's traditionally put in the garden as a transplant (tomatoes, peppers, and eggplants), the phrase means "85 days" (more or less) from a six- to eight-week-old transplant size. If you want ripe peppers (instead of less tasty and less nutritious green ones), then add another three weeks. That productive Gypsy hybrid sweet pepper I'm so fond of says "60 days" in the catalog. But that means 7 days to sprout, another 42 days for transplant size, 60 days until green picking stage, and then another 21 days to a red, ripe color. That's really a 130-day pepper!

Oh. And how come one catalog says "85 days" and another "72 days" for the same kind of plant? Does one have faster seeds? Nope. Those maturity dates are *averages*, and depend on the weather and soil as much as anything else. *Days to maturity* means generally how long the plant takes to grow from sprouted seed to harvest. These numbers are general, not specific guarantees.

For your other plants that are seeded directly into the garden (beans, carrots), the maturity date is the general guide to about when you should expect the harvesting to *start*. Things like pole beans will produce their first few beans about then, and you'll have more beans every week for the rest of the growing season. This also means that you can leave your carrots in the ground for a while after the 62-day mark.

Something to consider about maturity dates is whether you can reasonably expect to harvest your crop before a killing frost sets in! (See Chapter Four for frost date maps.) Thankfully, we live in a part of the country with a fairly long growing season, and few things are beyond our ability (although bananas come to mind).

MORE CATALOG TERMS

Here is a list of some other terms you're likely to see in your catalogs.

Bunching onion—An onion that does not form large bulbs, but rather multiplies itself into more onions; a perma-

nent form of scallion. Used in Chinese cooking.

Bush (bean, squash)—Bush plants are those that have been dwarfed or shrunken through breeding or that have a natural size limit. Bush beans do not need to be staked, and will produce their crop pretty much all at once. They were developed for the canning trade. Bush squash plants still get about 5 feet across, but do not "run" everywhere.

Determinate (tomato)—A "bush" form of tomato that grows only to a specific size, and produces only a specified amount of fruits. Some determinate tomatoes die after having done their thing. They are useful to the home canner, who may desire to put up tomatoes only once. They are also useful to gardeners who don't need lots of tomatoes, or don't want to cope with 6- to 7-foot-tall plants.

English pea—What Southerners call green peas, to distinguish them from cowpeas and black-eyed peas (both of which are really beans—go figure). English peas are the ordinary peas, distinguished from snow peas and sugar snap peas.

Indeterminate (tomato)—The tall, vining tomatoes that keep on growing until the frost hits them. Indeterminate tomatoes require cages or stakes for best results, or you can let them sprawl everywhere.

Loose-leaf, loose-head (lettuce)—A non-heading lettuce, useful for gardeners who want to continuously harvest a few leaves from each plant, or employ the "cut and come again" method of mowing part of a lettuce patch with scissors. These lettuces have more nutrients than the crisp-head (iceberg-type) lettuces.

Ornamental corn—A kind of pretty field corn, usually used for Thanksgiving decorations. Ornamental corn nubbins can be ground for homemade cornmeal. You can also strip the seeds off cobs that were dried on the stalks, and replant them next year. Some ornamental corns are popping corns.

Pelleted seed—Seeds that are coated (usually with a very fine clay) to make them easier to plant. Usually small seeds like carrot and petunia are pelleted. Pelleted seeds cost more, of course.

Pole (bean)—An indeterminate bean that does best when staked or trellised. Pole beans give a longer harvest than bush beans, with more production. Many people think pole beans have better flavor.

Popping corn/popcorn—A type of field corn bred to pop. You have to buy popcorn seed; sweet corn doesn't pop. Keep your popcorn and sweet corn 500 feet away from each other if they pollinate (tassel) at the same time, to prevent them from cross-pollinating. Or you can stagger the planting times to avoid this problem.

Savoy (spinach, cabbage)—The crinkly, puckered kind of leaves. Savoy spinach is slightly more difficult to clean, but easier to stab with a fork because it doesn't glue itself to the plate with salad dressing, like flat-leaf spinach does.

Scallion—An immature onion that has not formed a bulb. Or, a variety of onion (see bunching onion) that doesn't form a bulb.

Seed tape—A length of (dissolvable) paper tape with seeds (usually carrot or lettuce) that are evenly spaced down its length. These were invented for people who (1) grow their crops in rows, (2) have trouble bending over, and (3) don't want to thin their row of seeds after foolishly pouring the whole packet down the row. Seed tapes cost more, of course. You could make your own seed tapes with cheap paper toweling and flour paste, or simply use a wrapping-paper tube to drop your seeds down, and not have to bend over. You can also avoid excessive thinning by spacing the seeds the right distance and not planting the whole packet.

Size—Refers to how much room the plant needs at adult size. Unlike children and dogs that can be crammed together in the family car, plants need to be planted with spacing sufficient for their mature size.

Sow what you enjoy. More radishes are planted than are ever eaten.

Snap bean, snap pea—Snap beans and peas are those legumes that don't have a tough "string" running from stem to blossom that needs to be stripped off before eating. "Snap beans: The next generation" are distinguished from the older string beans.

Snow pea—A kind of Chinese pea that is eaten before the peas swell in the pod.

Untreated—Term describing seeds without chemicals on them. Some seeds have brilliant pink dust on them; these are treated seeds, best not handled barehanded unless you wash up well afterward. (*Never* feed treated seed to critters!) Captan and Thiram are used to help prevent the seed from rotting before sprouting in cold soils. A little patience also prevents this same problem. Some seed companies sell only untreated seeds.

Yield—Refers to how much you can expect the plant to produce, and whether it crops all at once (for example, bush beans) or over a period of time (pole beans).

THE NAME GAME

Often, old plant varieties have several names used in different parts of the country. When in doubt, ask the company if their green bean is your green bean. For instance, Catskill and Long Island Improved brussels sprouts are the same. Genuine Cornfield bean is called Crease-back in Texas. Scarlet Nantes, Nantes Coreless, Touchon, and Half-Long Coreless Nantes are all the same carrot. Simply saying Brandywine tomato isn't helpful either; there's a red Brandywine, pink Brandywine, yellow Brandywine, Suddeth Brandywine, and OTV Brandywine!

Names of imported varieties are sometimes translated. "Merveille des quatre saisons" lettuce in France is called Four Seasons lettuce in the United States. "Rotkapchen," a German lettuce, becomes Redcap or Red Riding Hood.

When in doubt, ask the seed company if they have your vegetable, or if it has more than one name.

FIGURING PACKET SIZES AND COSTS

Is more expensive seed better? Not necessarily. Seed pricing frequently reflects the size of the seed packet. Unusual seeds may cost more, because of lower demand or limited seed quantities available. Hybrid breeding also makes seed more expensive, due to the amount of labor that goes into the careful cross-pollination required to produce the seed.

Brand-new cultivars often cost more to help offset the cost of breeding, and because the company has an exclusive product and they simply *can* charge more. Once other companies can offer the new introduction for sale, the price will drop to a more common level.

Packet sizes vary from one company to another. For example, Pinetree Garden

Seeds sells smaller seed packets (except for standard-sized packets of beans and corn). Their aim is to provide seeds for the small home gardener, rather than the Amish farmwife who's putting up food for a family of nine. Hence, Pinetree's packets are less expensive.

On the other hand, there's *cheap*. Some seeds are only 10¢ per packet. This is because of two things: (1) small seed amount, and (2) these are nonhybrid, fairly generic seeds. Yes, they still grow and produce healthy food. (For a dime, you're not getting many bean or corn seeds, though.)

Packet size is given in both weight and number. I myself prefer number, because carrot or lettuce seeds weigh next to nothing. Minor variations in cost are usually due to seed packet size, rather than cost per ounce.

Are lots of color photos a sign of a better catalog? Nope. Some really fine catalogs, like Pinetree Garden Seeds and Garden City Seeds, don't rely on a lot of glossy pix. Instead, they give you plenty of descriptions, growing information, and some line-art illustrations. Even the glossy catalogs don't give pictures of every single item they sell.

PROVEN WINNERS

What's the fuss about AAS winners? Well, since 1932, All-America Selections have been tested over a wide range of growing zones by impartial judges. A plant has to be stupendous to earn the AAS award. The AAS is a nonprofit organization that tests new cultivars at over thirty flower and twenty vegetable test gardens throughout the United States and Canada. Only 5 percent of the new varieties tested merit awards, which are given to those items that are breeding breakthroughs, like the sugar snap pea.

Veggies with AAS certification are usually the cream of the crop of new varieties. AAS plants from years back are still living happily through catalogs, and are the standards by which new entries are judged. Some still in commerce are Honey Rock Cantaloupe (1933), Straight-8 Cucumber (1935), Comet Radish (1936), Early Prolific Straightneck Summer Squash (1938), Clemson Spineless Okra (1939), Jubilee Tomato (1943), Fordhook 242 bush Lima Bean (1945), Cherokee Wax Bean (1948), Victory Freezer Pea (1948), Iochief Sweet Corn (1951), Ruby Queen Beet (1957), and Jade Cross Brussels Sprouts (1959).

Look in your local newspapers and garden magazines in the December and January editions for articles about the latest AAS vegetable, herb, and flower winners. You can learn more about them on the Internet, at http://www.all-americaselections.org.

DISEASE RESISTANCE

Disease tolerance means that the plant won't absolutely keel over if hit by the creeping grunge. It'll still get set back, but it may at least give you a few more weeks of harvest before it dies. Resistance means that the seed carries the genes for immunity, as though it's had its shots. Not every plant has been rated for disease resistance, since this is a laboratory-intensive (and expensive) process. Older and nonhybrid varieties with comparatively low distribution don't have enough widespread interest to generate this process, even though they often harbor these lovely characteristics and were often the gene sources.

Here are some common disease resistance abbreviations:

A Anthracnose resistance in beans and cucumbers, or Alternaria stem canker in tomatoes

BMV Bean Mosaic Virus

CMV Cucumber Mosaic Virus; also affects squash, spinach, tomatoes, and peppers

DM Downy Mildew; affects many crops

F, FF, F2 Fusarium wilt; FF or F2 refers to a second type of Fusarium fungus

MTO Indicates that seed is free from Lettuce Mosaic virus

N Nematode; this parasitic worm affects the roots of tomatoes and peppers. Root Knot Nematode disease is found only in sandy soils in California, Florida, southern Georgia, and a few Gulf Coast areas, so it is of little concern to Heartland gardeners.

PM Powdery Mildew; affects cucumbers, squash, peas, and other crops

Se Sugar Enhanced; refers to a hybrid type of corn that is sweeter than regular sweet corn.

Sh2 Shrunken 2 gene; refers to a supersweet corn that should be isolated from other types of corn so they don't cross-pollinate

Su Refers to old-fashioned sweet corn; doesn't need isolation

T, TMV Tobacco Mosaic Virus; affects tomatoes and peppers. It is rarely seen outside of greenhouse conditions

V Verticillium wilt; a common killer of tomatoes and eggplants. This disease lingers in the soil

Y Yellows; a fusarium that affects cabbages

The value of something is not just the cost, but also what was given up.

HYBRID VS. OPEN-POLLINATED

Are hybrid seeds always better? Frequently they are, but not always. Hybridization often produces superior plants. Some plants are already excellent from years of genetic selection by garden-

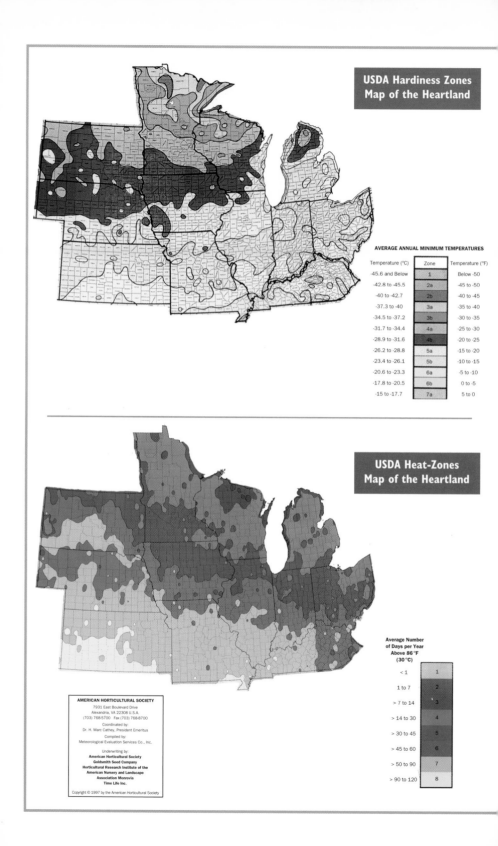

USDA Hardiness Zones Map of the Heartland

AVERAGE ANNUAL MINIMUM TEMPERATURES

Temperature (°C)	Zone	Temperature (°F)
-45.6 and Below	1	Below -50
-42.8 to -45.5	2a	-45 to -50
-40 to -42.7	2b	-40 to -45
-37.3 to -40	3a	-35 to -40
-34.5 to -37.2	3b	-30 to -35
-31.7 to -34.4	4a	-25 to -30
-28.9 to -31.6	4b	-20 to -25
-26.2 to -28.8	5a	-15 to -20
-23.4 to -26.1	5b	-10 to -15
-20.6 to -23.3	6a	-5 to -10
-17.8 to -20.5	6b	0 to -5
-15 to -17.7	7a	5 to 0

USDA Heat-Zones Map of the Heartland

Average Number of Days per Year Above 86 °F (30 °C)

< 1	1
1 to 7	2
> 7 to 14	3
> 14 to 30	4
> 30 to 45	5
> 45 to 60	6
> 50 to 90	7
> 90 to 120	8

AMERICAN HORTICULTURAL SOCIETY
7931 East Boulevard Drive
Alexandria, VA 22308 U.S.A.
(703) 768-5700   Fax (703) 768-8700

Coordinated by:
Dr. H. Marc Cathey, President Emeritus

Compiled by:
Meteorological Evaluation Services Co., Inc.

Underwriting by:
American Horticultural Society
Goldsmith Seed Company
Horticultural Research Institute of the
American Nursery and Landscape
Association Monrovia
Time Life Inc.

ers. What hybridization does for the seed grower is to give them a monopoly on a particular cultivar. If only they know who the two parents are, then no one else can breed and sell that particular cultivar.

What Are Hybrid Plants?

Hybrids are those plants whose seeds have been developed from the (male) pollen of one plant and the (female) flowers of another variety, to create a "bigger-better-faster-stronger" plant. You can't reliably save and grow seeds of hybrid plants, because the second-year plants will show off the motley collection of genes they inherited. Hybrids are noted in catalogs by the word *hybrid,* the letter *H,* or the term *F1.*

What Are Open-Pollinated Plants?

Open-pollinated plants are old-fashioned or nonhybrid varieties whose seeds you can save from year to year. If you save your own seeds from each year's best plants, you'll end up with a variety that produces well under your own local conditions. There are books available on saving your own seeds. Open-pollinated seeds are sometimes noted in catalogs by the letters *OP.* Open-pollinated seeds are sometimes "heirloom" seeds, meaning they originated before the Second World War (when hybridizing began), or someone's ancestors saved them.

USDA ZONES: WHAT THEY DO AND DON'T MEAN

The USDA hardiness map lays out different areas (zones) of the country according to the minimum winter temperature. Our zone 5 gets as cold as –20 °F. But it doesn't cover summer temperatures. Detroit and Kansas City are both in zone 5, but they obviously have different sorts of summers! When buying perennials, trees, or shrubs, you'll want to buy plants that are listed as being hardy in our winter climates. A shrub hardy in zones 4–9 would be hardy, but an herb hardy in zones 9–11 needs to be brought indoors during the winter lest it die of frost.

What the USDA zone map *doesn't* do is tell you how hot it gets in the summer, what your soil is like, when your average last frost date is in the spring or the average first frost date in the fall, or how much rainfall you get (again, on average).

The American Horticulture Society has put together a new *heat*-zone map (using USDA data). Compared to the USDA zones, this map shows entirely different geographic bands because it's divided according to the average number of 86-degree days (the point at which plants experience heat stress) in an area. I happen to be in heat zone 7, the same as northern Georgia! Plants are being ranked for heat tolerance, but the work is still devoted to ornamental rather than food plants.

Some cultivars are developed to grow in particular climates; an example is the Siberia tomato. Extension offices have lists of recommended vegetable varieties. Most catalogs use a bull's-eye, star, or other logo to point out varieties that do well in most areas of the country.

NARROWING DOWN VARIETIES

Oh dear, catalogs! What a dilemma—you want everything, and everything looks good. It's kind of like going through a buffet line or a cafeteria. Even seasoned gardeners have this problem.

Therefore, I recommend the following money-saving battle plan: (1) assess last year's seed stock to see what you have enough of; (2) choose what you want to grow *before* cracking open the catalogs; (3) stick to your list, allowing yourself only *two or three* fabulous new things that you can't live without!

What do you actually eat? Don't plant

radishes if no one likes radishes! (It's a mystery why children's gardening kits often include radishes; they grow fast, but few children like them.) If there are other gardeners in your neighborhood, do you really need to grow zucchini?

Try something new. Kids will often eat stuff from the garden—maybe chomp on raw asparagus stalks or nibble on chives—that they won't eat on their dinner plates.

Include a couple of herbs. Parsley is not just a garnish; it's packed with vitamins. If you grow tomatoes, grow basil. If you grow beans, grow summer savory. If you like to cook Chinese food, grow garlic, ginger, cilantro, and cayenne pepper.

Evaluate your "real life" schedule. Remember, life never gets simpler—it just keeps changing! Do you have time for spring crops? Will you be around to maintain summer crops? If you'll be in Colorado for two weeks during August, then maybe you should skip the summer squash. Or, find a friend to take care of your garden. Your house-sitter should harvest *every three days*. There's no glory in Hindenburg-sized zucchini, and tomatoes left to rot will make "weed" seedlings next year.

Do include flowers in your garden. There's no civil statute requiring you to segregate your flowers, veggies, and herbs.

FAVORITE VEGETABLE SEED CATALOGS

Good catalogs give you detailed growing instructions, include Latin names as well as common names (sometimes several different flowers have the same common name), suggest the best all-around varieties, tell you which varieties perform best in different climates, and so on.

Avoid catalogs that rely on exaggerated claims rather than figures, don't list Latin names, and don't have an easy way to call back if you have a problem with the merchandise. Likewise, avoid those places that advertise in Sunday newspaper supplements and make outrageous claims.

The companies listed here have proven their quality with years of good service and selection. I've added websites as well as phone numbers. However, a website is not exactly the equivalent of a catalog; you can't curl up with a website in the easy chair, bed, or tub.

Some catalogs have online ordering on their websites. If they have a secure server (there's that little padlock icon on the page), then I feel as comfortable giving them my credit card as I would reciting it to someone over the phone. If neither of these options is comfortable to you, continue to send your check through the mail (and wait longer for your order to be filled).

Websites are also excellent because you can request a paper catalog much more quickly than you can with a postcard. These addresses were current as of this writing, but companies do occasionally change them.

W. Atlee Burpee & Company
300 Park Avenue
Warminster, PA 18991-0001
phone 800-888-1447
www.burpee.com

Garden City Seeds
778 Highway 93 N
Hamilton, MT 59840
phone 406-961-4877
www.gardencityseeds.com
(quick-maturing varieties)

Johnny's Selected Seeds
Foss Hill Road
Albion, ME 04910-9731
www.johnnyseeds.com
phone 207-437-4301
fax 800-437-4290

J. W. Jung Seed Company
335 South High Street
Randolph, WI 53957-0001
phone 800-247-5864
fax 800-692-5864
www.jungseed.com

Nichols Garden Nursery
1190 North Pacific Highway
Albany, OR 97321-4598
www.nicholsgardennursery.com
(large selection of herb plants & seeds)

George W. Park Seed Company
1 Parkton Avenue
Greenwood, SC 29647-0001
phone 800-845-3369
fax 864-941-4206
www.parkseed.com

Pinetree Garden Seeds
Box 300
New Gloucester, ME 04260
phone 207-926-3400
www.superseeds.com
(smaller, cheaper seed packets)

Ronninger's Seed & Potatoes
Company & Greg Anthony's
Seed Company
"Irish Eyes with a Hint of Garlic"
P.O. Box 307
Ellensburg, WA 98926
phone 509-925-6025
fax 800-964-9210
www.irish-eyes.com
(vast selection of potatoes, all sorts of onions and garlic)

Seeds of Change
P.O. Box 15700
Santa Fe, NM 87506-5700
phone 888-762-7333
www.seedsofchange.com
(all open-pollinated, nonhybrid, seeds, organic gardening supplies)

Territorial Seed Company
P.O. Box 157
Cottage Grove, VT 97421-0061
phone 541-942-9547
fax 888-657-3131
www.territorial-seed.com

Tomato Growers Supply Company
P.O. Box 2237
Fort Myers, FL 33902
phone 888-478-7333
fax 888-768-3476
www.tomatogrowers.com
(hundreds of tomatoes and peppers)

Vermont Bean Seed Company
Garden Lane
Fair Haven, VT 05743
phone 888-500-7333
www.vermontbean.com
(lots of bean varieties)

CHAPTER THREE

Seed Starting and Garden Planning

It's like an itch. An urge to plant—*any-thing*—and it usually strikes way before the outdoor planting season begins. Fortunately, we have the resources to scratch these itches. Even better, you *don't* need to spend Big Buckos buying a seed-starting setup or a plant-growing rack of fancy lights. (Although you can if you really, really want to.)

The reasons for seed starting fall into several categories: There's the primal urge to plant *something*, which results in houseplants from avocado pits and compulsive fondling of free "wildflower" seed packets, even though you lack the requisite meadow for transplanting into. There's the frugal urge to grow a few flats of plants because you know you'll get all sweet peppers without any rogue hot ones, for a lot less than you could buy them at a nursery. And there's the sheer need to Grow Your Own because you know you won't find Aunt Ruby's German Green tomato transplants *anywhere*.

All are valid reasons for growing your own plants. Unfortunately, many novice gardeners end up repeating their grade school seed-starting methods with paper cups (or egg cartons) propped up against the windowsill. And then they wonder

why they're not having much success.

The disadvantages are many. The day-lengths during winter and spring are rather short. The light intensity during the winter and spring is low. And the light comes from the side, not above; so unless you turn the plants twice a day, phototropism sets in and they're all leaning sideways. Besides, most of us don't have windowsills of any reasonable size. Builders have realized that windows on the southern and western exposures are the sunniest, and those large windows make higher utility bills during the summer. Newer, more energy-efficient homes have smaller southern and western windows. Alas, builders are rarely gardeners. (Otherwise all that junk wouldn't have been graded up against the house—but that's a soapbox for another day.)

Consider the popular tomato. Tomatoes prefer soil temperatures around 80 °F for germination, followed by 60 °F for growing, with a high intensity of light and 14–16 hours of light per day. Your windowsill, if you're not living in Hawaii, will not provide this.

Well, now what?

SEED-STARTING EQUIPMENT

You need only five things to grow happy, healthy, inexpensive seedlings for your garden: light, air, water, nutrients, and soil. These five things spell out the word LAWNS, a handy acronym.

Light

Contrary to garden magazine advertising, you don't actually need expensive "grow" lights to grow plants and seedlings. For an initial investment of less than $25, you can start your vegetable, herb, and flower seeds. Each year you'll need to buy fresh bulbs and growing medium, and sometimes seeds. The light fixtures and containers just get recycled.

Incandescent lights, the round bulbs we have in our table lamps, are too hot. They also put out neither intense-enough light nor a broad-enough color spectrum. Remember that sunlight exists in the spectrum of colors: Red, Orange, Yellow, Green, Blue, Indigo, and Violet (that old mnemonic, "Roy G. Biv"). Plants look green because the chlorophyll reflects back the yellow and green light rays.

Simple fluorescent lights have the intensity and color spectrum. Those expensive, specially sold grow lights emit more blue and red light. These lights make the plants look prettier, and may help them bloom better (African violet growers swear by 'em), but are not any better for plain ol' seed starting.

Air

Next is air. NASA has learned that many common houseplants purify the air, removing toxins and increasing the oxygen levels. Growing your own transplants is not only cheap, rewarding, and gives you something to do after football season; it is also good for your health. (Smelling baby tomato seedlings is also good aromatherapy!)

Water

When you water your plants, don't drown them in cold tap water. It's best to let your water bucket sit out overnight, which allows the chlorine to evaporate and the water to reach room temperature. A rush of water will drown itty-bitty seedlings, so it's best to water your plants from the bottom until they have sprouted. Do you have a water softener? Check with the service company about which taps are not affected by the salts, or use filtered water.

This all means that you should have bottom trays for your containers. Any water your plants don't take up after the first five minutes should be drained off so you don't drown them. Nice in theory, but how do you do that? Well, I use an old turkey baster to suction off the extra water.

Every seed is alive; it breathes, and waits.

Nutrients

Once your seedlings have their second pair of true leaves (after the baby cotyledons), you'll need to start fertilizing them. Some soil blends have nutrients mixed in; but I prefer to do it myself, so I know when the feeding has been exhausted without waiting until the plant gets so bad that it's showing deficiencies. Instead of giving a full dose once a month or every two weeks (whichever is indicated on the back of the bottle), I prefer to give a half-dose twice as often. This avoids "shocking" the plants with vitamins. I'd rather have three sensible meals a day than have to stuff myself once a day. Wouldn't you, too?

For seed starting, you want to have fairly even NPK numbers, or even slightly higher PK numbers. Nitrogen makes things green and tall, but doesn't help develop the roots and fruits that the phosphorus and potassium do. Here are some of my favorite seedling fertilizers:

Roots Plus for Seedlings
Gardeners Supply Company
128 Intervale Road
Burlington, VT 05401
phone 800-863-1700
e-mail info@gardeners.com
http://www.gardeners.com

Neptune's Harvest
88 Commercial Street
Gloucester, MA 01930
phone 800-259-GROW

Or, you can ask for these products at your local garden center.

Soil

Lots of folks have tried to grow seedlings in garden soil, and have been disappointed. "But garden soil is so rich, dark, and full of nutrients!" they say. So it is. But garden soil has the whole world to help drain away excess water from the clay understructure. Garden soil also has plenty of microorganisms. Most are benign, or beneficial, but some are pathogens and will cause problems like damping-off, mold, or mildew. Ugh.

So we turn to clean seed-starting mixes. Note that I didn't say potting soil. Some potting soils are really great blends of sterile vermiculite, perlite, peat, and compost. Some, like an inexpensive bag I once picked up at a discount store, are nothing but gravily, clayey topsoil. Bummer!

You can buy or make your own seed-starting mix; there are several recipes out there. Here's one:

1/3 vermiculite
1/3 perlite
1/3 milled sphagnum moss

Vermiculite is mica (you may remember mica as the shiny flakes in granite) that has been baked at high heat and "popped" like popcorn. Perlite looks artificial, but is really volcanic ash that's been given much the same treatment. Sphagnum moss is harvested from bogs (*milled* means "ground up").

Interestingly, the moss may have an antibiotic effect to help reduce pathogens in your medium. Unfortunately, it sometimes also has a fungus that bothers some people. Wash your hands thoroughly after handling, or wear gloves, especially if you have any cuts in your skin. It's also not good to breathe in the dry peat dust; a pollen mask helps, or a bandanna. This is especially true if you have asthma or other pulmonary twitches.

If the mining of peat bogs is a concern to you, then consider bricks of *coir*, a substance made from ground-up coconut husks. Coir is great for seed starting, less so for potting soil. The bricks are dry, compressed coir, which need to be rehydrated and will plump up.

Whether your medium is store-bought or homemade, you'll want to wet the soil first (get it damp, but not soggy) before you pack it into pots and add seeds. Some peat blends, such as Pro Mix, tend to be water-resistant, and take a while to soak up water the first time. I crumble mine into a large mixing bowl and pour hot water on it, then let it soak in. If you start out with damp soil, then you also don't have to worry about washing your seeds out of their proper positions.

CONTAINERS

Resourceful and frugal gardeners have used almost every conceivable sort of container to grow transplants (including

APS unit

old shoes). Each has its benefits and drawbacks. After trying out a variety of containers, I've found my favorites to be APS units, the basic commercial flat of a tray with a dozen six-packs, and four-inch-square pots for growing larger transplants.

What is an APS unit? "Accelerated Propagation System" is one name for a variety of commercial products. Gardener's Supply sold them initially, and copycat versions are available at many garden centers now. Developed in the United Kingdom (where gardening is very popular), it's a nearly complete seed-starting setup.

The kit contains a bottom water reservoir; a stand that perches above the reservoir and holds up the tray; a wicking mat that drapes into the reservoir to bring water up underneath the tray; the bottomless tray of 40, 24, or 6 cells; and a clear lid to hold in moisture until the seedlings have sprouted. The unit is built

of polystyrene to conserve heat, and all the pieces cleverly nest together for storage. When it's time to remove the seedlings, you take the cell tray off the wicking mat, invert the stand, and set the cell tray onto the stand. The piers of the stand pop the transplants out of the tray! The unit is self-watering, so you can take a weekend trip without your baby seedlings keeling over.

Of course, nothing's perfect and even APS units have drawbacks: they're expensive initially; seedlings left too long in the cells will have roots that grow into the wicking mat; and the polystyrene is hard to wash clean without crumbling.

I am not impressed with peat pots and compressed peat pellets (Jiffy is one brand). Both dry out easily. The peat pellets are hard to label. Peat pots must be buried entirely into the ground, or else the resultant pot sticking above the soil level will wick away moisture and the plant will die in just a day's time. (Some

Cruciferous (cole crop) seedlings all look the same, so be sure to label them!

people tear off the extra bit on top.) I've also found that roots do not always grow out of these two forms of pots as well as they should, stunting the plants.

Don't confuse thick-walled fiber pots with peat pots. Peat pots are made of thin material, no thicker than the sheet of cardboard on the back of a legal pad. Fiber pots are one-quarter-inch thick, and plant roots will not break through. Fiber pots are fine for growing in, but you must remove the plant before transplanting.

Whatever container you select, it should have several qualities. It needs a drainage hole at the bottom so the seedlings won't get waterlogged and die. It also needs to be *clean*. As in, completely washed out and rinsed in a 10 percent bleach solution to kill any pathogens (like the dreaded damping-off fungus). Ten-percent solution means 1

cup of bleach with 9 cups of water. Also, don't recycle containers that have had inedible substances in them, such as herbicides, poisons, motor oil, and so on. Another tip: When washing out old pots, be sure to brush out all the extra peat medium before washing them in the sink. It's cheaper for you to learn this from me than from the person you call to unclog the drain!

A very important tip is to *label* everything that you plant seeds for. You can buy plastic or wooden labels; or many people cut their own from cottage cheese tubs, recycle old miniblinds, and so on. Hot pepper seedlings are identical to sweet pepper seedlings, and even the cabbage and broccoli transplants look the same for quite a while! If all the seedlings in a single six-pack are the same, one label for the six-pack is sufficient.

Benefits and Drawbacks of Various Containers

Container	Benefits	Drawbacks
Aluminum loaf pan	Reusable, large, reflects light, markable	Too large for small seedlings
APS units	Self-watering, space efficient, retains heat, reusable	Expensive, hard to wash
Clay pots	Picturesque, reusable	Dry out quickly, expensive, fragile, waste space
Dairy cartons (yogurt, cottage cheese, etc.)	Free, reusable, markable, good give-away pot	Not space efficient
Egg cartons	Free	Dry out too quickly, cells too small, single use (paper type, get soggy
Greenhouse flats (plastic tray and six-packs)	Reusable, can grow multitudes, inexpensive, come in different sizes	Hard to recycle
Jiffy pellets	Transplant whole ball	Single use, dry out easily, hard to label, small root ball
Peat pots	Transplant whole pot	Single use, dry out quickly, can wick away moisture and dry out in the ground
Quart paper milk carton	Space efficient, free	Single usage, gets soggy

SHELVES AND LIGHTING SETUPS

In real life, many of us don't have the perfect place to set up light fixtures. So we end up rigging up a variety of shelving units or hanging the lights around the house. Fortunately, the average Midwestern poured-concrete basement is about 60 to 65 °F, and that's just perfect for growing seedlings! (Hang up one of those cute Lucite thermometers if you're unsure.)

You will probably want a timer to turn your light on and off. I'm assuming you have better things to do than to run downstairs at 6 A.M. and plug them in and then run downstairs at 9 P.M. and unplug them. Set the timer to be on for 14–16 hours a day, which is the length of a summer's day. If you have several light fixtures, plug them into a power strip, and then plug the power strip into the timer.

You will need to keep the lights *no more than* four inches above the tops of your seedlings. If you've ever had plants that were tall, scrawny, guys, they were the results of insufficient light. Fluorescent bulbs are a "cool" light, and they won't burn your plants.

Lights Hanging from the Ceiling

In my basement there's a long workbench with my stacks of pots and the bale of Pro Mix underneath, and six shop lights hanging above. I hammered short nails with large heads (roofing nails that happened to be in my tool box) into the floor joists/ceiling rafters, and suspended chains from them. I can raise and lower the chains and lights as the plants grow.

Most brands of shop lights come with S-hooks and a chain. But for some silly reason, they think we're hanging our lights at the ceiling! Buy extra chain (the same light weight as what's included, like chain for a very small dog) so they'll hang down two to four inches from the tops of your seedlings. You'll also need to get some extra S-hooks, and use your pliers to cinch them mostly shut after you've hooked them to the fixture and the chain. Don't forget a pair of moderately priced wire snips for cutting said chain; you'll need them for cutting wire for trellises later in the summer anyway.

Of course, not everyone has a workbench handily built downstairs, or even a basement! If you don't want to hang lights under your kitchen cabinets, then you might want to get some shelves for growing your seedlings. And likewise, gardeners have developed various methods for shelving, depending on their skill and money levels.

Lights with Metal Shelving

The cheapest way to go is to get a plain, gunmetal gray utility shelving unit (some come in decorator colors like country blue and mauve). Assemble said shelving unit. Watch your fingers! Arrange the shelves so that one has a short space above it, one has a medium space above it, and another has a larger space above it, for short, medium, and tall plants.

On top of the fluorescent light fixture (near each end) are the holes where the original S-hooks loop through. Put an S-hook in through a pair of holes on each end of the light fixture. Squinch the bottom half of each hook shut with a pair of needle-nose pliers, just closed enough so the hooks don't keep falling out.

Next, attach a piece of chain (likewise included in the original kit, or you may need some extra chain of similar weight). Hook the *middle* of the chain onto the top half of each of the S-hooks attached to the light fixture. Do this to both ends.

Set the lamp onto the shelf (no plants should be on the shelf yet!). Drape four extra S-hooks from the each of the four vertical posts, from the underside of the shelf above. Mind you, the hooks should be on the *inside* of the angled vertical posts. Hook the ends of the chains onto the four S-hooks. Now your light fixture is hanging. You connect that stubby built-in plug into an extension cord.

Rotate the fluorescent tubes back into the correct "on" position (they invariably jiggle loose), or screw them into the fixture now if you've not done so already. Tip: If the bulbs are in and the fixture is plugged in, but there's no light, you may need to turn or rotate the bulbs until they're properly seated into the ballasts. There's a feels-right point and they hum and blink on when you've done it correctly. Failing that, check the timer setting.

Then, of course, you'll need to move your seedlings around as they "graduate" from one shelf to the next. The key is to keep the lights two to four inches above the tops of the plants. Another tip is to use aluminum foil on the shelves themselves and behind/on the sides for greater light reflection. Of course, you can set the shelves in front of a window for a little supplementary lighting.

Some Safety Considerations

A word of caution—the cheaper shop lights work fine for lighting, but they can have sharp corners on them. You might want to put some masking tape or duct tape there.

Another safety tip: Buy a smoke alarm, because after you plug all of your fixtures into a heavy-duty extension cord and/or power strip, and the power strip into the timer into the wall—well, it's sufficiently safe, but the sort of jerry-built thing that makes your local firefighter wince. Be sure to get a timer that takes a three-pronged plug, which all these fixtures use. "Adapters" are not safe.

SEED-STARTING SCHEDULES

Once you have the seeds, the lights, the pots, and the soil, it's time to get busy. You will need to know your last frost date. This time is not a set day, but rather a period of time when the last killing frost will occur. One of the most challenging things about gardening is the way the frost date waffles around. Here in the Heartland, it can be perfectly pleasant, warm, and sunny for two or even three weeks, and then there's a blizzard, just to keep you on your toes!

For absolute reliability (for instance, you're planting out a few really tender seedlings like basil), use the latest date. For hardier crops (kale and cabbage come to mind), you can plant at the earlier frost date, or even before, and use frost-protection devices (more on those in the next chapter.) When we talk about "*X* weeks before the frost date," I usually figure the middle of that four-week range.

If you live north or south of zone 5, you'll need to adjust your timetable accordingly (two weeks later in zone 4; two weeks earlier in zone 6). Our last frost date here in this part of zone 5 is sometime between April 15 and May 5. Figuring with the April 15 date, and using frost-protection devices, we have these schedules for vegetables:

8–10 weeks (early to mid-February) artichokes, eggplant, onions, peppers, tomatoes

6–8 weeks (mid-February to early March) broccoli, brussels sprouts, cabbage, cauliflower, kohlrabi, okra, parsley
4 weeks (mid-March) chard, Chinese cabbage, collards, kale, lettuce, spinach
2 weeks (end of March) cucumber, melon, pumpkin, squash, watermelon (many people just seed these directly outdoors)

Fill your containers with damp medium, put one or two seeds in each spot (just barely covered—don't *bury* them!), keep them someplace warm, and set the fluorescent lights two to four inches above the surface. Or conversely, keep the pot tops two to four inches below the lights. Once the plants sprout, keep moving the lights or the pots to maintain this distance and keep the plants from getting leggy. *Leggy* means that the stems are all stretched out of proportion, with long internodes between leaves or branches.

Tomatoes, peppers, and eggplants all need warmer conditions for sprouting than they do for growing. Although seedlings grow best at 60–70 °F, they sprout much quicker at 70–80 °F! Catalogs sell special seedling heating mats and cables to provide this warmth. There may be other places to find warmth. Most new refrigerators are too well insulated to provide much top heat, but older ones are often warm on top. There's always the TV, unless your honey just spent a fortune on one and would do something irrevocable to you, your seedlings, or your relationship! I've even set the pots on a stool above the bathroom heat vent, with a clear Lucite thermometer atop the pots to gauge temperature. It worked, but Andy was happier when I got a heating mat for them and quit parking the peppers and tomatoes by the shower. Once the seeds have sprouted their cotyledons (baby leaves), you can remove the heat source.

Cats and small children can be a problem, too, so think twice about where you leave pots of soft soil!

You can't make the plants grow; they grow of themselves.

HOW LONG DOES IT TAKE SEEDS TO SPROUT?

Some seeds are really enthusiastic and pop up in just four days, bless 'em. Others, like our night-owl children, are slow to awaken and get going.

Alliums: Leeks, Onions, Scallions, and Shallots—Because these grow into bulbs, they are monocots and have just one stringy seed leaf, not two. They take 7–14 days to sprout. When the seedlings are four inches tall, give them a haircut and cut them back to just two inches tall. This turns the seedling's attentions to growing a bulb instead of longer and longer "hair."

Artichokes—These large seeds are real sleepyheads and can take up to 20–30 days.

Beans, Corn, and Peas—These are rarely grown as transplants, but are seeded right out in the garden (direct-seeded). They normally take 6–10 days to sprout. If it's been really dry, then I soak the seeds in a bowl of tepid water overnight and then *very carefully* seed the tender things out in the garden. You'll see some runts or broken seeds that didn't do anything, and you can dispose of them without even planting.

Cole Crops: Broccoli, Brussels Sprouts, Cabbage, Cauliflower, and Kohlrabi—These dudes don't need any coddling, and will be up in 5–10 days. Be sure to label them; the cotyledons all look the same! Chinese cabbages are even quicker, showing up in 3–5 days.

Cucurbits: Cucumbers, Melons, Pumpkins, and Squashes—These seedlings are not fond of being transplanted, and they are usually direct-seeded. However, in areas with short growing seasons, that extra two or three weeks can make a difference, and people will grow them as transplants. I prefer the smooth plastic of a one-quart milk jug, cut down to half its height and lined with a paper towel. Two or three weeks after sprouting, gently slide the transplant out into warm soil. Warm soil temperatures (in the eighties) really make the seeds pop quicker.

Eggplants, Peppers, and Tomatoes—These all need heat to germinate happily. In 60-degree temperatures I've seen peppers take three weeks to sprout, but only one week at 80-degree soil temperatures. The same applies for eggplants and tomatoes. Once sprouted, they'll grow just fine—and even better, make nice stocky plants—at cooler temperatures (65 to 75 °F).

Greens: Chard, Collards, Kale, Lettuces, and Spinach—These sprouts appear promptly in 3–10 days. Lettuce and spinach transplants always look wimpy, but don't worry.

Okra—This vegetable is easily grown from seeds (although the lazy things take 6–17 days). They're intolerant of cold, so harden the seedlings off gently, and don't transplant until a week or two after your last frost. Okra also needs warm soil to sprout faster.

ADVANCED SEEDLING CARE: PRICKING OUT AND REPOTTING

Some folks like to sprout their seeds in a communal tray, and then after they've sprouted, transplant them into individual pots. This technique is called "pricking out." It's especially useful for seeds that have a naturally low germination rate, are slow to sprout, or are slow to grow.

Normally, though, you'll want to remove the seedlings as soon as you can see buds for the first pair of leaves. Waiting any longer will result in a long, thin taproot that's too easily broken.

Be sure to water the seedlings a few hours beforehand, so the medium is moist enough to stick together but isn't sodden. Have a pot all ready to go, with a large hole in the center that doesn't reach to the bottom. Despite owning all the tools in the world, I usually use a finger to poke the holes. Gardeners use a variety of instruments for plucking the little seedlings and their root balls, anything from special transplanting tools (long, concave metal tongue-depressor shapes), pencils, chopsticks, or my favorite, an old butter knife. This requires a delicate touch until you've acquired the trick, and then after you've done a few dozen you'll get rather nonchalant.

Try to avoid bending, pulling, stretching, tearing, snapping, or breaking the roots of seedlings when you pluck them out and pop them into individual pots. Keep as much medium as possible around the stringy little root ball. What you can't see well without a magnifying lens are the even tinier feeder roots that do all the work.

Firm the transplants in without squashing; I use the pads of my fingers, rather than the fingertips. I've found that most veggies can be planted a little deeper, up to the "armpits" of the cotyledons. This is especially useful for tomatoes (which will root along the stem) and for cole crops (cabbage is notorious for developing a giant head on a spindly stem).

The *most important* thing to remember is to hold or steady the seedling by its leaf. It can always grow another leaf, but if the stem gets broken or crushed, it's done for (and that's really annoying on those buck-apiece seeds!).

WHEN DO YOU *NOT* START THINGS FROM TRANSPLANTS?

Root crops like carrots, radishes, and beets should usually be sown directly into the ground. They don't transplant well. Cucurbit crops (cucumbers, melons, squashes, and pumpkins of all kinds) are just picky. They simply don't make peat pellets or peat pots in the pint size that's needed for a two- to three-week-old transplant.

HARDENING OFF

Well, it's a few weeks down the road, and you've been nurturing these pups all the way from birth to infancy. You've watched the winter-spring-winter-summer-winter-spring nonsense with anxiety. It's finally warm enough, the garden centers and groceries are bursting with plants, and so are your lighted shelves downstairs. It's finally time to take them outside and plant them.

Wait patiently. Wait impatiently. Wait you must.

Not! Where have your plants been living? In a generally breezeless place of constant temperatures, and lit sufficiently but without ultraviolet radiation. In other words, they've been in a household version of the space shuttle, and have never experienced weather! Take them outside, plonk them down in the wind and full sunlight, and I guarantee that they'll be wind-whipped and sunburned (a purply-white condition). I go through quite a bit of SPF 45 getting used to the spring sunshine, and your plants need help, too.

Of course, you can't slather gluey SPF

Harden off plants for two weeks before transplanting.

on your plants. Instead, take them "out for a walk." I set my seedling trays of pots into boxes or old laundry baskets ('cause my seed-growing space is down in the basement, and heaven forbid I should dribble damp medium in a trail to the back door!). This not only makes the lugging easier but also provides a much-needed windbreak. Then I set the box in

Lettuces pout when transplanted. Children pout when made to walk three blocks to school. Give them food and drink, put on their jackets, tell them you love them, and nudge them out the door.

a semi-shaded location, out of the wind (a northern or eastern location against the house, for instance). They're only out there for an hour, and then they come inside back under the lights, where they start building stronger stems, darker leaves, and other coping mechanisms.

The next day, presuming it isn't pouring, hailing, or other Heartland weather abominations, I take them out again, for a little bit longer. Over two weeks' time, you can gradually increase the exposure to life in the real world. Don't be in a hurry to rush wimps like basil, peppers, and eggplants out of doors! Transplant them after the last expected frost date.

For hardier plants like pansies and cabbages, I harden them off for only a few days, then lay a piece of Reemay or other brand of spun-bonded polyester over them for added protection. These vegetables are planted **a month before the last date in your frost range**.

ASEXUAL PROPAGATION

Essentially what we're doing here is cloning, not from the DNA or cellular level, but from chunks of plants. This goes faster than by seed, and for a few plants, it's the *only* way to make more that have any resemblance to the original plant. For example, you'll get French tarragon only by cuttings; the tarragon seeds sold are the dreaded, tasteless, and invasive Russian variety. (I had one of these once, and had to prune it back hard, expose most of the roots that eventually ran annoyingly under a stone wall, and let it *winter kill*. Worse yet, it reseeded everywhere, and had no flavor. So watch out!)

Other kinds of plants are so promiscuous that you would have to hand-pollinate to get anything close to ideal seeds, and sometimes not even then! Potatoes are a good example. That's why although the plants flower, we don't collect flower seeds, but use eye-chips or small tubers for "seed." I save my golf-ball-sized tubers and use them whole for seed. I also plant them 4 to 6 inches deep, in the late fall, figuring that plants are smarter than I, and they'll come up when it's time. Which they do, and then I know I can plant my peas. The reason I use whole taters instead of pieces cut off is that they *don't* rot from cold and *don't* need antifungal powders and other nonsense. Now the catalog world has caught onto the idea of "mini-tubers" and is starting to sell them, too.

Cuttings are usually taken from stems and leaves or sometimes roots. Select stems of soft, younger growth, and make a clean cut after the third leaf branching. Never break or tear cuttings; always cut with a sharp knife.

Dip in rooting hormone, knock off the excess, and press the stem 2 to 3 inches deep into seed-starting medium—and press firmly. Keep the medium moist, but not soggy. Cuttings can take up to four weeks to root. If you see any sign of mold or fungus, trash the plants and their medium immediately.

Willow water is an old-fashioned ingredient that contains the same plant hormone as the synthetics. Get a handful of any type of willow twigs and chop into pieces an inch long. Make a sun tea of the pieces, soaking them for two days in water a few inches deep, and then remove the twigs. You can use the willow water for watering flats of cuttings.

Some people prefer to root cuttings in a greenhouse made from an inverted canning jar, or a 2-liter soda bottle. Cut the top of the bottle off at the "shoulders." These miniature greenhouses provide constant humidity that makes it easier on the cuttings.

The following plants are suitable for taking stem cuttings: bay laurel, French tarragon, lavender, rosemary, sage, scented geranium, tomatoes (no rooting hormone necessary), and winter savory.

DIVIDE TO MULTIPLY

When your herb plants get large after several years' growth, you can divide them. You will need a shovel (freshly sharpened on the inside curve), a sharp gardening knife, and a good pair of gloves.

Be sure to select where you want the new plants to go *before* you start cutting everything up. It also helps if you've already dug the hole, so the divisions don't have time to dry out in the hot sun. Keep the hose ready for soaking them into their new locations. Also keep several sections of newspaper on hand, in case you discover that you have too many, and need to pawn off—um, give them to your friends and neighbors.

Divide spring- and early-summer-blooming perennials in the autumn. Divide late-summer-blooming and autumn-blooming perennials in the spring. In other words, in their "off" season. It's

GET RED, RIPE TOMATOES IN MAY!

Most years I pick my first ripe, red tomato out in the garden the last week of May. Other gardeners in my city feel they're doing great if they pick fruits by the Fourth of July. Getting early ripe tomatoes is a hobby of mine, and I've compared different early types for production and flavor.

How can you achieve this? You need just two things: a quick-maturing variety of tomato, and an earlier start in your transplant growing.

I start my tomatoes indoors under lights in mid-February. Long-term transplants like tomatoes will need to be potted up before it's time to set them outside. This means that by the time the plant gets its second pair of true leaves, move it from the 2-by-2-inch container into a pot 4 inches wide. Pinch off the baby leaves (cotyledons) and plant your tomato lower, up to the armpits of its first pair of real leaves. Don't pot it up in topsoil, but continue to use the seed-starting medium because it is free from disease and easier for the roots to grow in. Tomatoes will grow roots along their buried stems.

Three weeks later, pot up the tomato into a quart-sized pot, once again pinching off the bottom pair of leaves and transplanting it up to the armpits of the next pair of leaves. Feed with an organic liquid fertilizer at half strength, twice as frequently. I start feeding as soon as three true leaves are visible in the growing point; otherwise, you get that purple haze on the undersides from insufficient phosphorus.

Outdoors, I plant in a raised bed that's been sun-warmed to 70 °F (a soil thermometer can tell you if the soil is warm enough). I dig a nice foot-deep hole, and guarantee sufficient ground moisture by dumping in a bucket of warm water. Then the bottom leaves are once again pinched off (third time), and the plant goes into the ground. I now have a tomato plant with a quart-sized root ball that is 10–12 inches deep, assuring that the plant will be drought- and wind-hardy. Don't fertilize yet. You don't want lots of vine production; you want fruits.

Last, of course, comes the Wall O' Water to protect them from late-April snow or frost. Wall O' Waters are water-filled vertical tubes in a moat around the plant. They absorb solar energy during the day, and give it off at night. I've even had them protect plants from freak late-spring snows.

To fill a Wall O' Water *easily*, invert a bucket over the young plant, to protect it from squishing, and hold up the empty Wall O' Water. Fill the tubes alternately, not sequentially, or it will get heavy on one side and flop over to splash all over your shoes!

My favorite early and tasty tomato cultivars are Matina, Prairie Fire, Stupice (Stoo-PEACH-ka; it's from Czechoslovakia), and Jaune Negib (a yellow one).

Pinch off the cotyledons (baby leaves) and transplant the tomato deeper. It will root along the buried stem.

Invert a bucket over the tomato, slip on the Wall O' Water, and fill tubes alternately, not sequentially.

Early tomato plant after first transplanting.

Wall O' Water in snow.

Pot of leaf lettuce and spinach.

that simple. Most herbs can be moved in the spring or the fall.

Start digging several inches away from the clump. Each root chunk should have stems/leaves growing from it. Replant at same depth. The following plants are suitable for dividing: chives, horehound, horseradish, lemon balm, lemongrass, mints, *Monarda didyma* (bee balm), roman chamomile, and thyme. Any horseradish root left behind will regrow, whether you want it to or not!

OUT-OF-GROUND EXPERIENCES: CONTAINER GROWING

All but the very largest of vegetables can be happily grown in containers. Asparagus root systems are way too large, sunroots are way too tall, and it's hard to get a good sweet-corn crop even in a barrel. But roll out the (tater) barrel, and let's

have a barrel of fun!

Top tips for containers: Think big. Think bigger! The larger the container, the happier the plants will be. There's more room for the roots, the pots will dry out slower, and you can get a larger harvest. Five-gallon pots are useful for growing larger plants. Half-whiskey barrels work too, and you can seed in small plants like lettuces and radishes around the perimeter of the larger plants in the center. Harvest the perimeter veggies as the center plants grow and need more space.

Some people find that really large containers can get too heavy on balconies. You can crush foam packing peanuts and mix them in the bottom half to lighten the load, but watch out for those biodegradable kind that dissolve in water!

Any sort of seed-starting medium

Good Cultivars for Growing in Containers

Good Cultivars		Number of Plants and Pot Size
Beans	Any bush types	Plant 4 inches apart.
Beets, Radishes	Any types	Thin seedlings to 4 inches apart.
Broccoli	Any type	One plant per 12-inch pot
Cabbage	Any quick-maturing type	One plant per 12-inch pot
Carrots	Any type; be sure that container is 3 inches deeper than expected size of roots	Thin seedlings to 4 inches apart.
Cauliflower	Any type	One plant per 12-inch pot
Cucumber	Any bush type, such as Spacemaster, Salad bush, or Bush Crop	One plant per 5-gallon pot
Eggplant	Any type	One plant per 12-inch pot
Kale, Lettuces, Spinach	Any type	Plant or thin to 4 inches apart.
Melon	Any bush type such as Minnesota Midget, Sweet 'n' Early cantaloupes, or Garden Baby watermelon	One plant per 5-gallon pot
Okra	Any of the shorter types, such as Burgundy or Clemson Spineless	One plant per 5-gallon pot
Onions	Any type, especially scallions	Thin or transplant scallions 2 inches apart; bulbing onions to 5 inches apart.
Peas	Any short types, such as Novella, Little Marvel, Sugar Bon, or Maestro	Seed 2 inches apart.
Peppers	Any types, use wire 3-ring "tomato" cage for support	One plant per 5-gallon pot
Potatoes	Any types	Seed small taters 6 inches apart; best done in a barrel; keep adding soil and/or straw as the vines lengthen.
Squash	Any bush type such as Spacemiser Zucchini, Gold Rush yellow zucchini, Starship Pattypan, or Table King Acorn Squash	One plant per 5-gallon pot
Tomatoes	Any bush type, such as Martino's Roma, Green Grape, Rutgers, Bush Beefsteak, or Prairie Fire	One plant per 5-gallon pot

makes a fine base for growing in containers. But with such a high peat content, once the "soil" dries out, it's *really* dry, and then the plants are *really* dead. Plus, it doesn't have any nutrients. A good solution is to use equal amounts of sterilized (or purchased) compost and peat or coir mix. The organic matter of the compost makes a good binder and holds onto moisture, and it adds some nutrients. How do you sterilize homemade compost? Preheat your oven to 275 °F, spread compost in a shallow baking pan (like a lasagna-baking dish), and bake for half an hour. However, it *really smells*. Hence the popularity of purchased mixes.

Some people prefer just to buy potting soil. Unfortunately, there's a wide variety of stuff out there labeled as such, and some of it's dreadful. Read the content label and feel the bag; don't go paying for gravel or clay!

There's no way around it; container gardens need supplementary fertilizer. Once again, I prefer the half-strength, twice-as-often approach. If your containers get a white buildup on the surface and pot rim, it's caused by chemical salts from fertilizers. Select liquid organic fertilizers to prevent this problem. Feed when the transplants begin new growth, and when plants begin flowering.

Herbs of all types can be grown in containers, and tender perennials such as rosemary and bay laurel must be. You can mix salad crops and herbs together for an attractive, edible display.

HEY, ARE THESE SEEDS STILL ANY GOOD?

Here's a common dilemma: While cleaning up after Christmas, you find *lots* of old seeds. Some are from a few years back. Some aren't even opened! Are they still good?

Yes, they probably are! Only onion, parsley, and parsnip seeds lose vigor in just a year's time. Here's an age-old useful tip: Place ten seeds of one kind in a row across a damp paper towel, roll it up, and stick it in a baggie atop your television or refrigerator. After 7–14 days, see how many have sprouted (germinated). The count is your "percent germination rate." Depending on the variety, anything less than 60–70 percent isn't too spiffy. Of course, then you have those sprouted seeds. . . . If it's too early to start them, just chuck them into the trash before you start agonizing over heavy moral questions!

We'll discuss more about saving and storing seeds in Chapter Ten.

PLANNING YOUR GARDEN LAYOUT

The urge to go out and get planting gets so strong that often we spend an exhausted two days plonking plants and seeds into the ground until we're cross-eyed and brain-dead. Unfortunately, this can lead to those fatal gardening errors.

You don't notice it at first, but after a couple of months, you realize that the once-sweet garden has turned into an impenetrable jungle of plants, and you can hardly get in to weed and harvest. Apathy sets in, and *another one bites the dust (boom-boom!)*.

Smart gardeners plan their layout according to what they want to grow and how much room they have. Or rather, how much room there is, and what you can fit in. If you don't know how much room there is, then grab a big tape measure and measure it! Remember, the space has to be in full sun, all summer long. Don't plan to grow veggies anywhere near a tree, especially those rude Black Walnuts, which emit hostile juglone from their roots.

After you know how much room you have, decide precisely what you want to grow, and how much of it. Unless you're

The old-fashioned row method requires four times as much water, weeding, and tilling.

on the northern edge of the Midwest, where the frost-free season is short, a half-dozen tomato plants is really quite enough for the average family. Unless you're putting up a barrel of sauerkraut, you probably don't need 30 cabbage plants to produce all at once! If you're not putting up, then you really don't need large quantities of anything at all.

Okay, given a fixed amount of space, and a general idea of how much produce you want to achieve, the next step is to determine the amount of space each one requires.

Over the centuries, several methods have evolved for spacing crops in home and truck-farm gardens.

Traditional Row Planting

There's the row method traditional to twentieth-century America, the "Victory garden" style of plowing up half the backyard and planting everything in long, straight rows spaced 2 to 3 feet apart. Modeled after farming, the row method allowed for the use of a tractor to rototill and plow. As mentioned before, it's not the most efficient method. A newer twist on row planting is wide-row planting, where a double or triple row of plants is seeded in a wider, long block. For people who want to maximize production and minimize work but are still attached to their tillers, this is an excellent method. Either way, the plants are still spaced at the same distances.

Intensive Planting

In the back-to-the-earth movement of the 1970s, we were willing to try all sorts of novel things, and quite a few people grew most of their own food and put up large amounts for the rest of the year. But lacking large machinery or a village to help, the wonders of the "French Intensive" method quickly became apparent.

These same space-efficient methods are also used in only slightly different form by Asian truck farmers and home gardeners. Instead of planting in rows with plants spaced *x* inches apart, the plants are spaced on a hexagonal grid (alternating rows) in a raised bed to maximize production.

Square-Foot Planting

A retired engineer named Mel Bartholomew also noted the inherent problems of row gardening, especially in community garden situations. In the early 1980s he published his book *Square Foot Gardening*, which detailed a likewise space-efficient method, but with a square grid overlaid on the garden to provide structure for spacing and prevent overplanting. Doubtless "Square-Foot Mel" has saved many a home gardener from hours of frustration.

If you look on a package of carrot seeds, you'll note that it says to "thin to 3 inches apart." This implies seeding a row (often using the entire contents of the seed package) and then ripping out the extra plants that sprouted until the remaining ones are 3 inches apart. I don't know a soul who enjoys ripping out perfectly happy plants that they've just managed to sprout! It's a real waste of seed and time. Instead, you can just plant a couple seeds every three inches.

So which method should you use? Well, one thing I noticed after lots of research is that each kind of plant needs a certain amount of room (be it 3 inches, 12 inches or 4 feet). It doesn't matter whether you're planting in one long row, in a hexagonal grid, or in a square grid. Plants need a consistent amount of room to grow well, and they need it from the very beginning.

Over the years I've used a combination of intensive and square-foot gardening. I have long, large raised beds rather than Mel's absolute 4-foot-by-4-foot

beds. Sometimes a whole bed is filled with just potatoes or tomatoes, and sometimes it's a collection of different plants going in and coming out.

So regardless of which geometry you prefer, here's the necessary spacing:

3 inches apart, or 16 per square foot
- Root crops: beets, carrots, radishes
- Alliums: garlic, leeks, onions, scallions, shallots
- Trellised crops: tall-vining peas, pole beans

4 inches apart, or 9 per square foot
- Bush legumes: peas, beans
- Leafy greens: loose-leaf lettuces grown for cut-and-come-again method, but not head lettuces

6 inches apart, or 4 per square foot
- Cole crops: kale, kohlrabi
- Leafy greens: mustard, spinach, Swiss chard

12 inches apart, or 1 per square foot
- Cole crops: broccoli, brussels sprouts, cabbage, cauliflower
- Corn
- Trellised cucumbers
- Eggplant
- Head lettuces
- Peppers
- Potatoes

Gimme space, lots of space!
- Large watermelon and squash vines can easily fill an area 10 feet square. Plant just two or three seeds in the center. Sweet-potato vines also spread over a large area of ground.
- Tomatoes can be caged and spaced 2 to 3 feet apart. Or, let them sprawl and space 5 feet apart.
- "Bush" type melons and squashes can be given an area 4 to 6 feet in diameter.
- Perennials such as asparagus and sun-

roots should have their own permanent patch.

PLAYING AROUND WITH SPACING

All these different spacings can be confusing at first. You draw out a plan, discover a problem or two, and redraw it— oops again, redraw it, and so on. My cat loved garden-planning time because there were lots of pieces of paper floating around!

Some people prefer using a computer to design their bed layout. Others prefer a more hands-on approach. It's easy to make your own garden-layout planning kit with poster board and index-card paper. (Kids really enjoy playing with this!)

On a piece of poster board, sketch your garden beds. Use 1 square foot per square inch, for a smaller garden. You can then cut out pieces of index card in one-foot squares to represent different crops, and "rearrange the furniture" to your heart's delight. The little squares can have the name, a drawing or photo cut from a catalog, and the number to be planted on it.

Sometimes I don't plant just 1 square foot of something. For instance, my potato bed is usually 4 by 6 feet, so I'll have a 4-by-6-inch card for potatoes.

Here are some things to keep in mind:

- Put the tall things along the north side (corn, okra, climbing beans and peas, indeterminate tomatoes) so they don't shade out the other crops.
- Sort plants by growing season. You'll first plant your cool-season crops (beets, broccoli, cabbage, carrots, cauliflower, lettuce, onions, peas, potatoes, radishes, spinach, Swiss chard, and turnips). Then a couple months later you'll plant out your warm-season crops (beans, corn, cowpeas, cucumbers, eggplant, melons of all kinds, mustard, okra, peppers of all kinds, pumpkins, squash, sweet potatoes, and tomatoes).
- Large, sprawling plants like squashes do better in a bed of their own; otherwise, they try to creep into the adjoining crops.
- There are two rules for planning: (1) *Always* plan your garden, and (2) the garden *never* goes exactly according to plan!

MAXIMIZING THE HARVEST: INTERPLANTING AND SUCCESSION PLANTING

Interplanting is planting fast-growing crops (lettuces, radishes) in between slow-growing crops (corn, tomatoes, squash). Native Americans interplanted corn, beans, and squash, which they called the Three Sisters. The pole beans were seeded after the corn was a few inches tall, and climbed up the corn for support and to provide extra nitrogen for them. The squash vines shaded the ground and helped keep down weeds.

Days are perfect for what we have done, not for what we might have done. Planning goes so far; then planting must take over.

Succession planting involves keeping the garden ground employed through the whole frost-free season. Many folks make a great rush in May, planting everything they're going to grow, but leaving ground unused in the early spring and autumn. To be more efficient, when some of your ground comes empty, add some more compost and plant something else in. Not only will you have your enthusiasm refreshed for a new crop, but you won't have old crops attracting pests.

If you have favorite spring crops, you can usually replant them again in the autumn. Be sure to add two weeks onto the maturity time because of the shortening days. For greens and cole crops that are planted in September, I start them as transplants indoors, at the beginning of August. It's just too hot here for direct seeding in August!

Some successions
- March beets by May lima beans
- March broccoli by May corn
- March pak choy by May eggplant
- March cabbage by May zucchini
- March peas by July kale
- March peas by July carrots
- March potatoes by July rutabagas
- March onions or garlic by August lettuce
- April lettuce by June kale
- April lettuce by June carrots
- April bush beans by August spinach
- May bush tomatoes by August beans
- September garlic by (next year's) June baby corn

All right! You have your seeds, your transplants, and your plans; you're all ready and raring to get going. But is it time to plant yet?

CHAPTER FOUR

Moving out of Doors

LABOR PAINS: IS IT TIME YET?

So how *do* you know when it's safe to plant outside? Well, you could follow the "one fell swoop" approach and not plant anything outside until after your last frost day in May or June. But doing that would deprive you of weeks of potential growing season, and limit harvest by depriving you of succession planting.

When determining planting time, you need to take into account several factors: the cold hardiness of the plants, how cold the soil is, what the weather is likely to do, and what you can do to protect plants from the weather. With all these factors, it's no surprise that planting time falls somewhere between an art and a science. But forewarned is forearmed, so off we go!

Some crops do quite fine in cooler (but not freezing) weather. These are discussed in Chapter Five, and include leafy greens, root crops, alliums, peas, and cole crops.

Soil temperature can be measured with a soil/compost thermometer. Cool-season crops will sprout in 50- to 60-degree soil, although they'll certainly sprout much

quicker in 60- to 70-degree soil. If the soil is too cold the seeds just sit there and can even rot. Fungicide-treated seeds are sold (that pink dust), but I prefer to just wait a week or two more before planting.

Trying to predict the weather is always entertaining and frustrating. The accumulated wisdom of previous meteorological history helps us to understand what sort of risks we're taking. As mentioned before, spring is not a gentle, easy transition from cold to cool to warm to hot weather. It's really a roller-coaster ride. Just because you're having balmy, summerlike temperatures one day doesn't mean you can't have more winter weather and frosts ahead of you.

FROST DATES

Frost dates are taken from *Climatography of the U.S. No. 20, Supplement No. 1* published in 1988 by the National Climatic Data Center, National Oceanic and Atmospheric Administration, U.S. Department of Commerce.

Illinois

The following dates are generally the latest in

spring and the earliest in fall your region experiences frost.

City	Spring	Fall
Aledo	5/8	9/25
Cairo	4/6	10/29
Chicago	4/25	10/22
East St. Louis	5/1	10/5
Peoria	5/8	10/6
Rockford	5/13	9/25
Springfield	5/1	10/6
Windsor	5/7	10/7

Indiana

The following dates are generally the latest in spring and the earliest in fall your region experiences frost.

City	Spring	Fall
Evansville	4/23	10/12
Ft. Wayne	5/15	9/25
Gary	5/17	10/2
Indianapolis	5/9	10/7
Muncie	5/15	10/1
Princeton	4/30	10/4
Scottsburg	5/10	10/1

Iowa

The following dates are generally the latest in spring and the earliest in fall your region experiences frost.

City	Spring	Fall
Ames	5/12	9/26
Cedar Rapids	5/13	9/25
Clarinda	5/10	9/24
Davenport	4/25	10/13
Decorah	5/26	9/18
Des Moines	5/9	9/21
Le Mars	5/18	9/17
Mason City	5/20	9/16
Ottumwa	5/3	10/5

Kansas

The following dates are generally the latest in spring and the earliest in fall your region experiences frost.

City	Spring	Fall
Dodge City	5/7	10/11
Goodland	5/16	9/23
Independence	4/26	10/13
Phillipsburg	5/14	9/23
Salina	5/4	10/9
Topeka	5/4	10/1
Wichita	5/1	10/10

Kentucky

The following dates are generally the latest in spring and the earliest in fall your region experiences frost.

City	Spring	Fall
Bowling Green	4/28	10/7
Ford's Ferry	4/15	10/18
Frankfort	5/5	10/10
Lexington	5/3	10/10
Middlesboro	5/15	10/5
Owensboro	4/24	10/5
Paducah	4/18	10/15
Vanceburg	5/14	9/27

Michigan

The following dates are generally the latest in spring and the earliest in fall your region experiences frost.

City	Spring	Fall
Cheboygan	5/30	9/25
Detroit	5/12	10/9
Evart	6/14	8/28
Kalamazoo	5/15	9/29
Lansing	5/31	9/18
Marquette	5/25	10/4
Muskegon	5/24	9/24
Pontiac	5/16	9/29
Sault Ste. Marie	6/10	9/12
Traverse City	6/9	9/17

Minnesota

The following dates are generally the latest in spring and the earliest in fall your region experiences frost.

City	Spring	Fall
Duluth	5/21	9/21

City	Spring	Fall
Minneapolis	4/30	10/13
Willmar	5/4	10/4

Missouri

The following dates are generally the latest in spring and the earliest in fall your region experiences frost.

City	Spring	Fall
Canton	4/27	10/7
Charleston	4/17	10/10
Hannibal	4/19	10/9
Jefferson City	5/13	10/1
Joplin	4/26	10/13
Kansas City	4/30	10/9
Macon	5/3	10/5
Maryville	5/10	9/26
Springfield	5/2	10/8
St. Louis	4/30	10/8

Nebraska

The following dates are generally the latest in spring and the earliest in fall your region experiences frost.

City	Spring	Fall
Ainsworth	5/21	9/24
Falls City	5/3	10/3
Grand Island	5/16	9/26
Lincoln	5/9	9/30
North Platte	5/25	9/10
Omaha	5/12	9/23
Scottsbluff	5/25	9/14
York	5/10	9/30

Ohio

The following dates are generally the latest in spring and the earliest in fall your region experiences frost.

City	Spring	Fall
Akron	5/21	10/2
Athens	5/31	9/19
Cincinnati	4/29	10/13
Cleveland	5/18	10/5
Columbus	5/9	10/3
Dayton	4/27	10/16

City	Spring	Fall
Lima	5/19	9/24
Sandusky	4/29	10/14
Toledo	5/16	9/29
Youngstown	5/24	9/29

South Dakota

The following dates are generally the latest in spring and the earliest in fall your region experiences frost.

City	Spring	Fall
Castlewood	5/30	9/4
Custer	7/3	8/17
Gettysburg	5/23	9/14
Huron	5/27	9/15
Ludlow	6/6	8/31
Mobridge	5/19	9/20
Pierre	6/2	9/8
Rapid City	5/26	9/14
Sioux Falls	5/24	9/17

Wisconsin

The following dates are generally the latest in spring and the earliest in fall your region experiences frost.

City	Spring	Fall
Ashland	6/18	9/6
Eau Claire	5/26	9/15
Green Bay	5/26	9/18
Lacrosse	5/15	9/29
Madison	5/13	9/25
Milwaukee	5/20	9/26
Solon Springs	6/10	9/7
Wausau	5/22	9/6

Microclimates within your yard and neighborhood can have an effect on whether your garden will be hit by frost. The valley bottom and the north side of a hill will be colder. Cold air can also "puddle" above a solid wall on a hill. All these result because cold air sinks. Frost is less likely if there has been rain (this is why citrus growers sprinkle their orchards). Windless nights are also more prone to frost. Urban areas are often warmer than surrounding rural areas because the buildings and pavement retain heat. Bodies of water also retain heat and offer some frost protection. For the best location, pick the south side, halfway down the hill, below wind-catching trees or fences, and preferably all three of these factors if you can.

Wind is an important factor to consider in the choosing of frost protection. A microenvironment that cuts down on or eliminates wind will reduce the stress on the plant and enable the air to warm up more around it. Hay bales can be blocked on three sides around the more tender plants. Snow fencing or specially made wind fencing is also available at hardware and garden centers.

Predicting whether you'll have frost tonight can be tricky. Your local weather forecast can be quite helpful. Lots of gardeners are Weather Channel junkies! But because of local microclimates, your actual overnight lows can be greater or lesser than the forecasted amount.

Normally we worry about killing frosts in the autumn more than in the spring, when we don't have our crops out yet. If you have frost-sensitive seedlings, you can monitor the mid-afternoon dew point. This gives you an approximation of the overnight low temperature *if* there are clear skies and calm wind conditions.

For example, if the afternoon dew-point temperature is 28 °F, and you have a clear sky and light winds that evening, then you can probably expect the overnight/early morning minimum to be around 28 °F. Twenty-eight degrees is an important number; for tender plants, the temperature must be 28 °F or lower for three hours or more before the plant is damaged.

Salads and cole crops can be started indoors as transplants, and then put outside into raised beds (which warm up faster than flat ground) and given some protection. This gains you a month of maturity in just the transplant size alone, and you will have a nearly guaranteed number of plants growing. Generally you can transplant these and seed your root crops and peas a couple weeks before the last frost date or within the first half of the last frost date range, soil willing. Of course, the best time to seed is the day before a rain is predicted. And cloudy days or chance-of-rain days are best for transplanting because of the reduced sun intensity.

I tell my children, "If the soil is like chocolate cake, you can dig. But if it's like Play-Doh, then you must wait." This is because we have clay soil, which warms up slower than sandy soil or loam. And you really don't want to try digging into wet clay, or you'll compress it into bricklike clods.

Another way to warm up the soil earlier (in addition to creating raised beds) is to cover it with heavy, clear plastic a couple weeks before planting time. This also helps the weed seeds germinate earlier, and you can get rid of some of them.

SOME HOMEMADE FROST- AND WIND-PROTECTION DEVICES

Gardeners everywhere have tried a wide variety of materials to protect plants during late, light frosts. All of these work, some better than others.

- Newspaper tents folded atop tender seedlings; weigh edges down with soil to keep them from being blown about.
- Plastic or paper grocery bags (they have to be staked on sticks).
- Straw tent: Make a teepee with branches, wind string around it a few times for stability, and stuff with straw. You can use this method to protect roses and other tender shrubs during the winter. In Minnesota, I've

Eggplants under cold frame.

seen entire rose gardens that are fenced off and filled in with straw. Presumably, all that straw is mixed with spring grass clippings for compost.

- The famous plastic milk jug (with the bottom cut off) is less inclined to blow away if you run a stick through the handle.
- Translucent corrugated fiberglass panels can be bent to form open tunnels, like Quonset huts. Use string or wire to run between the corners of the open ends to stabilize, and set the panel's bottom edges into the earth. The ends can be sealed off.
- Wood shingles may be stuck in the ground between plants to cut down on wind or to provide shade in the summer.
- The English have long used glass tents made from panes of glass. Wire connecting supports were used to hold the panes together in A-frame or barn shapes. Of course, these are fragile,

heavy, and sometimes sharp.

- Cut the bottoms off gallon glass jugs, such as cider jugs, to make your own glass cloches.
- If you have one of those deep, clear plastic umbrellas, stick the bottom half of the handle into the ground, to cover larger plants.

THERMODYNAMIC AND OTHER COLD FRAMES

A cold frame is a bottomless box that's topped with plastic or glass. Unlike greenhouses, cold frames are unheated. Gardeners use them to protect crops that are being overwintered, to grow quick-maturing seedlings, and to have a safe place to park seedlings later in the season.

A cold frame can get pretty toasty on warm spring days, so you'll need to prop the lid open a bit to vent warm air. You can also buy a regulating mechanism that will open the lid for you above certain temperatures.

Thermodynamic cold frame.

A standard cold frame can be constructed like a bottomless box, 9 inches high in the front (southern exposure) and 15 inches high in the back (northern exposure). Here are some things to remember in making a cold frame:

- Use rot-resistant wood—cedar, locust, or redwood—for longer life.
- Avoid using wood containing creosote (as in railroad ties) or "penta" (pentachlorophenol), both of which emit plant-toxic fumes.
- A catch to hold the lid up is essential, especially if it's a heavy glass lid.
- If you decide to paint your cold frame, use a reflective color (such as a gloss white) on the inside.
- You want your cold frame to face south preferably.

In my own garden I use a special type of insulated cold frame to overwinter kale and spinach. With this thermodynamic cold frame, I can harvest fresh greens all the way through the winter, even with cold fronts that drop temperatures down to -24 °F.

The cold frame is built of a 2-inch-thick sheet of polystyrene, which is usually sold in 4-by-8-foot sheets. You will also need a 6-by-6-foot sheet of heavy plastic (garden supply catalogs sell clear greenhouse plastics that are more UV resistant than common plastics). You will also need four clean, empty gallon milk jugs and two 1-by-2-by-4-inch laths. [Note: A *lathe* is the machine for turning table legs, etc.]

Use a pruning saw or a long-bladed serrated knife to cut the sheet of polystyrene into four 2-by-4-foot lengths. Since you can't glue or nail the sheets together, I simply bury them 8 inches deep into the ground. The soil displaced can be used inside the cold frame. To make the clear top slant toward the low-slung winter sun, bury the south wall 10 inches

Reemay for crop protection.

deep and the north wall 7 inches deep.

In late autumn, fill each milk jug with water, leaving the cap off, and set one in each corner. Then transplant kale and spinach into the cold frame. Cross the two laths, and drape the plastic over the top (anchor with bricks, rocks, or more laths). If desired, you can trim the corners, but I decided that a little overlap was more secure.

Check the cold frame every two or three weeks to water as necessary. Brush snow off the top so it doesn't weigh down the plastic. As the days get shorter, the plants quit growing and just hunker down for the winter. You can harvest whenever you want, and come next spring, any remaining plants will start growing right away, providing a harvest for St. Paddy's Day, when other gardeners are still contemplating seeding their spinach.

ANOTHER COVER-UP JOB

A lighter variation on the cold frame is the row cover. Row covers are various fabriclike materials that cut down on wind but allow sun and rain through, providing a protected environment for plants to grow. Sealed in around the edges, they also keep out flying insects, such as the cabbage moth. However, they do not protect plants from pests within the soil! So if you use some of these, don't forget to peek underneath every week for pests and weeds. Most row covers have a heat-retentive quality that gives crops a few degrees of frost protection.

There are three different basic types of floating row covers: polypropylene, polyethylene, and polyester.

- Woven polypropylene is known as Agronet. One brand of spun-bonded polypropylene is called Garden Quilt. This is a 10-mil-thick material used to

Reemay over wire hoops.

cover strawberry beds and garden-stored crops in the winter.

- A type of woven polyethylene is called VisPore; this fabric is used for trapping heat and extending the gardening season.
- The Reemay fabric you may have used to keep bugs off plants is spun-bonded polyester. There are summer-weight types used to keep insects off crops without the heat-retentive qualities.

Of the three, the Garden Quilt material is used for overwintering plants, or you can put a layer of straw on top of Reemay to add insulation.

No matter which fabric you choose, you need to secure it. You can bury the edges in, lay down pipes or timbers along the edges, or staple the material to laths. The last method is the easiest because it allows you to inspect growing crops and harvest mature ones most easily. When covering your beds, be sure there's plenty of drape and "give," so the plants will have room to grow. You can also drape the material over arched pipe, "hardware cloth" fencing, or wire supports.

My favorite catalog sources for cold frames, frost-protection devices, row covers, and row cover supports include

Charley's Greenhouse and Gardening Supplies
17979 State Route 536
Mount Vernon, WA 98273-3269
phone 800-322-4707
fax 800-233-3078
www.charleysgreenhouse.com

Gardener's Supply Company
128 Intervale Road
Burlington, VT 05401
phone 800-864-1700
www.gardeners.com

Peaceful Valley Farm Supply
P.O. Box 2209
Grass Valley, CA 95945
phone 888-784-1722
www.groworganic.com

MULCH, TWO, THREE, FOUR!

Gardens are mulched for several reasons, and your reason determines the mulching material and how you use it:

- Mulch to suppress weeds.
- Mulch to keep the soil cool.
- Mulch to retain soil moisture.
- Mulch to make beds attractive.

And last, but not least:

- Mulch to prevent muddy blossoms.

A wide variety of mulches are used in flower gardens. But we rarely use these in vegetable gardens because we're constantly harvesting and turning over the soil. So the mulch of choice needs to be readily available, preferably free, not harmful to vegetable plants, and organic so it will break down and enrich the soil. Fortunately, grass clippings fulfill all these requirements!

However, using grass-clipping mulch carries a few caveats. Here they are, along with some other tips:

- Be sure not to apply grass-clipping mulch greater than 3 inches deep, or it will mat up and develop that obnoxious ammonia odor. Otherwise, grass clippings dry to a nice straw color and nourish your plants with a gentle amount of nutrients.
- If your lawn is treated with herbicide (weed killer), you must wait for three mowings before using the clippings. This allows the treated portion to grow and be cut off. Otherwise it could poison your plants.
- Do not cover the tops of plants. Three

inches is also enough to suppress the seeds you're trying to grow, so *don't* mulch newly seeded areas!

- For squashes and melons that are grown on the ground and take up great amounts of space, I like to lay down several sheets of newspaper and cover them with 3 inches of grass clippings. Now I don't have to weed that patch!
- Three inches is enough to suppress weeds but not smother the plants. Spread the mulch around the plants, leaving an inch or two of space around the growing base.
- Because mulches help cool the soil, they're great for hot summer droughts. Conversely, don't mulch in the early spring when you want the soil to warm up.

Other good mulches for the vegetable garden are shredded leaves, straw, and hay. Unfortunately, hay contains grain seeds, and they can sprout everywhere after a rain. But grain sprouts in thickly applied hay are usually easy to knock over.

TRELLISING: OH, GROW UP!

Now you know how to protect your plants and reduce weeding. But there are other garden chores you can reduce! By trellising, you're growing all those vines upward, so you use less ground space. This increases your yield per square foot, since only the roots need room. There's also less weeding, especially if you mulch! Monitoring and controlling pests is easier—they're right in front of your face. Harvesting is also easier—no stooping or hunching over. Trellising also means less waste resulting from missed and overripe fruits hiding under the lush growth. Raised beds with trellises are easier for gardeners with disabilities; you can tend and pick from a chair or garden seat.

Raised beds and trellises allow you to maximize garden production in the least space.

Vegetables Suitable for Trellising

Vegetables that grow well on trellises are legumes (pole beans and peas), cucurbits (non-bush cucumbers, gourds, smaller melons, and squashes), and indeterminate tomatoes. What do the words *bush* and *indeterminate* mean? Bush cucumbers and squashes are those with shorter vines, usually only 4 to 6 feet

> *Don't ask the broccoli to climb the trellis; everything has its own journey in life.*

long. Bush types don't need trellising, but the longer sorts often do.

Tomatoes also come in bush types,

also known as *determinate,* which means that they grow shorter and produce a finite number of fruits. Indeterminate plants are the ones that keep on growing and growing until the frost hits them. (Cherry tomatoes are apparently super-indeterminate, and often have visions of world domination.)

The stems and vines of the cucurbits tend to stray, leaning away from the trellis and trying to wander off toward their neighbors. So stop by every couple of days and gently tuck the growing tips back onto the trellis.

But what about melon and squash fruits? Do they really need those panty-hose hammocks? Granted, anything larger than a volleyball should be grown on the ground. But trellising allows all the smaller winter squashes and pumpkins (Jack Be Little, Baby Bear, acorns, buttercups, and such) to "grow up." All but the largest melons can grow on trellises. Many home gardeners are now

Melon growing on "W" trellis.

Bean vine winding onto netting.

growing smaller "icebox" watermelons anyway, and I've had excellent success with those and other sorts of melons on trellises. I've also found that most vines grow strong enough to support the weight of the fruits on them. (An exception was when I walked by one day and a ripe melon fell to my feet, begging, "Eat me! Eat me!" So I did.)

One note: If you are growing melons on a wire trellis, watch out for fruits growing where they can get stuck between the wires. Otherwise you'll have to do your Hercules/Xena impression to bend the wires apart and free the developing fruit!

Not all plants climb trellises the same way. Cucurbits have vines with tendrils (modified leaves). Whenever the tendrils touch something, they wind around it. Beans don't have tendrils, but their stems wind around the trellis. This winding is called thigmotropism.

You know those small, conical metal

wire supports they sell as "tomato cages"? Well, they won't hold anything but tiny "patio" tomato plants. However, they *are* excellent for holding up peppers and eggplants!

BUILDING A TOMATO CAGE

There are as many different ways to build tomato cages as mousetraps, but the simplest method is taking a piece of hog wire or concrete-reinforcing wire. Both of these have the necessary 4-inch-square grid, so you can get your hand in and the fruit out.

For a cage 2 feet in diameter, cut a 6-foot-long piece of wire; for a cage 3 feet in diameter, cut a 9-foot-long piece of wire. Cut the section off the roll so the wire ends are sticking out. After rolling the wire into a tall cylinder, bend those wire ends over to secure the cage. You will also want two metal fence posts or other stakes, put 1 to 2 feet into the ground and

Pepper 'Big Chile' grown in conical wire cage.

Staked tomato ring made of concrete-reinforcing wire (CRW).

secured to the cage. This holds the cage down when the plant is tall, loaded with fruits, and a big summer storm comes through! Cage your plants at planting time; it's really hard to do after the plants get gangly.

You would think that the wire would get hot and burn the plants, but it doesn't. I've grown my tomato plants attached to metal stakes, within metal wire cages and against metal wire fencing. On none of them have I had any problems with stem, leaf, or fruit burn due to the wire. And trust me, Kansas can get pretty dang hot!

TRELLIS-BUILDING SUPPLIES

Resourceful gardeners use everything they can scrounge for trellising material. Some of the better materials are PVC pipe, half-inch electrical conduit pipe (the galvanized stuff is "Square-Foot Mel" Bartholomew's favorite), bamboo, cedar 2-by-2-foot stakes, and any available fences and posts. I've grown Jack Be Little pumpkins on the neighbor's chain-link fence, with the understanding that all the fruits growing on their side belong to them.

What sort of material do you wind or hang on the framework? Several years ago I bought a 50-foot roll of hardware cloth (galvanized 2-by-4-foot fencing) at the lumberyard, and it has been serving me faithfully ever since. (I even had the furniture movers load it onto the truck to my current house!)

You can also buy nylon netting (sold folded in a package or rolled on a tube). I like the nylon netting for growing Super Sugar Snap peas or cucumbers. I leave the nearly indestructible nylon netting on during the winter. This is much easier than trying to untangle the stuff every spring, a practice that made me feel like a fishwife.

Many gardeners are fond of using jute

TOMATOES: STAKE, CAGE, OR SPRAWL?

Tomato vines don't have tendrils but are often grown upward. Tomato growers have debated for decades about whether to stake or cage their plants. But in all fairness, there is no one "right" way, merely different methods to produce different results. It's up to you to decide what your goals are and which method works best for your garden.

On the other hand, I might point out that a University of Missouri study found that staking (pinching off suckers to maintain just one main stem) yielded an average of 8 pounds of fruits per plant, while caging yielded 20 pounds of fruits per plant. If you want to reduce your yield by half, that's your business. The study, "G6370 Fresh Market Tomatoes," can be found at http://muextension.missouri.edu/xplor/agguides/hort/g06370.htm

SPRAWLING is the original and natural method. You tend to lose a few fallen fruits to rot; but this number is low, the method is truly effortless, and the plants don't care. Just be sure to space them about 5 feet apart. You will get a large number of fruits with this method.

STAKING tomatoes requires gardeners to pinch the suckers off their indeterminate plants every week or two, and reduces the number of fruits produced—although the remaining ones are a bit larger. "Pinching off suckers" means to snap off the new branch that's sprouting between the main stem and existing branch. This reduces the plant to one or two main stems for tying to the stake, and prevents tomato jungles. Staking is also good for bush or determinate tomato plants that don't get very large (you don't need or want to pinch suckers on determinate plants). Select stakes that are 7 to 8 feet tall, so 2 feet of their length can go into the ground for storm and weight resistance. Put the stake in the ground at the same time you plant your tomato, so you don't stab the roots. Some gardeners in our hot climate allow two main stems to grow, for some extra foliage to prevent sunscald. Space staked tomatoes 1 to 2 feet apart.

Should you pinch off suckers, or not? I say not, unless you're staking your tomatoes. Photosynthesis is the biochemical engine that

Staking tomatoes requires pinching out suckers and reduces yield by 50 percent.

drives growth. Leaves are needed for the number of chloroplasts that do the photosynthesis. The plants use the nutrients from fertilizer for growth; but without enough chloroplast engines, the plant can't do much! A sufficiency of leaves is needed to run the engines that will produce the tomato fruits. Decreasing the numbers of chloroplasts by pinching off suckers reduces the number of flowers as well as the number of leaves, producing a smaller number of fruits (although the remaining ones will be a bit bigger, just like when thinning tree fruits).

CAGING requires building and storing cages, but the cages last for years. Most gardeners simply leave the cages out in the garden, or off to the edge so we can clean up and then improve the soil. Caging is excellent for indeterminate tomato plants that keep growing larger all summer long. Caging produces the largest number of fruits from a plant.

Cucumber vining on trellis made from netting and electrical conduit.

Sugar snap peas on A-frame trellis.

string wound up and down between two horizontal supports. The handy thing about jute string is that it can go right into your compost pile along with the bean vines. Otherwise bean vines are a pain to strip off of metal or nylon trellises, unless you let them turn dry and brittle before snapping them off.

Situate your trellises along the north side of your garden to prevent shading other plants. Do be sure to have some kind of wind anchorage; sink trellis posts in 24 inches deep, and stake tomato rings.

Ring trellis is used for tomatoes or melons. Clip a 10-by-6-foot or a 10-by-8-foot length of galvanized fencing (with a 4-inch-square grid), and bend prongs over the other end to secure into a ring. Push two stakes 15 to 24 inches deep into the soil on each side and secure. Watch developing melons so they don't get stuck between two wires.

"W" trellis is great for squashes or short peas. Clip a 24-by-24-foot length of galvanized fencing, lay it on the ground, weave a 6-foot electrical conduit pipe or bamboo pole along an end, and again every 6 feet. Bend into a "W" shape, and plunge pole ends into the ground. Or, tie to standard fence posts.

Arch trellis is perfect for tall bean vines or indeterminate cherry tomatoes. Mine arches a pathway between two beds and is 10 feet high (just the right size for those overexuberant Chinese Yard-long beans). Weave 8-foot electrical conduit pipe through hardware cloth at each corner, stand, and push pipe ends 24 inches into the ground. Weave tomato vine tips where *you* want them to grow.

Panel trellis can be used for cucumbers or peas. This a netting hung from a framework. Weave a pole along the bottom of the netting and anchor with "U" pins (row-cover type). Or string jute up

Squash on "W" trellis.

Bean teepee.

Yard-long beans on arch trellis.

and down a framework made of laths (the sides should be 24 inches longer at the bottom for staking).

Teepee trellis is traditional for legumes. Tie together 6–8 bamboo poles 6 feet from the top, and spread the legs in a circle 3 to 4 feet in diameter. Plant a few seeds around the base of each pole. Space two poles a little wider to allow small children access into the fun, edible interior. Watch out for those bamboo poles dyed peacock green; the stain will rub off on your hands (you can figure out how I know this).

Ready to get growing?

CHAPTER FIVE

Spring and Autumn Crops

HOW TO GROW COOL-SEASON VEGETABLES

Local gardeners often find spring vegetable gardens to be challenging because of the highly changeable weather. Yet folks who wait until May or June to do all their planting are most likely to be disappointed; for some crops, the season is nearly over!

Seed root crops 4–6 weeks before the frost date, and transplant your leafy and cole crops around your early frost date. Germination requires consistent moisture, so be sure to water seeds on the days that it doesn't rain.

See color photographs of vegetables in the center section.

PEAS

Peas are ancient to cultivation; mummified remains in Thailand were radiocarbon-dated to 9750 B.C. In later times, peas found their way to Bronze Age Europe. Small and starchy, they were the food of peasants, finding their way into rhyme as "pease porridge."

Peas are legumes, related to a variety of beans, peanuts, carob, clover, mimosa, and other interesting plants. All of these can "fix" nitrogen in the soil with the aid of symbiotic rhizobia bacteria, turning the free atoms into molecules useful to the plant. Thus, farmers often have a year of soybeans or other legume crop to improve the nitrogen level in soil. Home gardeners can do the same thing with various leguminous cover crops. Austrian monk Gregor Mendel did his pioneering genetic research with smooth and wrinkled, and green and yellow, peas in his mid-1800s monastery garden.

It used to be that peas were just peas, all "English" or shelling peas. Nowadays we also have snow peas and sugar peas, both of which have edible pods. Snow-pea pods are eaten at "slab," before the peas inside swell. Sugar snap peas (introduced to market in 1979) can be eaten in any stage of pea growth. Sugar snap peas rarely make it to the dinner table—children and adults both snack on them because they are so sweet, crunchy, and tasty.

Peas take about ten weeks from seed to table. You can plant them 2 inches apart for climbing peas and 16 per square foot

Presoaking pea seeds.

for the bush type. If it's been a dry spring, you can soak the peas for a few hours in plain water to speed up and guarantee germination.

If you've never planted peas or beans in that location before, then sprinkle the seeds with *inoculant*, which provides beneficial microorganisms to help them utilize nitrogen in the soil. Pick snow peas when the pods are the length of your little finger, but before the pea seeds show. Sugar snap peas can be picked when the peas inside the pods are very small. Shelling (English) peas are picked when the peas inside start to touch each other, but before the pod gets leathery or tough. Peas have vitamins A, B1, and C, and the minerals phosphorus and iron.

Recommended cultivars for various peas include

- English/shelling pea—Alaska, Green Arrow, Knight, Tall Telephone/Alderman, Lincoln, and Maestro
- Snow peas—Oregon Giant, Oregon Sugarpod II

- Sugar snap peas—Super Sugar Snap, Sugar Ann, Sugar Sprint

CRUCIFEROUS OR COLE CROPS
(BROCCOLI, BRUSSELS SPROUTS, CABBAGE, CAULIFLOWER, KALE, KOHLRABI)

Cruciferous crops are so named because their flowers grow in the form of a cross. They are highly nutritious but have a terrible reputation because people boil them to death. Many children and adults prefer their cruciferous veggies raw or blanched. People have been eating cabbages for thousands of years, since Greek and Roman eras. The Chinese have bred many interesting variations on the cabbage family, including loose-leaf types, long-stalked bok choys, and salady tall-heading types. Builders of the Great Wall of China were fed wine-pickled cabbage. Members of the Mongol horde salted their cabbage and brought the resultant sauerkraut with them as they invaded Eastern Europe, where it became entrenched in the local cuisine. So strongly was sauerkraut identified with German cooking that during World War II the domestic pickle was renamed "Liberty Cabbage." Sauerkraut happily has a good concentration of vitamin C, which prevented scurvy in winter diets of both sailors and landlubbers alike. Cole crops are also rich in calcium and iron, as well as vitamin A.

Brassicas (the botanic family name) are usually grown from transplants to ensure maximization of garden space, and because they will bolt (go to seed) in hot weather. There are many Asian variations in this group. I've found that the Asian types usually grow quicker than many of the European kinds.

When transplanting cole crops, be careful of the fine feeder roots. Most of these plants will produce large plants and heads on stringy stems, and it's perfectly OK to transplant deeper for extra stability, as long as you do not bury any of the leaves. Cole crops require soil of good fertility to produce well. Cabbage is more cold-tolerant than broccoli or cauliflower.

Broccoli takes about 16 weeks from seed to table. You can plant them one per square foot, or 12 inches apart. Harvest the broccoli by slicing the stem at its base when the head has grown large (4 to 6 inches wide), but before the buds turn a lighter green and then open into yellow flowers. (You can eat the yellow flowers.) Many varieties will grow side shoots or "broccolettes" if you leave rest of the plant in the ground. Broccoli contains vitamins A, B, C, calcium, phosphorus, and iron. Good cultivars include Green Goliath, Premium Crop H., Primax, Green Comet H., Early Dividend H., and Packman H. More interesting purple and chartreuse broccolis are being reintroduced into the seed market.

Brussels sprouts have had a lot of bad press. This is partly because they have a murky, or mustard taste before being hit by a frost or two. Brussels are a longer-season crop, with plants for harvest after the first autumn frost. After this treatment, the flavor perks right up and the cute little mini-cabbages are really tasty. I microwave-steam mine with a tad of molasses and butter.

You can plant Brussels sprouts one per square foot, or 18 inches apart. They also come in purple varieties. Just plant them early, about mid-July, and grow them for the fall harvest. Brussels sprouts are the only vegetable with the distinction of being named for their place of origin: Brussels, Belgium. Unfortunately, early-maturing varieties of Brussels sprouts have not been developed, as is true of broccoli, cabbage, and cauliflower. We now have 60- to 65-day cabbages and broccoli, yet we're still stuck with 90- to 120-day sprouts. Once autumn starts, snap off the top of the plant stalk to prevent more new growth. This directs the remaining growth into plumping up the existing sprouts.

Cabbage takes about 16 weeks from seed to table, but maturity dates range from 60 to 105 days. You can plant them one per square foot, or 12 inches apart. Harvest the cabbage when it reaches a size you like by slicing it off the stem and removing any raggedy leaves. Cabbage has lots of vitamin C. There are many varieties of Chinese cabbage, including a heading kind called Mei Quing Choi, or the non-heading Tat Soi. I've found that generally the purple cabbages (called "red" for reasons that escape me) seem much less attractive to the cabbage white butterflies who lay the eggs that hatch into Very Hungry Caterpillars (the "cabbage loopers"). Or, the green caterpillars stand out like a snowball in a coalfield on purple leaves, and the birds eat them up! Here are some recommended cultivars:

- Early cabbages—Tastie H., Headstart H., Emerald Cross
- Midseason cabbages—Bravo, Grand Slam
- Red cabbage—Ruby Ball, Red Acre
- Chinese cabbage—Jade Pagoda H., Early Hybrid H., China Doll H., China Pride H.
- Chinese greens—Joi Choi, Pak Choi Lei Choi, Tyfon (Turnip x Chinese Cabbage)

Cauliflower takes about 14 weeks from seed to table. Some cauliflowers are "self-blanching," which means the leaves cover the curds or flower head and keep it white. Otherwise, tie leaves over the head to keep the curds a creamy color. There are also purple and green cauliflowers, which don't need to be covered. Cauliflower doesn't produce side shoots like broccoli does, but if you leave the plant in the ground, it often sends out new growth from the root. Pinch off these volunteers to just one or two, and you'll get a second harvest of smaller heads later on. Cauliflower is loaded with vitamin C. Mark Twain dismissed cauliflower as "nothing but a cabbage with a college education," but his were probably served to him over-boiled. Recommended cultivars include Snowball and Snow Crown H.

Kohlrabi looks like a vegetable sputnik, with the stem swelling into a ball, and leaves sprouting around the sides and top. It takes about 9 weeks from planting to table, and you can plant kohlrabi 4 per square foot, or 6 inches apart. Care for it like any other member of this family, and harvest when tennis-ball size. Kohlrabi is rich in protein, calcium, potassium, and vitamin C. Cultivars are generally limited in domestic catalogs, but are nearly all worth pursuing.

ROOT CROPS
(BEETS, CARROTS, PARSNIPS, POTATOES, RADISHES, RUTABAGAS, AND TURNIPS)

All of the root crops described here, except for the potato, need the same treatment. They grow best in cooler weather, making them spring and autumn plants. Space all roots (except for potatoes) 16 per square foot, or 3 inches apart. They are grown from seed because they're quick-maturing, and because root crops don't like to be transplanted. For optimum root crop soil, amend with 50 percent sand. With root crops, it's very important to keep the soil moist; they take one to three weeks to sprout!

Beets are peculiar, because each beet seed is really a cluster of seeds. They *always* need thinning, or else you'll get stringy roots. Some new varieties with the prefix "mono-" in their name (such as Monopoly) are single seeds. Beets, or beetroots, are a good source of iron and B vitamins. The beet leaves are also quite edible and nutritious. Recommended cultivars are Early Wonder, Detroit Dark Red, Little Ball, Ruby Queen, Cylindra, and Perfected Detroit. Chioggia beets have concentric rings of red and white. Burpee has also introduced the Burpee's Golden beet (sold in several catalogs), which comes in a lovely gold color. It tastes pretty much the same, but doesn't bleed cerise juice all over your plate. Pick beets when they are golf-ball size; most get "woody" when they get huge.

Carrots—People want to grow foot-long carrots because that's what they buy at the market, but in soils with lots of clay or those riddled with glacier gravel, the shorter types do much better. If you're fond of the European "peas and carrots" dish, then follow the European method and grow the round, ping-pong ball carrots. Smaller carrots mature faster, so maturation dates for carrots are all over the calendar. Pick carrots when they are

1/2 to 1-1/2 inches in diameter; you can brush a little soil away to feel the carrot top. To prevent green carrot tops, hill up some soil over the top of the root, but don't bury the leaves. Of course, carrots are a good source of vitamin A, as well as B1, thiamine, and calcium. Recommended cultivars are Caroline (less prone to that soapy taste, and a good longer carrot), Red Cored Chantenay, Gold Pak, Royal Chantenay, Gold King, Scarlet Nantes, and Tendersweet.

Celeriac goes by several other names: celery-root or celery-rave (Germans call it Sellerie; Austrians call it Zeller). This is not the root of everyday celery, but a slightly different plant. This tan, slightly knobby vegetable is a star in European recipes, but less commonly grown here. The edible part is the swollen crown from which the stems grow. They can grow up to 5 inches across, but are best picked at 2–4 inches. Celeriac is most easily grown from transplants. Start your seeds 10–12 weeks before your frost date and then transplant in late spring, when the soil has warmed to 50 °F. Space one per square foot. Celeriac needs consistent moisture; mulching helps. In areas with hot summers, try planting it to the north of taller crops for some shade. The roots taste even better after a light frost, but should be picked right afterward.

Parsnips look like white carrots. Many folks nowadays have no idea what a parsnip is. Please try them, because they don't have that "twang" common to carrots. They take 18 weeks to maturity, and taste better after a frost, making them an ideal autumn garden choice. Parsnips are one of the few veggies that you really need to buy fresh seed for every year. Recommended varieties include All-American, and Model.

Potatoes are not native to Ireland; they are native to Peru. When this vegetable was first brought back to Europe from the New World, no one wanted to eat it, because the potato is a member of the nightshade family. It took some urging and a bit of sneakiness before the vitamin-packed, easily grown tuber became an indispensable part of every European cuisine.

The biggest question I get about homegrown potatoes is, "Why bother, when I can buy a ten-pound bag at the market real cheap?" Well, why do people grow their own tomatoes? Because of the flavor! The same applies to potatoes. I grow a variety called Yellow Finn. It's not as large as a russet, and it's not a baker. This yellow boiling potato has a waxy texture, like new potatoes, and it has a lovely flavor. My father-in-law was surprised the first time he ate homegrown potatoes.

To grow potatoes, you start from "seeds," which are actually small potatoes or sections of larger tubers. Potatoes are not generally grown from real seeds, because they won't grow true from type. Place one "seed" 3 or 4 inches deep, one per square foot or 12 inches apart. Potato seeds are actually chips of potato, cut so that each piece has an eye to sprout from. Or plant golf-ball-sized taters into the ground, whole. There seems to be less trouble with rot by this second method. Either way, it helps if the pieces already have sprouts growing; otherwise, they are prone to sitting around for a few weeks before sprouting in the garden.

Aside from weeding, the taters pretty much take care of themselves. Like other vegetables, they do better with consistent moisture. Once the potato plants flower, you can reach under and pull out a few new potatoes for eating if you're impatient. The flowering is also a sign that the plants are entering their second growth phase, and won't be needing as much water.

Adding extra soil (by "hilling up" or hoeing soil onto the plants) or by adding successive layers of compost and straw will give the plants more room to grow more tubers in. You can hill every week or two, covering up the plant stems as they grow. Larger quantities of potatoes can be grown in "potato rings," by making a 4-inch-diameter ring of small-mesh wire (such as quarter-inch mesh hardware cloth). The ring will hold the successive additions of soil/compost/straw mixture. Come late summer when the plants die down, remove the wire ring and the taters will tumble out of the light filling material. This is also an excellent way to improve poor garden ground, if you hill up with alternating layers of straw and compost!

You can seed potato pieces or small whole tubers in the spring or the fall. St. Patrick's Day is a traditional potato- and pea-seeding day, but the soil is often too cold and wet to actually plant on March 17. Wait until the soil has dried out enough to dig in before planting.

One trick I've found to be nearly foolproof is to seed my taters in the fall. In September or October I'll put those golf-ball-sized, whole spudlets a foot apart in the garden, and then cover them with a foot-deep layer of shredded leaves. Shredding the leaves with the lawnmower keeps them from blowing around and helps them break down quicker. The potatoes remain outside all winter under their layer of mulch. Once the soil warms up enough, the potatoes will sprout leaves through the mulch. That's the sign that I can go outside and plant my peas. (Gee, the potatoes are smarter than I am!)

Come mid to late summer, the leaves and stems will die back. This is your signal to dig up the tubers. Start forking a foot or two away from the plants, or just pull on the vines. Any tubers you don't find will hang around and grow back next year to provide another crop.

Most of the potatoes you get at the grocery have been treated with sprout inhibitors. Instead, buy seed potatoes from the same places as your other vegetable seeds. The following mail-order company specializes in potatoes (plus lots of different onions and garlics). Reading the catalog is interesting and informative. The company carries red, pink, russet, yellow, white, or blue potatoes; big bakers and small boilers, quick-harvest potatoes, and long-keeping kinds.

Ronninger's Seed & Potato Company & Greg Anthony's Seed Company
"Irish Eyes with a Hint of Garlic"
P.O. Box 307
Ellensburg, WA 98926
phone 509-925-6025 fax 800-964-9210
www.irish-eyes.com

Potatoes are not fattening unless you load them down with dairy products. They have plenty of protein, iron, niacin, phosphorus, potassium, and calcium as well as vitamins B and C.

Radishes are popular in seed kits for children because they mature in only 4 weeks, making them the closest thing to "instant gratification" you'll find among veggies. Funny thing is, I don't know any small children who *like* radishes! Seed companies are always coming out with new cultivars, and given consistent moisture and a cool growing season, the varieties all seem to be equally good. The Easter Egg mix features round radishes in white, pink, red, and purple, which is fun. Longer white radishes are also popular and do well in improved soils. The Japanese daikon radishes need both deep, rich soil and the full growing season. Spring-planted daikons are harvested in the summer, and summer-seeded ones are harvested in the fall. Space them 1 foot apart. Unlike regular radishes, daikons don't get hot-tasting when the weather warms up. The seed pods of bolted radishes are also edible, and used stir-fried with spices in East Indian and other cuisines.

Rutabagas are also called swedes, or swede turnips (mainly in England). If you find turnips too strong, I highly recommend growing sweet, orange-fleshed rutabagas. Both rutabagas and turnips are cruciferous vegetables, but I grow them like root crops. Rutabagas grow larger than turnips, and keep better, too. They take about 18 weeks to mature, and they're another great autumn vegetable that tastes sweeter after a light frost. Thin to 4 per square foot or 6 inches apart. Rutabagas are high in vitamin A.

Turnips are fast-growing roots, taking only 5 to 10 weeks, so the quick ones are ideal for spring gardens. If left in the heat, they get strong and woody. Turnip "greens," or leaves, are used as a potherb in Southern cooking, such as boiled with a piece of salted fatback or bacon. Thin spring turnips to 16 per square foot (3 inches apart) and autumn ones to 4 per square foot (6 inches apart). Turnips are also high in vitamins A and C.

ALLIUMS
(GARLIC, SHALLOTS, POTATO ONIONS, LEEKS, ONIONS, WALKING ONIONS)

Life would be pretty dull without alliums. They have spanned the globe and have been grown since the dawn of civilization. The overworked builders of the Egyptian pyramids were fed onions, radishes, and garlic to keep up their strength.

Garlic is best started in the autumn for the largest heads, although spring is OK, too. Separate a head of garlic into cloves, and plant the fat cloves 2 inches deep and 3 inches apart, or 16 to a square foot. All alliums prefer rich soil, and do not compete well against weeds. Autumn-planted garlic cloves will grow and hang around most of the winter, then spring back to life with warm weather. Side-dress your garlic with compost when the leaves come back in the spring. By midsummer,

when the leaves are half-dead, pull them up, brush off the extra dirt, and let dry in the sun for a couple of days before trimming off the leaves a couple inches up the neck.

Hardneck-type garlics have several large cloves, while softneck garlics are better keepers, and the sort that are braided into swags. Hardneck types are inclined to put up a seed stalk with bulblets at the top. Snap off the seed stalk at 6–8 inches tall, to encourage a larger bulb instead.

Shallots are grown just like garlic, except each bulb will multiply into a clump of seven or more. Separate the bulbs when the leaves are mostly dead. Shallots are a bit less expensive in catalogs than in the stores, and you can start them from seed or "sets" (bulbs). If you're really frugal and patient, replant this year's harvest in the early autumn for a large crop next year.

Multiplying onions are grown just like shallots, and are sometimes called "potato onions" because of their multiplying quality. They are onions, not potatoes. They don't grow as large as some types of onions, but do save you the effort of growing or buying sets every year.

Leeks are biennial plants started from transplants or seed. When transplanting, space them 6 inches apart, or 4 per square foot. To get the desired long white bottom of the stem, there are two options. You can plant your leeks in a trench, adding dirt around the seedlings as they grow. Or you can mulch them deeply with earth, shredded leaves, or straw as they grow. I prefer to mulch leek transplants with shredded leaves, since they grow cleaner.

Leek transplants are definitely the easier way to go. I usually get mine from Piedmont Plant Company, which specializes in mail-order transplants of popular garden crops (sweet potatoes, tomatoes, peppers, broccoli, onions, shallots, and so on). Piedmont's plants are grown in the sandy, warm Georgia soil, and then quickly shipped bare-root. Although the seedlings look puny for a couple of days, they will perk up and be happy by the end of the week. Piedmont's chosen leek cultivar tends to change from year to year, but you can get a bundle of 100 for less than $10—a bargain compared to the two-for-$3 leeks at my local grocery (Piedmont's price per 100 decreases when you buy more bundles). The stringy things never look very promising, but I just dibble them in, water them, and they always grow to give me a long winter's supply of leek tarts and potato-leek soup by the end of summer.

Piedmont Plant Company
807 North Washington Street
P.O. Box 424
Albany, GA 31702
phone 800-541-5185
www.piedmontplants.com

When putting in a large number of transplants (be they leeks or annual flowers), I *highly* recommend purchasing a dibble (tool). Back in neolithic times, the dibble was originally a hollow cattle horn. Modern versions are made of heavy aluminum, with curved or T-handles. You simply go along and easily *punch, punch, punch* a line of holes and then *drop, drop, drop* in the transplants, followed by a good soaking. It sounds frivolous until you have more than a dozen holes you're levering up with a trowel, and then the wisdom becomes apparent.

Onions are also grown from seed or transplants. The baby onion sets you buy in mesh bags were started last summer. Growing from sets is the easiest method for the beginning home gardener. Yellow onions will keep better than red ones. To grow from seed, select day-neutral or long-day onions (short-day onions are best grown in the South). If you are fond

of the really sweet and mild onions, try Walla Walla seed. The "heat" in onions depends on the level of sulfur in your soil, but the cultivar makes a significant difference, too.

Start your seeds in late February or early March, planting them just a quarter-inch deep. The small, black, geometric seeds look like miniature coal for my HO-scale model train set. If you have trouble seeing where you've sown onion seeds, try sprinkling the top of the seed-starting medium with a layer of nice white perlite to make the seeds more visible and avoid undue thinning. You can sow them in a wide, 3- to 4-inch-deep pot, spacing the seeds an inch apart. When the leaves (tops) get 6 inches tall, give them a haircut down to half-height. This encourages development of the "bulb" instead of long, stringy leaves. Transplant your onions to 6 inches apart in the early spring, and keep them weeded.

Feed everyone garlic, and no one worries.

Harvest onions when they develop the familiar papery "tunics" or skins, and the tops shrivel up and fall over. Pull them from the ground, knock the soil off the roots, and let them air-dry out of direct sunlight for a week to cure. (Old window screens supported by extra pots, buckets, or paint cans in the garage work well as drying racks.) Then clip off all but 2 inches from the tops, and store your onions someplace cool and damp. Recommended cultivars: Walla Walla sweet, Copra H. storage, Early Yellow Globe keeper, Ebeneezer yellow keeper, Granex yellow, Mars Red H., Ruby red, Red Burgundy.

Another kind of onion is known variously (same vegetable, several names) as the **top onion, tree onion, Egyptian onion,** or **walking onion.** This plant produces smaller onions at the stem base, and clusters of small bulbs at the top of the thick, often twisted stem. The bulbils often sprout into new plants, and the weight causes the stem to bend over. The bulbils then root into new plants and can even sprout a bulbil stem of their own, which in turn forms roots, and so on—hence the name, walking onions. The walking onion is a perennial, so it deserves a patch all of its own. You probably don't want it waltzing all over the rest of your lettuces and such.

Suppliers usually ship onion bulbs of all types in the autumn. Onions are quite hardy, overwintering well and taking care of themselves, aside from needing you to keep down the weeds. You can harvest them in the middle of the following summer. The smaller onions and their greens are good picked at almost any size, and are just right for stuffing roast bird or for an early spring vegetable.

LEAFY VEGETABLES

Kale, lettuces, spinach, and other greens are all grown in the early spring and fall. They can be directly seeded or started as transplants. When you have a really rainy spring, transplants (in a raised bed) stand a better chance, since they won't be washed away.

Leafys must be grown quickly, before summer's heat makes them bolt (make flowers and go to seed). Leafys have shallow roots, and need consistent watering and nutrient-rich soil. Most leafys take about 7 weeks from seed to table. You can plant them (or thin out the extra seedlings) to 4 per square foot, or 6 inches apart.

Lettuces come in different varieties, known as loose-leaf and head lettuces.

Given our temperature fluctuations, leaf lettuces are easier to grow than head lettuces. Spinach comes in two types: savoy or crinkly, and plain. Leafys contain vitamins A and B, calcium, and iron (greener leaves have more vitamins).

Turn Over a New Leaf

Who's Who in the world of Lettuce: Crisphead lettuces include the familiar iceberg and other tightly packed lettuces. Batavians are loosely headed. Romaine lettuces have upright leaves with crisp ribs and are familiar for their use in Caesar salads. Butterhead or Bibb lettuces have loosely packed heads with tender, wavy leaves. Endives are frilly loose-leaf heads often included in blends for their piquant flavor. (Loose-leaf lettuces do not make a solid head, but rather a clump of leaves.) Leaf shapes and colors of loose-leaf lettuces vary, including red and green combinations.

Crisphead lettuces like the familiar iceberg are sometimes trickier to grow. That's why the catalogs offer such a greater variety of loose-leaf lettuces. And what a variety! Although I can't predict which cultivars each catalog will sell from year to year, discerning companies know to stock not only lettuces that like the cool spring and autumn weather but also those that tolerate warmer summer weather and those that will overwinter under covers.

Growing Better Lettuces

Leafy greens grow best in loose soil with good nutrient levels and even watering. Lettuces are shallow-rooted plants. Irregular watering, especially during hot weather, results in toughness and bitterness. If your garden is in a windy area, you can reduce the hardship to your plants by putting up a windbreak. (Wind stress also makes greens tough.) A 50-percent-permeable windbreak fabric will slow down the wind. Solid barriers simply lift the wind and drop it a ways further down, without reducing its speed.

Heat-tolerant summer lettuces need a little shade. There are several ways to do this:

- Plant them in a location that has shade during the hotter afternoon hours.
- Grow them underneath a lattice.
- Place them on the north side of trellised crops such as pole beans.
- Stretch a shade cloth in a tent over the lettuce patch.

Cold-tolerant winter lettuces can be transplanted out in a cold frame, in the early autumn, so they can reach most of their mature size before the temperature drops (around November 1 in zone 5). Do not fertilize heavily; excess nitrogen creates weaker cell walls. Then harvest as needed through the cold months. Lettuces do not really grow under these conditions, but merely hibernate, kept in perfect condition. Be sure to whisk snow off the tops of cold frames to let in light. Actually, snow is a great insulator on the sides of cold frames, and it reflects lots of light, so snow is beneficial.

Winter cold-tolerating lettuce cultivars for overwintering include

- Loose-leaf—Arctic King, North Pole, and Selma Wisa
- Romaine—Winter Density
- Butterhead—Brune D'Hiver, Rouge D'Hiver, and Winter Marvel

Because lettuce is an annual, it's prone to bolting, or going to seed. This is fine if you're planning on saving those dried seed fluffs; but if you want salad, it's a problem. Bolted lettuces taste bitter because they have more sap. (The botanic name for lettuce is *Lactuca*, referring to the milky sap.) To avoid this, don't plant all your lettuces at the first spring sowing.

Instead, sow just a 4-foot-by-4-foot or 2-foot-by-4-foot block every two or three weeks. This ensures an ongoing supply of young plants. Lettuces sprout best at 70 °F, and grow best at 50–60 °F. Transplants will work best in warm weather; quick in and quick out. Fertilize plants with nitrogen-rich cottonseed meal, liquid seaweed/fish emulsion, or well-rotted manure, whichever is most commonly found in your area. What do you do about the bolting plants? Rototill them under, yank them, and chuck into the compost pile; or better yet, let them produce free seeds for your taking!

Summer heat-tolerating lettuces are less quick to bolt. Some cultivars are

- **Butterheads**—Buttercrunch, Continuity, Divina, Ermosa, Mervielle des Quatre Saisons (also known as Four Seasons), Optima, and Ovation
- **Batavians**—Cardinale, Nevada, and Sierra Blush
- **Loose-leafs**—Bronze Guard, Brunia, Deer Tongue, Fire Mountain, Green Saladbowl, Oak Leaf, PomPom, Red Riding Hood (Rotkapchen), Red Sails, Red Saladbowl, Simpson Elite, Slobolt, and Two-Star
- **Crispheads**—Centennial, Loma, Mission, Sierra, Summertime, and Vanity
- **Endives**—Rosalita Red (romaine) and Traviata
- Heat-tolerating Perpetual Spinach cultivar is actually a cousin to chard and beets.

Picking Once, Picking Twice

You can pick a whole head of loose-leaf lettuce, such as a romaine, or you can pick just the outer leaves and leave the inner heart of the plant. This means that you pick no more than you need for that meal's salad, not only ensuring the freshest lettuces for the table but also preventing the other half of the head from withering away in the crisper drawer. Instead, it's living happily out in the vegetable garden and continuing to produce.

Some gardeners like to plant a solid block of loose-leaf lettuces, especially Mesclun, and "mow" a portion of the block with sharp scissors, leaving behind 1- or 2-inch stubs that will regrow. These are the same tender mixed leaves as sold in supermarkets. Cut-and-come-again harvesting guarantees just the right amount of fresh, mixed greens for the bowl, and is a quick operation.

Spinach lovers can sow in the autumn, harvest the succulent leaves, and leave behind 1- to 2-inch hearts that will regrow for a lush, tender March harvest.

THIRD TIME'S THE CHARM: AUTUMN CROPS

Are you ready to "throw in the trowel" by the end of summer? Feeling overwhelmed by the heat and humidity? Thankfully, it'll be cooling down. And if you spend a little time cleaning up the dead, the bad, and the ugly, you'll find that the garden looks welcoming and full of promise again.

Most gardeners plant their vegetables in the spring and summer, not realizing that autumn is the perfect season for growing those cool-weather lovers all over again. You will need to select quick-maturing cultivars that will produce in 45–60 days. Then add two weeks to that maturity date to make up for shortening days. To avoid late-summer heat, start your transplants indoors to optimize germination.

First select vegetables you can grow in the autumn:

- Lettuces, spinach, and other leafy greens like Swiss chard—Grow some in a cold frame, and you can be picking through the end of the year.

CREATING THE CUSTOM HOUSE-BLEND SALAD

Just as green salads are not limited to crunchy, pale iceberg lettuces, they're also not limited to lettuce! Alternative greens include the Mache (also known as Corn salad, Nusslisalat, or Feldsalad), along with the kales and spinaches that do great in cold weather. During the growing seasons, you can also round out your salads with arugula (roquette), Malabar spinach, purslane, nutrient-rich beet greens, carrot greens, lovage, lemon balm, as well as bits of parsley, basil, cucumber-tasting borage, and chervil.

Many catalogs offer one or more types of Mesclun, which is merely a French term for mixed salad greens, or in Italian, Misticanza. You can make your own "private label" Mesclun of lettuces for the different seasons by mixing your favorite lettuce types and thinly broadcasting the seed where it is to grow. If you keep your packets of seed cool and dry, they will keep for four years.

- Cole crops, including broccoli, cabbage, cauliflower, bok choy and kale—Watch those maturity dates! Often the Asian cultivars are especially quick-maturing.
- Peas; select snow peas and sugar snaps over shelling peas—These can be eaten without waiting for the pea seeds to develop.
- Root crops, such as short or ball-shaped carrots, radishes, beets, and turnips—Avoid slow-growing daikon-type radishes. Beet leaves (or greens) are also good in salads and are loaded with vitamins.
- Garlic for next summer's harvest—Just unpeel the paper jacket on a head of

Snow is an insulator in the garden.

garlic, break off the cloves, and plant the cloves pointy-end-up, 2 inches deep and 4 inches apart. They will sprout, winter over, and produce larger heads by midsummer next year.

The second step is to get your transplants of leafy greens and cole crops ready. Some nurseries will grow a limited variety for autumn planting, so call around to those near you. To grow your own, you can clean out and reuse leftover six-packs from this spring. Once the seeds have sprouted, thin to one per little pot, and set outside in full sun, on the north or east side of your house. This exposure will give your plants sufficient light without baking them in the hot afternoon sun. A tray underneath the pots will aid in watering. Bottom watering—pouring

water in the tray rather than the pot—prevents the seeds from splashing around. After 4 weeks in the vegetable nursery, put your plants out into the garden.

The third step is to improve your garden soil by turning under some compost and vegetable fertilizer, to make up for nutrients lost during this summer's growing season.

The last step is remembering to water when it doesn't rain. Unlike springtime, when frequent rains are guaranteed, in autumn the rains are more erratic. Be sure to water the seeds of root crops daily until they've sprouted. Then slowly cut back on watering as the plants become established. Peas can also be direct-seeded. I've gotten excellent results from presoaking pea seeds in a shallow dish of water overnight, and then carefully dribbling them into the garden.

Here are some good cultivars for autumn crops:

- **Lettuces**—all loose-leaf types, especially red ones
- **Swiss chards**—all types
- **Broccoli**—select types that mature in 65 days or less
- **Cabbage**—Columbia, Red Express, Dynamo, Tastie, Bonanza, and other 45- to 60-day cultivars

- **Cauliflower**—Early White, Milky Way, White Corona, Snow Crown, and other 45- to 60-day cultivars
- **Bok choy**—all types
- **Snow peas**—nearly all types
- **Snap peas**—Sugar Ann, Sugar Bon, Sugar Pop, and Sugar Snap
- **Beets**—nearly all types
- **Carrots**—Thumbelina, Short & Sweet, Little Finger, and Scarlet Nantes
- **Radishes**—nearly all types
- **Turnips**—nearly all types

Pea 'Super Sugar Snap'.

Broccoli 'Packman'; the single head is 6 inches wide.

Brussels sprouts taste better after a couple of frosts.

Cabbage 'Red Express'.

Asian cabbage family member, 'Tah Tsai' pot green.

Cauliflower 'Early Snowball'.

Kohlrabi 'Early Purple Vienna'.

Beets 'Burpee's Golden' and Italian 'Chioggia'.

Carrot 'Healthmaster'.

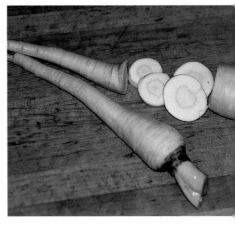

Parsnip 'Giagantic'.

A colorful harvest of red, blue, and yellow potatoes.

Potato 'Yellow Finn' growing.

Potatoes grown in a wire-mesh ring.

Radish 'Red Beret'.

Turnips 'Purple Top White Globe'—pick them small and sweet!

Garlic in June, nearing harvest time.

Shallots ready for harvesting; plant one and it multiplies into many.

Leeks 'Large American Flag'; deep mulching makes long, white stems.

Onion 'Ailsa Craig'.

The Egyptian/walking onion produces bulblets atop the stalks.

Bed of 'Mesclun' lettuces.

'Green Forest' and 'Outredgeous' Romaine lettuces.

'Ovation' Butterhead lettuce.

Spinach 'Bloomsdale Long Standing'.

Wax beans 'EZ Gold'.

'Black Turtle' soup beans at dry, ripe stage.

Sweet corn 'Kandy Kwik' doesn't even need cooking!

Asian eggplant 'Diamond'.

Flower on okra 'Lee'.

Just the right picking size for okra.

Assorted sweet peppers.

Assorted hot peppers.

Sweetpotato slips 'Porto Rico'.

Sweetpotato vines.

Mixed tomato harvest.

Cherry tomatoes—red 'Cherry Baby' and 'Sweet Gold F1'.

Sweetpotatoes grown by Miles Raymond.

Anna and her 'Voyager' tomatoes.

Yum! Tomato sandwiches.

Slicing cucumber 'Burpee's Burpless'.

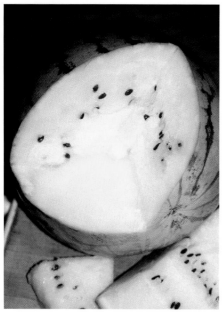

Watermelon 'Cream of Saskatchewan'.

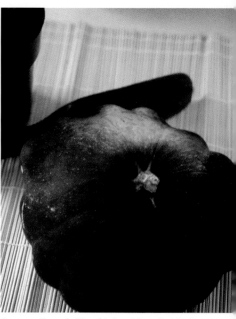

Summer Squash 'Starship'—pick at 3–4 inches diameter.

Zucchini 'Ambassador'.

Baby summer squash and edible flowers.

Crookneck summer squash 'Butterstick'.

Pumpkin 'Jack Be Little'.

Pie pumpkin 'Baby Bear' produces a "just right" amount for recipes.

Tomato press is great for preparing cooked pumpkins for recipes.

'UC157' asparagus sprouting.

Seven-foot-tall flower stalks bloom on sunroots in September.

Cut off the stalks, let rest for a couple weeks, and then fork up the sunroots.

'Stampede' sunroots—a prolific perennial crop.

CHAPTER SIX

"Squashes and Corn and Beans, Oh My!" Warm-Season Vegetables

BEANS

Be they ever so humble, beans are wondrous things. Most of the beans we grow are legumes native to the New World. Fava (or broad) beans are European, and soybeans are Asian; but all the rest—from green beans to navy beans—hail from their South American ancestors. Peruvian beans, which have been radiocarbon-dated to 8000 B.C., have a long and venerable history.

Beans fall into two general categories: those eaten fresh, and those cooked as dried (shelling) beans. Green beans, yellow wax beans, purple beans, string beans, and snap beans are the fresh type. These can be bush or pole beans, with the pole types giving a much longer harvest. Otherwise, seed a new patch or row of bush types every two or three weeks to extend your fresh bean harvest.

String beans have a fibrous filament that runs from stem to blossom end. This filament is zipped off before the beans are cooked. Snap beans don't have this filament, a nice breeding advance that gave them the snide name "lazy wife beans" upon introduction. Traditionally, the ends are snapped off of string beans; but if you're eating snap beans, you can leave your beans whole. French green beans (haricots vert) are picked before the bean seeds develop inside the pods, when the pods are "pencil thin." These are quite tender and delicious, and require picking every few days.

Dried beans are usually bush-type bean plants. Some are eaten young like green beans, but most are left on the plants until the pods are a dry, papery brown. The bean seeds must be completely dry before storing. It's a good idea to put them into the freezer for two or three days to kill any lurking bugs. Bean seeds keep for years. Fresh dried-bean seeds cook quicker than those that have been sitting on the pantry shelf for a year or two.

There are hundreds of varieties of dried beans, ranging from large to small; from spotted to streaked or splotched; and from black to brown, tan, purple, burgundy, red, orange, yellow, white, and pink. Seed Savers Exchange (a non-profit organization committed to preserving the seed diversity of all types of vegetables) maintains an incredible

94

collection of historical beans. The seeds are available to members; non-members can select some varieties from the organization's public catalog. The Vermont Bean Seed Company also sells a wide variety of fresh and drying beans.

Seed Savers Exchange
3076 North Winn Road
Decorah, IA 52101
phone 319-382-5990
www.seedsavers.org

Vermont Bean Seed Company
Garden Lane
Fair Haven, VT 05743-0250
phone 803-663-0217
www.vermontbean.com

To grow beans, be sure to let the soil warm up. Old-timers say that when the apples blossom, it's warm enough to plant your beans. If you plant the bean seeds "eye" side down, they will be able to bring their leaves up most easily, though this isn't critical. If you wish, you can soak the bean seeds for a few hours in tepid water, or even go so far as to pre-sprout them in vermiculite, to eliminate the duds. To presprout, lay the seeds on a tray spread with damp vermiculite, and keep the tray someplace warm (such as atop the fridge) for a couple of days. When the seeds have *just* put out their roots, plant immediately. Long roots are fragile for planting.

Lima beans (yes, they are from Peru) are especially picky about warm soil. Wait until a week or two past your last frost date. Combined with sweet corn and a bit of onion sautéed in butter, Lima beans make a delightful dish called succotash.

Bush beans can be grown 16 per square foot (in a block of 4 seeds by 4, each one 3 inches apart from the other). Pole beans, which need a trellis or some-

thing to climb on, are also placed 3 inches apart. Pole-bean stems will wind clockwise upon contact with the support trellis, a phenomenon called *thigmotropism*. Like peas, beans need to be dusted with a legume inoculant if you're never grown them in that part of the garden before. Pick string and snap beans when the seeds inside are just noticeable, about 8 weeks after planting. (To easily remove old pole-bean vines from trellises, let them dry until they're crispy-critters, and then you can snap them right off.) Beans are a good source of protein (best eaten with corn, dairy, or grain products for a complete protein) as well as vitamins A, B, and C.

CORN

Corn is an ancient crop of the Americas (scientists are still debating whether it was bred from the native teosinte grass). Various types of corns are used in an extraordinary number of products. Home gardeners commonly grow sweet corn and sometimes popping corn. Field corn (flint or dent corn) is used commercially for more than just cornmeal and corn flakes. Corn syrup, corn starch, corn oil, corn whiskey, corn charcoal briquettes, shoe polish, soap, corncob bottle stoppers, corncob smoking pipes, and other imaginative uses have turned field corn into a major crop in the Heartland. Settlers used the ubiquitous husks to stuff their mattresses. Pilgrim children ate popcorn with milk and maple sweetening for breakfast. Ornamental "Indian corn" is flint corn, which comes in an amazing display of colors, from black, purple, and blue to white, yellow, gold, orange, red, maroon, and brown.

The word *corn* can be confusing; traditionally it meant a kernel, such as the peppercorn or salt grains used to make corned beef. *Corn* has also been used to mean the grain commonly grown in a country, be it wheat, oats, or barley. The word *maize* always refers to America's native corn. Corn is high in carbohydrates, but short in amino acids. A diet high in corn but lacking in meat, milk, and eggs (which provide the complementary amino acids) produces a niacin deficiency called pellagra. Boiling the corn kernels in wood ash or lime before grinding increases the nutritional quality of corn tortillas compared to ordinary cornmeal, and prevents pellagra.

Corn seed can be presoaked or presprouted just like beans. Traditionally corn is planted "when the oak leaves are the size of squirrel ears." Keep the seeds covered with Reemay or chicken wire, arched high to keep the birds away until the grassy leaves are a few inches tall. Corn is a heavy feeder and roots along the stem, so be sure to mulch with compost to provide nutrients and support. Short (3 to 4 feet tall) corn plants can be grown 4 per square foot. Most sweet corn varieties are taller; space them 1 per square foot. Because corn is wind-pollinated, growing a single row of corn often results in poor kernel fill. Instead, plant corn in blocks of 4 by 4 seeds or larger, or in four rows of 4 seeds or longer. The pollen structures on top of the plant (they look like TV antennae) will drop the heavy dust onto the silks. Each silk leads to a kernel, so if no pollen lands on that silk, you have a dud kernel. In a small patch of corn, you can even lean the pollen over and shake it onto the silks of the edge and corner plants.

If you want more than one harvest of corn, consider planting a new block every two or three weeks through the early summer. Or, you can plant early-, mid-, and late-maturing varieties at the same time. Most stalks produce two ears of corn; short stalks generally produce only one ear.

Once the silks (string atop the corncobs) get brown, start checking your corn every day. When it's ripe (18–24 days after silking), the ears feel full and bumpy. When you puncture a kernel with your thumbnail and it's milky, the corn's ready. Clear juice means it's not ready. Pick regular cultivars right before cooking so they don't lose flavor. Super-sweet Hybrid (S2) sweet corns can be kept in the fridge without losing sweetness. Sugary Enhanced Hybrids (SE) have even higher sugar levels that allow the kernels to remain tender a week or two after harvest. Shrunken (SH2) types must be physically separated from other corn types or planted with a time delay to prevent tasseling at the same time; the cross-pollination messes up the flavor and texture.

If you want "baby" corn (the miniature kind used in Chinese stir-fry), then grow sweet corn. Simply pick the cobs when the corn is 2–3 inches long, before it is pollinated. You can either plant a patch of closely spaced stalks, or pick off one stalk of regular sweet corn early for baby corn, and leave the other stalk for regular sweet corn.

Sweet corns come in yellow, white, and bicolor types, as well as multicolored Indian Summer and a new red sweet corn called Ruby Queen (but it requires another sugary enhanced [SE] cultivar for pollination). Recommended cultivars include old-fashioned Silver Queen (white corn), the newer Kandy Korn (yellow corn), and Northern Extra-Sweet (SH2). New cultivars come out every year. Corn is a source of carbohydrates and some protein, but is short on other vitamins.

Popping corns are grown like field corns. Let the plants and husks mature until the plant is papery dry. Many people leave them outside for a frost or two. After harvesting, spread out the ears someplace dry to cure for a few weeks.

Popping quality is related to the amount of moisture in the kernels. Test a few kernels to see how they pop, and when the results are satisfactory, twist the kernels off the cob. Popping corns come in yellow, red, pink, and blue types. Ornamental Indian corns are grown the same way, but not removed from the cobs. Instead, pull the husks back and wire into clusters for hanging. In the garden, you'll have to separate the popping and Indian corns from your sweet corns, or else the sweet corns will end up really chewy. Either stagger plantings so they won't be tasseling at the same time, or separate them by 500 yards to two miles.

EGGPLANTS

OK, so why are those purple things called "egg plants"? Because some of them are small, white, and ovoid and look very much like eggs! (Those aren't the tastiest cultivars, though.)

Eggplant, like lima beans, is really picky about the soil being good and warm. Wait until two weeks after the last frost date before transplanting them. In fact, eggplants can tolerate much more heat and drought than can other crops (not surprisingly, they're native to the Middle East). The "madde apple" made its way into Europe in the sixteenth century; but being a member of the deadly nightshade family, it was not well accepted for ornamentation, much less table use. Today eggplants are sometimes known in English and French references as aubergines, a name that also refers to purple or purple-brown clothing in pricey catalogs.

Eggplants grow better in warm soil. Cool soils make them prone to both blossom-drop and verticillium wilt. If you've been bothered by verticillium wilt (on eggplants or tomatoes) in the past, consider planting your eggplants in three-gallon pots filled with a mixture of potting soil and compost (in equal amounts). In places with cool summer nights, containers might be "the" way to go, since you can bring in your beauties when the weather's inclement.

Taking 20 weeks from seed to harvest, eggplants come in the familiar purple as well as pink, green, and orange—and the namesake small, round, white ones. The slender purple Asian types have fewer tendencies toward getting seedy, pithy, or bitter than the bulbous sorts. Do not fertilize eggplants until after they've begun flowering and setting fruits.

Pick the fruits when they are a size you like. They should be firm, shiny, and colorful. Young, small fruits are fine for picking. Purple ones that have turned brown are way overdue. Be sure to use garden shears or a sharp knife to sever the tough stems, lest you rip the plant. You might also want gloves, because the plants can be thorny, too. Small, conical "tomato cages" make great eggplant cages.

Eggplants have carbohydrates and a little protein, but could not be considered nutritional powerhouses. Indeed, with their capacity to sponge up cooking oil, eggplants can be a caloric hazard.

OKRA

Okra is also known as gumbo. Plant the seeds 2 feet apart, and keep well mulched. In northerly zones, transplant seedlings into the garden at 4 weeks. The edible part of the plant is the seedpod that develops from the hibiscus-like flower. Use pruning shears to cut off the pods when they are a few inches long, and still tender. Watch out for thorns! The Clemson Spineless cultivar has none.

Okra is heat- and drought-tolerant, if you give it a deep soak now and then. Okra is not a heavy feeder and doesn't require extra fertilizer. When the plant is 3 feet tall, you can use a pair of pruning shears to cut the plant back to 1 foot tall, and it will sprout a new, fruiting stem for continued harvest.

Here are some recommended okra varieties:

- **Clemson Spineless**—no thorns
- **Emerald**—rib-free
- **Annie Oakley II H.**—a high-yielding variety
- **Burgundy**—attractive red pods make it a good candidate for edible landscaping or inclusion in a "tropical" garden
- **Cajun Delight H.**—a 1997 AAS winner especially good for the north, with semi-dwarf plants

PEPPERS

In ancient Mexico, the Aztecs cultivated the native annual peppers and helped develop dozens of variations. These zingy fruits have since become popular all over the globe, especially in hot climates. (Spicy food helps you sweat, which in turn helps you stay cooler.) The world would be a dull place without Cajun gumbo, Texan Chile Con Carne, Indian Curry, Hungarian Goulash, or Szechuan dishes.

The heat in **hot peppers** is regulated not only by the genes of the variety but also by the climate. A habanero pepper grown in Minnesota won't be quite as hot as one grown in Oklahoma. Peppers are traditionally rated on the Scoville Heat Scale, with units ranging from 0 to 300,000. This being a little unwieldy, editor Dave Dewitt of *Chile Pepper* magazine came up with the Chile Heat Scale: hottest are the habaneros at 10; mildest are the sweet bell peppers at 0. For the curious: Chile piquin 9; cayenne 8; Thai chile 7; serrano 6; cascabel 5; pasilla 4; poblano 3; mulato 2; New Mexico 1.

The seeds and veins are the hottest part of any spicy pepper, and removing these will tone down a recipe. The active ingredient is capsaicin oil, which is why slugging down a Dos Equis beer or margarita does not cut the fire in your mouth. Instead, try dairy products or carbohydrates (tortillas, rice, potatoes) to sop up the offending oil. When handling hot peppers, be sure to wear gloves (wash the gloves with soap and water afterward), and do *not* get your hands anywhere near your eyes. Otherwise it's quite easy to get capsaicin oil underneath your nails, and any oil not washed off will come back to haunt you next time you scratch an itch or blow your nose. Capsaicin oils are also used in arthritis creams and in rabbit/insect repellents.

Peppers often have different names when fresh and dried. Poblanos allowed to ripen and dried are referred to as ancho peppers. Poblanos are the mildly zingy kind used for *chiles rellenos*. The dried anchos are used in making *mole* sauce.

Here are some popular types of hot peppers:

- **Cayenne peppers**—the long, skinny type used for hot sauces
- **Cherry peppers**—resemble their namesake fruits, and are generally pickled
- **Jalapenos**—figure prominently in many pepper-eating contests; also appear on nachos and pizzas, or are stuffed with cheese
- **New Mexican peppers**—ripened to a red color and then dried and hung in *ristras* (strings). Anaheim is a type of New Mexican pepper that often goes into chile sauces.
- **Paprika peppers**—although prominent in Hungarian goulash (more than forty types of paprika peppers are grown in Hungary), the paprika

pepper also originated in the New World. Some paprikas are sweet; others are spicy. Paprika pepper pods are likewise ripened, dried, and then ground into powder. You can use your coffee grinder for this job, as long as the pod is dried to a crispy state and you are sure to wipe out the coffee grinder before and after.

- **Pimientos**—the peppers that are slivered and inserted into green olives, or sometimes used to make paprika spice
- **Serrano peppers**—used, in addition to jalapenos, in fresh salsas

Bell pepper is another name for **sweet peppers.** For some reason, Americans eat a lot of green, unripe peppers. I'm not sure why, because peppers are much sweeter, more nutritious, more attractive, and produce fewer "burps" when allowed to ripen to another color. Bells can ripen to chocolate brown (the Chocolate cultivar is only that color, not that flavor), purple, lilac, red, orange, golden yellow, ivory, and chartreuse. Mexibell is a faintly spicy sweet pepper. My favorite sweet pepper is Gypsy Hybrid, which outproduces the old standard, California Wonder, by 300 percent (that's four times as many). Gypsy H. peppers start out chartreuse and ripen to a rich red.

Peppers are fragile plants; don't whack hoses against them or try to pull the fruits off. If you don't have a pair of garden scissors or a garden knife, invest in one and keep it sharp for harvesting. A short, conical tomato cage also makes a great cage for pepper plants. Pepper plants can be anywhere from 12 inches to 5 feet tall! Peppers are rich in vitamin A, and the ripe ones are an especially good source of vitamin C.

SWEETPOTATOES

The sweetpotato is not a potato at all; it's related to the morning glory. It's also not a yam, which is an African vegetable sometimes found in Latin or international produce markets. The tropical vines of the sweetpotato will spread over a wide area of ground to produce the tubers, which require a long, hot growing season.

To grow your own transplant "slips," find a jar that will hold two-thirds of a whole, raw tuber and keep the bottom inch of the root under water. Most people insert a few toothpicks around the widest part of the root to suspend it in the jar. Keep it in a warm, bright place, and in 2 to 4 weeks rooted shoots will appear on the top half of the root. Break these off and transplant outdoors in May or June, a couple weeks after your last frost date.

Avoid using high-nitrogen fertilizers, or else you'll end up with lots of vines but few roots. Sweetpotatoes are not only a heat-loving crop, but they're also drought-tolerant, too. At the end of summer, dig up the roots. Sweetpotato slips can also be bought from Piedmont Plant Company or from your local farmer's market.

Sweetpotatoes have a long growing season, so gardeners in the northern states will want to stick with a quick-maturing cultivar, such as Georgia Jet (90 days), Vardaman (100 days), Bush Porto Rico (110 days), or Centennial (120 days). Most others take 150–160 frost-free days to maturity. In the northerly parts of the Heartland, where the nights can be chilly, consider putting sheets of black or clear mulching plastic on a mounded or raised bed. You just cut holes in the plastic 24 inches apart, make a slight depression or well to catch rainwater, and plant a slip in each hole. The stuff traps and retains heat, giving you leafier vines and larger roots.

When harvesting your sweetpotatoes, fork up the roots very gently. They have thin skins and, like potatoes, need to be "cured" in a warm (80 °F), humid place out of direct sunlight (the garage comes to mind). They'll be done curing after a week, and can simply be kept on the upper pantry shelf, away from the tumble of cereal boxes and cans that can bruise them. Do not refrigerate raw sweetpotatoes; like bananas, they turn gross quickly. Sweetpotatoes are a good source of carbohydrates (they're calorically denser than potatoes) and a good source of vitamin A.

TOMATOES

This champion of the American garden has been popular only in recent history, but nowadays many people consider themselves gardeners even when they grow nothing but a few tomato plants.

Bush (also known as determinate) tomatoes grow only so big, and produce a limited number of tomatoes. These varieties are often used by the canning industry, because once the tomatoes are harvested, the field can be stripped and replanted with something else. Pole (or indeterminate) tomatoes keep on growing vines and fruits until the frost gets them.

Anxious gardeners can put transplants out (in a Wall O' Water) at the earliest last frost date, as long as the evening temperatures are above the fifties. (Remove the Wall O' Water after the last frost date.) The soil should have warmed up to 70 °F, or else the plants will just sit there and sulk. Pick off the bottom pair of leaves, and bury the plant up to the armpits of the next pair of leaves, because it will root all along the stem. This deeper planting gives extra drought and

wind tolerance. Growing early tomatoes is discussed in Chapter 3 on seed starting.

Those short, conical tomato cages will hold up only tiny patio tomatoes. Larger bush tomatoes are better contained by hog wire or concrete-reinforcing wire (CRW), bound into a tube around the plant. Cut wire to a length of 9–10 feet, and bend over the wires along the side to secure and create a ring 3 feet in diameter; or cut a 6-foot length of wire to make a ring 2 feet in diameter.

Do not prune bush tomatoes (pinch out suckers), or you'll cut fruit production to half of what the plant is capable of producing. Despite some old gardeners' tales, bush tomato suckers *do* grow fruits on them!

For pole tomatoes, you do need to prune off the suckers, which are stems that grow from the joints of the side branches. Keep pole tomatoes pruned to just one or two "leaders," or main stems. If you stake them, bury the stake at least a foot deep for sturdiness. For pole tomatoes, you'll need a stake 7–8 feet tall. (Those 5-foot stakes are for bush tomatoes.) You can also let them sprawl, climbing fences or mesh netting. More on different types of tomato supports is discussed in Chapter 4 (see the section called "Tomatoes: Stake, Cage, or Sprawl?").

Pick the tomatoes when they're purple, red, orange, gold, pink, or whatever color the variety is supposed to get. (Pink tomatoes are the same as red tomatoes, except they lack the yellow coloration in the skin; pink tomatoes have clear skins.) Do not refrigerate tomatoes; they lose their flavor. Do let them ripen to a deep, rich color on the vine. If you pick them when they're just "breaking pink" and let them ripen on the kitchen counter, they will have no more flavor than supermarket 'maters. When a heavy rain is forecasted, you'll probably want to pick all the ripe tomatoes to avoid cracking later.

Cherry tomatoes are the small sort served on salads. Most cherry tomato plants, despite producing small fruits, grow into overenthusiastically long vines. One greenhouse owner said that the supported vines eventually reached the other end of the structure! If you like really sweet tomatoes, try orange Sungold H. or Sweet Gold H. Sweet Million and Cherry Baby are very productive red cherry tomatoes.

Large slicing or "beefsteak" tomatoes ripen later in the harvest season, due to their large size. Male gardeners are especially fond of these, perhaps feeling that their gardening skills (or machismo) are reflected in the giant quality of the fruit. If you're going for competition-size 'maters, try Big Beef H., Better Boy H., or Delicious and let only three fruits grow on the entire plant.

Paste-type tomatoes are simply those that are less juicy than the cherry or slicing types. In the cooking pot, they take less time to cook down to a thick sauce. In truth, any shape or color of tomato can be used to make sauce! And frankly, sauces made with good-flavored tomatoes are better than those made with mealy, insipid tomatoes. Roma may be a popular paste tomato, but this plant is determinate (produces only a limited number of fruits), and I don't find it to be the tastiest 'mater on the block. I prefer Italian Gold H., which grows larger, golden-orange fruits, and more of them. Opalka is a Polish red paste tomato with few seeds. It also has "wispy" foliage, which is normal to the cultivar, and not a health concern for the plant. You'll find more information about saucing tomatoes in Chapter 7.

Heirloom tomatoes have lately become all the rage, which is kind of funny because they've been around a long time!

Heirloom is a somewhat imprecise word that can have various meanings: a cultivar that predates the 1940s, when hybrids appeared on the scene; a cultivar that came "from the old country"; or a cultivar that's been handed down for several generations. Modern hybrids are created by taking the pollen from one cultivar of tomato and using it to fertilize a different cultivar. This hand pollination is the reason for higher seed prices. Hybrids often exhibit better disease resistance or larger fruits. However, they are not always "better" than open-pollinated or heirloom tomatoes.

If you are interested in heirloom tomatoes, check out a book by Carolyn Male, a recently retired professor of microbiology who has grown over a thousand types of tomatoes. *100 Heirloom Tomatoes for the American Garden* was published by Workman Publishing in 1999, and the volume is chock-full of photos of real tomatoes, with great descriptions of the history and growth habits. I owe most of my knowledge of heirloom tomatoes to Carolyn Male's expertise.

In her book, Male explains that for those of us who've tried to grow the famous Brandywine tomato, the common pink strain has difficulty with pollination due to malformed blossoms. This problem can be helped by flicking your finger across the tomato blossom, or by brushing plants with a broom. Male recommends either the OTV or Suddeth (Quisenberry) strains of Brandywine for cultivars that have a much better pollination record as well as fantastic flavor.

In addition to Seed Savers Exchange, another good source for hundreds of hybrid and heirloom tomatoes (and peppers, too) is Tomato Growers Supply. You can probably find a family favorite here!

Tomato Growers Supply Company
P.O. Box 2237
Fort Myers, FL 33902
phone 888-478-7333
www.tomatogrowers.com

Or try Chuck Wyatt's heirloom tomato website:

Charles A. Wyatt
5421 Princess Drive
Rosedale, MD 21237
phone 410-687-8665
www.heirloomtomatoes.net

Here are some recommended tomato cultivars:

- **Early tomatoes**—Matina (from Germany), Prairie Fire (bush type), Stupice (stoo-PEACH-ka, from Czechoslovakia), or golden Jaune Negib
- **Midseason**—Better Boy H., Big Beef H., Celebrity H. (bush type and 1984 AAS Winner), Jetstar H., Supersonic H., or Rutgers (an old favorite and bush type)
- **Late season**—Arkansas Traveler (heat-tolerant)
- **Colorful**—Aunt Ruby's German Green (goes from olive drab to bright chartreuse with gold blush when ripe; very tasty), Black Krim (purple beefsteak type from Russia), Flamme (orange salad tomato from France), Garden Peach (sweet, fuzzy, and peach-colored), or Italian Gold H. (golden paste type)
- **Cherry**—Sweet Million, Sungold H.

Tomatoes are low in calories (being watery), but are a source of vitamins A and C.

CUCURBITS
CUCUMBERS, MELONS, SUMMER SQUASH, WINTER SQUASH, PUMPKINS

Like beans and tomatoes, cucurbits come in bush and vining types. Bush types produce fewer fruits and take up less space. They can all be started by transplants or by direct-seeding 1 inch deep in the garden. Cucurbits are picky about being transplanted, so if you really insist on transplants, start the seeds in an 8-inch, plastic- or newspaper-lined pot that will allow the root ball to slide right out. Otherwise, direct-seed them after the ground is thoroughly warm in May or June, about the time the peonies bloom.

Cucumbers

Cucumbers have been grown since antiquity and are native to India, from which they spread to Egypt and China. Vining (non-bush) cucumbers do best crawling up trellis netting. Cukes are thirsty plants, so keep them well-watered. Some gallon plastic milk jugs, with a couple of pinholes in the bottom, are handy for watering. Just fill up the jugs after burying them halfway, and they will slowly drip water into the cuke's root zone without taking up your time, or splashing the leaves. Cut the fruits off with a sharp blade—don't pull on them and risk ripping up the vines. Keep the cukes picked (starting at about 9 weeks) when they're no longer than your hand, or finger-length for pickling. If a cuke goes from green to yellow, it's an over-ripe seed case, and is overdue for the compost heap lest the plant cease production of new fruits.

Cucumber wilt is spread by both the spotted and striped cucumber beetles, which look like yellow ladybugs. These are discussed in depth in Chapter 8. However, I've found two types of cucumbers that are very resistant to this virus, mostly because the plants are unattractive to the beetles. These are County Fair H. pickling cucumbers (also good eaten fresh) and Marketmore 97, a glossy, long, slicing cucumber. Garden City Seeds and Territorial Seed catalogs have carried these varieties; check the current catalogs. Cucumbers are nutritional duds, but are cool and juicy and make excellent pickles.

"You know," this young fellow said to me, "I never seem to get many cukes off my plants. But I keep them well-watered and fertilized!"

"I bet you have an insect problem!"

"No way!" he protested, "I always spray 'em with Sevin. Knocks the bugs flat!"

Ouch. I bet that's his problem. Unlike tomatoes, which have "perfect" flowers that are self-pollinating, cucurbit flowers require the extra help that pollinating insects (honeybees, bumble bees, squash bees, and others) provide. To improve your own harvest, you need to make sure that your own horticultural practices do not offend or destroy these beneficial insects. The popular chemical pesticide Sevin is *deadly* to bees! If you must use it, use the liquid type at dusk when the bees have gone home for the night.

Common cucumbers produce both male and female flowers growing on the same plant. These are called *monoecious*, and are known as "standard type" cukes. If you've delved into very many catalogs, you'll have noticed there's a dizzying array of standard, greenhouse, monoecious, gynoecious, and self-fertile cukes.

Greenhouse-type cucumbers for sale can be grown either inside a greenhouse or outdoors. But watch out what you're getting here. Greenhouse cucumbers come in two types: mostly female, or all-female flowers. If they're mostly female, then most of the flowers on each vine are female, fruit-producing flowers, which in-creases your crop production. They still have a few male flowers to ensure pollination.

The *real* all-female cucumber cultivars are called *gynoecious*, and have exclusively female flowers. Some gynoecious cukes are sold with the seed of a standard cucumber included in the package, to provide pollen-producing male flowers. The standard seeds will be colored or specially packaged within, so you can be sure to plant them. Look at the package or the catalog for telltale words such as "seed of pollinator included." This means the plant is not capable of self-pollination. You must be sure that you have room to grow at least two separate cucumber plants.

Some catalogs sell true greenhouse cucumbers that produce their fruits through a sort of "virgin birth" process. The ovary (the fleshy part of the cucumber that we eat) grows and develops, even though there are no viable seeds within them. These *parthenocarpic* cucumbers are seedless. If grown outdoors and pollinated, they can actually become coarse and inedible. A single packet of parthenocarpic cucumber seeds, developed in Europe exclusively for greenhouse growing, can set you back several dollars. Of these parthenocarpic cukes, there are new varieties that can be grown outdoors without bad results. Again, unless otherwise specified, most cucumbers are the standard type.

The male flowers are the first to bloom, standing on long stems, but without ever growing into cukes. This fact has caused many an unwitting novice gardener to suspect either their growing methods or the plant itself. (And no, adding more fertilizer won't make those male flowers bear cukes!) But don't panic. Think of the male flowers as simply an early warning signal to the bees, so they will gather their forces for the riches to come.

Male cucumber flower.

The female flowers are recognizable by their shorter stems and the "microcuke" (or micromelon or microsquash, depending on which cucurbit you are growing) that grows behind the blossom. These are the ovaries that will grow into the fruits after pollination and fertilization take place. (Botanists call cucumbers, tomatoes, peppers, and eggplants "fruits" because they have seeds inside them.)

Bees don't pollinate flowers on purpose. This intentional "accident" of nature occurs because bees collect pollen for a foodstuff (storing it on "breeches" on their legs), and because pollen naturally sticks all over the bee's fur. When the bee stops by another flower to get more nectar and pollen, some of the pollen is transferred to the sticky stigma part of the flower. This part of the process is called pollination, and only the correct type of pollen grains will work on a flower. Once the pollen grains reach the

egg cell in the ovary, then fertilization occurs. The right amount of pollen must land on each flower for each of the seeds to be fertilized. If there isn't enough, the plant creates underdeveloped, misshapen fruits.

Don't let old gardener's tales frighten you; you can't grow "melocumbers" or "cukermelons." The pollen simply won't be accepted on the wrong plant. What can happen is the cross-pollination of different kinds of melons, or different kinds of squashes. You won't notice the results this year, since you're eating the fleshy ovary that was already genetically determined. What you would notice was if you saved the seeds from crossed plants and planted the seeds the next year. Then the mixed genes would express themselves in the second (F2) generation of fruits.

Female cucumber flower.

Melons

Melons take about 12 weeks from seed to harvest. Muskmelons (also called cantaloupes) develop a pronounced netting on their surfaces when ripe, and many other melon types will "slip" or fall off the vine when ripe. Native to Persia, melons have long, sprawling vines that can reach lengths of 6 to 8 feet. Mulching the ground in your melon patch with straw or grass clippings will save you much weeding time. Be sure not to pick fruits too early; once picked, they will not sweeten anymore.

Melon cultivars are always changing, but Burpee H., Minnesota Midget (compact), and Ambrosia H. muskmelons are popular; Earlidew H. is a quick-maturing (80 days) green honeydew. The French Charentais melons are exquisite, with faintly ribbed green skin and deep orange, sweet flesh. Savor H. does well, and

is ripe when the leaf next to the fruit stem turns pale. Melons have vitamins A and C as well as carbohydrates.

Watermelons are native to Africa. Most of them take up quite a bit of space, and all but the smallest of Japanese-bred "icebox" melons have to be grown on the ground instead of a trellis. When ripe, watermelons change from white to yellow on the bottom, and the little tendril nearest the melon stem withers. Moons and Stars is an heirloom type with rounded fruits of a dark green skin spotted with yellow dots (the stars) and a few larger yellow spots (the moons). Watermelons can have red, pink, orange, or yellow flesh. Watermelon rind is also made into a sweet pickle, and of course the seeds are optimum for spitting contests. And no, watermelon seeds do *not* sprout in your stomach, no matter what the neighbor boy said.

WHERE DO THEY GET THE SEEDS FOR SEEDLESS WATERMELONS?

How do they get the seeds for seedless watermelons? Well, first of all, the part you're eating (the fruit itself) is the ovary, and this is created as part of the development of the flower. Whether the ovary develops into a nice, large melon—or falls off as a dud—is dependent on pollination. Once the pollen reaches the female flower, one grain migrates to meet up with the egg cell to create the embryonic seed, and the other grain becomes part of the endosperm (the part of the seed that provides food for the seed when it sprouts). This second step is known as fertilization (not to be confused with fertilizing the soil or plants). Pollination does not automatically guarantee fertilization; melon pollen can land on cucumber flowers, but nothing else happens. Seedless watermelons occur because the female flower-bearing plants were specially treated to have a different number of chromosomes than the plants that will be used for their male flowers.

When you get your packet of seedless watermelon seeds, you need to look for specially packaged or painted pollinator seeds. These must be planted as well as the treated female-flower seeds. The pollen from those male flowers is close enough to ensure fruit development, but sufficiently different that the fruits cannot produce viable second-generation seeds. Seedless watermelons are the mules of the cucurbit world.

Squashes

Summer and winter squash (including pumpkins), native to the New World, are part of the Native Americans' "Three Sisters" trinity of squash, beans, and corn.

Traditionally, the corn was planted before the beans, so the stalks would have a height advantage and provide a climbing support for the pole beans. The squash vines ran amuck around the patch, shading the ground and making a prickly barrier against critters. Squashes kept the Pilgrims and other colonists alive during the long winters. They remain a popular winter vegetable in the Northeast, where the growing season can be too short or cool for sweetpotatoes. Pumpkin seeds are roasted and salted as a snack, and like other seeds, are full of nutrition.

Squashes are started from seed. Plant a few seeds into a "hill." A hill is a small, raised mound of soil (not a giant pitcher's mound) that will warm up quicker than the surrounding garden. Water the seeds and stand back. Smaller vining squashes, including the Jack Be Little pumpkins, do great on trellis netting. Larger types will have to be grown on the ground, easily taking up 100 square feet of space.

You could eat a watermelon all by yourself, but who would want to?

Summer squashes are nearly all bush type, and they include crooknecks, pattypans, and zucchinis. At 8 weeks from seeding, keep an eye on zucchini and other summer squashes *every day*; they can double in size during a rainy night! There is no glory in growing Hindenburg-sized zucchini. Pick them small, about hand size. New varieties of "more productive" summer squashes are released every year. Summer squashes that are ignored and turn into hard squashes are edible, but not tasty. They have some car-bohydrates, but no major vitamins to speak of.

Winter squashes should be harvested before the heavy frost in October. Cut the stems 2–3 inches from the fruit, leaving a "handle" that helps the fruit resist rot. You can be sure the fruits are ready for picking when you can no longer scratch the skin with your thumbnail. Store them someplace with cool, even temperatures, such as under the bed, atop the china hutch, on the guest-bedroom dresser. . . . Many types of winter squashes exist, including the smaller green, ribbed acorn types; round butter-cups; long with a knob butternuts; giant warty Blue Hubbards; and yellow, oval spaghetti squashes whose flesh cooks into spaghetti-like strands. Squash blos-soms are also edible and find their way into Zuni and Italian recipes. Choose the male flowers (with the longer, straight stems) and remove the sex parts (some-times bitter) before preparing. Winter squashes can be eaten as immature "summer-type" squashes, but don't taste as good. They are rich in vitamin A and carbohydrates.

Pumpkins are grown just like other winter squashes. Some pumpkins are grown for jack-o'-lantern use, and they are stringy and not very tasty. (In me-dieval times the pumpkin had not yet been introduced to Europe, and jack-o'-lanterns were made out of hollowed turnips.) For pie pumpkins, look for the word *sugar* or *pie* in the name or catalog description. Consider Baby Bear, a 1993 AAS winner and a good producer of two-pound fruits, each of which cook down to two cups of squash squish, *just right* for recipes. Small Sugar produces larger 5–8 pound cooking pumpkins.

Lumina is a white-skinned pumpkin; Jack Be Little or Wee Be Little are orange miniatures, and Baby Boo is a white-skinned miniature. The classic Cin-derella's carriage pumpkin is the French heirloom Rouge Vif D'Etampes. You can personalize your pumpkins by gently scratching names, slogans, or pictures into the outside layer of skin on green pumpkins, once they've reached softball size. The scratches will grow into corky scar tissue and become permanent tattoos on the fruits.

Do your pumpkins scream "Unfair!" when you don't water them as much as the cucumbers? Do your carrots complain, "You pay more attention to her!" when you attend your tomatoes by caging them? Their needs are different.

For growing competition-size pump-kins, get Atlantic Giant seed, and check out Don Langevin's book, *How to Grow World-Class Giant Pumpkins* (1993, Annedawn Publishing, Norton, MA). Wayne Hackney from Connecticut has used his 700- to 800-pound wonders for outboard boats! In recent years, these giant squashes have passed the 1,100-pound mark, and growers around the world meet at various locations to offi-cially weigh in.

These giant pumpkins require prodi-gious amounts of room, soil preparation, and attention (they can gain 20 pounds a day!) but are lots of fun. Growers get rather involved in their specialized grow-ing methods. Some even go so far as installing heating cables in the soil, building a greenhouse over the patch in September to extend the season, or using PC-based programs to track daily growth, weather conditions, feeding schedules, and more. Visit the World Class Giant Pumpkins website for more information, seeds, and books: www.backyardgardener.com/wcgp

PERENNIAL VEGETABLES
ASPARAGUS, RHUBARB, SUNROOTS

You can start an **asparagus** patch by seed, but then you'd have to wait four years for the first harvest. Better yet, you can start with two-year-old roots and wait just two years. Once established, the patch will live for years. Simply spread the crowns out 6 inches deep and 18 inches apart. If the crowns are dried out and stiff, soak them in tepid water for a couple hours before planting. Each crown will have perpendicular buds, which are the stem points that indicate the topside of the plant. The ground should be well tilled or dug deeply and loosely for the plants to establish easily. Unlike the Herculean efforts Victorian gardeners went through to plant their asparagus in 2-foot-deep trenches, modern gardeners find that they're easily grown when planted only 6 inches deep.

Eat none of your asparagus stems the first year after transplanting. You can pick a few the next year; the third year, you can cut stems for nearly a month, or until all of the sprouting stems are coming up pencil-thin. You can cut stems with a knife at just below ground level. The cook should then snap the stalk where it will—near the bottom—separating the tough from the tender part. Be sure to keep your asparagus patch mulched to avoid stressing new plants, and save yourself some work! Salting the ground is neither necessary nor beneficial. Asparagus has carbohydrates and some vitamins A and C, calcium, phosphorus, and riboflavin. Try UC157, Purple Passion, Jersey Giant, or Mary Washington.

Rhubarb is also called "pie plant," because the tart stems are so often found in sugary pies, generally mixed with strawberries. Stems come not only in red versions but also in pink or green. The leaves of rhubarb are poisonous and should be avoided. Select a planting location in full sun, with rich, well-drained soil. Because rhubarb is a perennial, don't put it in garden areas subject to tilling.

Plant the roots outside in the early spring, 4 or 5 inches deep and 2 feet apart. Mature plants can be divided, cutting the roots into several pieces and replanting. Be sure to improve the soil with 3 to 4 inches of compost (the plant will be there for years), especially if you have heavy clay soil. Good drainage is important to rhubarbs, so raised beds are also an excellent choice. Mulch the plants to keep weeds down.

Do not harvest until the second year. Instead of cutting, *pull* the stems off. After the second year, you can pull stems for as long as 8 weeks. Once a flower stalk grows out, that's the signal that the plant is done giving up stalks for you. Quit pulling stems. Do pull off the flower stalk; otherwise it'll spend its energy making seeds instead of fortifying itself for next year.

Sunroots are also known as Jerusalem artichokes, or sunchokes. Sunroots are the edible tubers of a native perennial sunflower (*Helianthus tuberosus*). Like many of our natives, it has become more popular in Europe than here, and its curious moniker was a bastardization of the French name for the sunflower (girasole).

This lumpy tuber has many fine reasons for gardeners to take up cultivation: high yields, ease of growing, hardly any pests, no need to repurchase seed stock in successive years, and its particular carbohydrate form. Sunroots do not contain starch, but rather have "inulin" carbohydrates. Inulin breaks down into levulose rather than sugar, making it useful in diabetic diets (do not confuse *inulin* with *insulin*). Sunroots are a good source of potassium, phosphorus, calcium, iron, and vitamin A; and they have as much protein as soybeans.

You can purchase sunroot tubers in the mail, or at the groceries and garden centers. Plant the tubers 4–6 inches deep and 12–18 inches apart, in April or May. Sunroots are not picky about their soil, being a native. But because they're a root crop, your yield will be substantially increased if you give them fertile, compost-enriched soil (do not use fresh manure to improve soil for root crops). Of course, vegetable crops need full sun.

From the tubers grow 6- to 10-foot-tall yellow sunflowers. The shortening days of late summer trigger the flower and tuber production. Sunroots are a 120- to 150-day crop. Mulch around the stalks to prevent weeds from growing. You might want some fence stakes and twine around the patch to keep the tall flowers from falling over. Otherwise, they need no maintenance.

Oh, and one more thing: Sunroot tubers *spread*. They're very *productive* and *vigorous*, two key words that careful catalog readers are watchful for. It's impossible to find *all* the tubers when you harvest, so the ones you leave behind will become next year's "seeds," whether you want them to or not. Don't even *consider* rototilling them! So what do you do to contain your ever-productive patch? I recommend 12-inch-wide aluminum roof flashing, inserted vertically in a ring moat around the area. Install the moat before you make the initial tuber planting. Rototilling to loosen the earth for planting will also make slipping in the moat easier.

Prepare to harvest your bucketsful of tubers in the autumn, after a light October frost. Cut down the flower stalks (whose hollow stems are great for allowing air into the center and bottom of the compost pile), and then *leave the tubers in the ground* for two to three weeks. During this curing time, the inulin breaks down and the flavor improves. Uncured, freshly dug tubers can have a "green" taste, and give some people gastric upset.

Sunroots are thin-skinned, and they can dry out quickly. Many people prefer to store them in plastic bags in the refrigerator, or right in the ground (lacking a more sophisticated root cellar). Use a spading fork to fluff up and loosen the soil while lifting the tubers near the surface. Then cover the top of the ground with nylon burlap or an old polyester bedsheet, and spread straw mulch a foot deep on top. This will keep the ground from freezing, and you can easily lift the fabric and pull out a few roots whenever needed during the winter. The next spring, simply pull out the fabric and leave the straw there for a weed-preventing mulch (the plants will have no trouble growing through it, believe me).

Several different cultivars of sunroots are available: super-productive Stampede, a rounder and slightly knobby sort. French Mammoth White is another common, knobby cultivar. Although sunroots are easy to wash off, some people prefer smoother tubers for peeling. Try the spindle-shaped Golden Nugget, long sweetpotato–shaped Fuseau, or red-skinned Smooth Garnet. Dwarf Sunray has shorter stems for more ornamental edible landscaping.

THAT COVER-UP JOB

Once you've started harvesting and pulling out stuff in the late summer and autumn, there is one more thing you can do to help improve your soil and cut down on weeds.

First put away the support cages, clean off the old vines, and pull the weeds and old plants. Once the garden's cleaned up and "virgin" again, the view is liberating, and you'll have fewer pest problems next year. Of course, the sight of bare ground makes any gardener twitch, and there's probably a good reason for that. Bare ground is subject to ruin by erosion and weeds!

So take the second step, and choose an annual cover crop to plant in. If you can, time the seeding before a rain is supposed to come through. If the ground has been baked hard from pounding rains followed by endless hot days, you may want to rototill, but usually just scribbling the top surface with a garden rake will suffice. Remember, *never* rototill wet clay soil, or you'll have terra cotta clods that remain so for several years.

So what are cover crops, and what do they do for your soil? A cover crop (also called "green manure") is a crop grown on currently unused ground. It's a crop that puts large amounts of nutrients back into the soil—often it's a legume, which has the ability to "fix" nitrogen from the air into a plant-usable form down in the soil. (Avoid using fungicide-treated seed; the fungicide kills those living inoculant organisms.) Legumes are an especially good choice for a cover crop to follow heavy feeders, such as corn and salad greens. A good rule of thumb is to seed half a pound of grass-type cover crops per 100 square feet, or a quarter-pound of leguminous-type crops.

Seeds for cover crops are ridiculously cheap—less than the price of a cup of coffee per pound—and well worth the little effort required. You don't need to use a turf-grass spreader to apply them, either. Seed autumn leguminous cover crops 6 to 8 weeks before your hard frost, and grassy cover crops 4 to 6 weeks before the hard frost. Just broadcast the seed by hand, scattering it in swoops down the beds or rows. After a few swoops you catch onto the rhythm, and will find your aim improving. It's a very archaic and gentle activity, shared by hundreds of generations of our ancestors. Compared to flowers and vegetables, cover crops are nearly foolproof! A sheet of Reemay or other row cover will keep the birdies from munching down on the yummy seeds until they're sprouted and on their way.

Cover crops are cut down before the flowering stage and turned under to decompose right back into the ground. (Do yourself a favor; cut down the cover crop and let it die for a week or so before trying to rototill the matter in.) It's a form of on-site composting. Clay soils are usually rich in nutrients, but their wedgy texture leaves something to be desired. Green manure provides organic matter to loosen up the clay, and it encourages the population of earthworms, those "knights in slimy armor" that are nature's own rototillers. Cover crops also suppress weeds, control erosion, and help trap rainfall and snowfall.

Dutch clover and hairy vetch are leguminous cover crops, and the flowers provide pollen for bees. Those bees need to get their larders filled before winter comes, so they will be able to come back and fertilize next year's fruits and cucurbits. The first time you plant a leguminous cover crop in an area, it will require a special inoculant. The inoculant dust is mixed with the seed before planting.

Alfalfa is a grain cover crop with deep-growing roots that can bring up the nutrients found in our deep prairie soils. Be sure to get an annual alfalfa, such as

A cover crop of buckwheat.

Nitro; otherwise, those deep roots can come back to haunt you later on. Annual alfalfa dies during the winter, and then you can easily turn it under come late winter or before the spring rains. Oats and annual ryegrass will germinate even when temperatures are in the forties. Annual cereal rye is an especially good choice for acidic soils or just generally poor soils. (*Do* be sure to cut it down before it goes to seed.)

If you choose buckwheat for its weed-smothering qualities, be *very* sure to mow or hoe the stuff down before it goes to seed, or you'll be pulling buckwheat for the rest of the summer. Buckwheat is planted in the spring, and it's a good choice for new ground you want to open up to cultivation later on in the summer.

Wait 2 to 3 weeks for the material to decompose before planting again.

If you are trying to recover really worn out or abused ground, take a one-year rehab approach by seeding in the large white lupine (*Lupinus albus*) in the spring. Turn under in the fall and seed in winter rye. Turn that under the next spring, and the soil will be much improved.

Cover crops also serve another purpose. If you plant perennial Dutch white clover in your orchard, it smothers the weeds and produces a large number of flowers to attract the bees. You can mow Dutch white clover as well (it becomes somewhat weedy without mowing). I have this type of clover between my vegetable beds instead of grass. Buckwheat is also a good draw for bees.

CHAPTER SEVEN

Growing and Cooking with Herbs—
No Icky Veggies, Only Icky Recipes

WHY GROW HERBS?

Why not grow herbs? They're fun; they make your meals taste better without adding extra fat, salt, or sugar; and they are easy to grow! Some people shy away from growing them because herbs seem mysterious, difficult to grow, or require specially designed gardens. Others shy away from herbs because they're not sure what to do with them. Fortunately, vegetables and herbs are old friends that go hand in hand.

When considering your garden site for an herb bed, you will want to consider the same factors you did for your vegetable garden. Most herbs need full sun, although some will tolerate some shade. You will want your herb garden nearby the kitchen door if possible, because then it's easier to pick herbs for cooking, it's easier to keep an eye on for weeds, and you'll be able to enjoy it more and give it more attention. Herbs are rather care-free plants, but they still need watering and weeding, like anything else.

You can separate the herb garden from your vegetable garden, or you can plant the herbs with your vegetables. Or, you may want to plant annual herbs with your vegetables and have a separate bed for the perennial herbs. Many people find that planting basil in front of the tomatoes (give it a good 3-foot distance, since tomato plants do get huge later on) and dill near the cucumbers is just good common sense. You can go and pick both at the same time.

Most herbs are not hybridized. They are essentially the same plants used for thousands of years to season foods, dye clothes, and prepare potpourris and medications. In this book, I'll focus on the culinary herbs.

In this chapter I've divided my descriptions of herbs into four sections: perennial plants, tender perennials, annuals and biennials, and "volunteer" annuals and biennials. Most perennial herbs will have to be bought from a nursery or grown from cuttings of a friend's established plant. Rarely does anyone start them from seed.

Common Chives, Chinese/Garlic Chives

Chives are a quintessential ingredient on baked potatoes, along with sour cream or yogurt. Their light onion flavor goes with lots of things. Chives look like skinny onions, but their bulbs at the base of the plant never get fat. Chives multiply by growing more bulbs and by self-seeding, and often in the early spring you'll see a dark, hollow-stemmed "grass" growing in weedy yards; this is often wild chives. (You'll know this plant if you've ever mown over it.)

Common chives.

Chinese chives differ from common chives because their stems are flat, rather than round. Chinese chives are also known as garlic chives. I sometimes substitute Chinese chives for scallions in recipes. They come back every year, like all perennials. Chives are one of the few perennial herbs that are easy to grow

A DISCUSSION BETWEEN THE COOK AND THE BUTLER

"Erb" or "Hhherb"—which is correct? Actually, both are correct. And both pronunciations are used in the U.K., too. The only time you must say Hhherb is when it's a guy's name.

What's the difference between an herb and a spice? Herbs are usually the leaves or seeds of temperate-zone plants, while spices are the seeds, stems, roots, or bark of tropical plants. Columbus was seeking a quicker way to the Indies because he was after a cheaper path to buying the now-common black pepper! Herbs have been common in kitchen gardens since Greek and Roman times, but it was the rarest spices shipped in from far-eastern countries that brought great prices.

from seed. In fact they're almost too easy. Be sure to cut off the flower heads before they go to seed, unless you want chive plants sprouting everywhere. Plain chives have purple or pink flower heads. Chinese chives have white flower heads. Set plants 12–18 inches apart, in full sun. Chives can tolerate some light shade. Chives are 12–24 inches tall.

Horseradish

The horseradish plant is grown for its root, which is dug up in October or November, then peeled and shredded with great amounts of weeping. To grow horseradish, select an area in full sun, with rich soil that stays fairly moist throughout the year. Buy young roots that are plump and feel heavy, about 8–9 inches long and about a half-inch wide. Plant the root at a 45-degree angle, with the crown 5 inches below the soil surface, and space the plants 18 inches apart. Dig up and re-plant after two years, as you harvest the horseradish. Any root not dug up will grow back (whether you want it to or not). Two-year-old plants are 2–3 feet tall.

Lavender

Lavender flowers are used in potpour-ris and recipes. English lavenders (such as Munstead or Hidcote) are the hardiest, and French and English lavender have the best scent. Lavender is best from rooted cuttings, since the seeds do not al-ways grow true to the parent. One no-table exception to this is Lady lavender, a 1994 AAS Winner. Lady lavender grows true from seed, blooms a rich lavender-blue the first year, is winter-hardy, and smells wonderful. Its only downfall is that it doesn't have the long stems that florists require, shucky-darn. All laven-ders require excellent drainage; many gardeners grow them in raised beds, and those in areas with clay soils dig 50 per-cent sand into the soil!

Lady lavender grows true from seed and blooms the first year.

Lovage

Lovage is an essential vegetable/herb in the garden, because its leaves and stems taste just like celery! The only time I need to buy "real" celery is for making "ants on a log," that kid fodder decorated with peanut butter and raisins. Give your lovage plant some room; it grows 5 feet tall. Be sure to cut off the flower heads before they go to seed, or else you'll be pulling out lovages *everywhere*!

Lovage.

Lemon Balm

The leaves of lemon balm have a strong lemony scent. The fresh leaves are good in iced tea, for making tea, or any time you want a lemon flavor. You can take cuttings from older plants, and you can also plant this one by seed. The plant blooms during the summer, self-sowing readily (the children call it the "Lemon Bomb"). Take that as a warning! When the small white flowers begin to bloom along the stems, gather the plant and shear it to half-height, or just below

Lemon balm.

Mint in pot.

where the flowers begin appearing. The plant will grow back and fill in. You can dig up the baby plants for friends, or weed them out. The plant gets 2 feet tall and spreads as it matures. In the fall, cut it back down to a couple inches from the ground, and it'll come back in the spring. Lemon balm does best in full sun, but will take partial shade.

Mint

All mints are invasive. There are many varieties of mints, such as apple or pineapple mint; Corsican mint, which is a short, creeping mint with a crème de menthe flavor; eau de cologne mint, with a lemony tone; Japanese mint, used for menthol; peppermint, like candy canes; and spearmint. Mints can also grow in partial shade. You would do best to keep them in large, frost-proof pots. Mints spread by seeds, roots, and sometimes by rooting branches. Keep mints pruned, or they'll get woody and scraggly. Catnip is related to mint. All mints can be mown if they escape to the yard; it's a heady experience, though. Otherwise, mints grow 1–3 feet tall.

Oregano.

Oregano

Sweet marjoram is botanically known as *Origanum majorana*. Oregano is known as *Origanum vulgare*; in Latin the word *vulgare* means "common," in the older sense of the word. These two herbs are closely related, and sometimes it's hard to tell them apart. Marjoram can grow to 2 feet tall, and is sometimes called annual marjoram or knotted marjoram. Everyone knows oregano as the seasoning in pizza sauce. Oregano comes in several varieties, and grows just as tall as marjoram. Oregano is also known as wild marjoram or pot marjoram, just to make things even more confusing. There are some rather blah-tasting oregano plants out there. If you want one with really good flavor, get Greek oregano (it also has better manners and doesn't spread so aggressively).

Sage

Sage is an herb you'll definitely have to buy at the garden center or through a catalog. Sage grows into a small shrub that needs room for air circulation and full sun. The herb grows 3 feet tall. Golden sage has variegated yellow and green leaves and grows to only 18 inches tall. Tricolor sage has purple, cream, and green splotches on the leaves, but is not very winter hardy; it's generally grown for ornamental effect.

Sage.

Sage is prone to getting "leggy" after two or three years, meaning that the branches become bare on the bottom half and the plant looks unattractive. Prune the leggy branches back in the au-

tumn (much the way one does to rose bushes), being sure to leave small leaf buds on the remaining branches for the plant to grow back. Hang your sage prunings upside down to dry for this year's harvest. (Our ancestors probably pruned their sage when they slaughtered the piggies in the autumn, and turned the two into sausages.) The sage plant will re-sprout along the lower branches and retain its tidier form the next year. Sages sometimes decline after a few years and may need replacing. As with all herb blossoms, bees love sage blossoms. Herbs are a good way to attract these beneficial pollinators to your garden.

Thyme.

Thyme

Pronounced "time" or "thime." Thyme is a low-growing perennial that needs room at the front of the herb bed. Thyme does best in full sun. Plant thymes a foot apart; they'll grow 6 to 15 inches tall. The flowers are teeny-tiny pink or white. There are several varieties of thymes. There's regular garden thyme, Blessingham thyme, creeping red thyme and its blossoms, silver thyme, and woolly thyme. The latter sorts are lots of fun in rock gardens or collector's herb

Winter savory.

gardens, but often don't have quite the flavor of the common thyme. Harvest thyme by clipping off a stem or two, and stripping off the leaves from the top of the stem downward. There's no need to chop the tiny leaves.

Winter Savory

Winter savory is called *bohnenkraut*, the bean herb, in German. It is used not just to flavor green and dried beans, but also for its antiflatulent effect. There's also an annual kind, called summer savory, that grows 12–18 inches tall. Both savories resemble tarragon, so be sure to label what you have.

POPULAR TENDER PERENNIAL HERBS

Tender perennials will love our hot Heartland summers, but are not hardy during our harsh, varying winters. You will need to keep these herbs in pots, bringing them in before the first frost and then taking them out again after the last frost.

Bay Laurel

Bay grows into a small tree. Pruning for harvesting will keep it contained, be-

cause it grows slowly. Potted bays rarely get taller than 6 feet. Bays are propagated by rooting cuttings, so the small plants cost several dollars. Plant into a 5-gallon pot, and it will grow to fill the pot in just two or three years.

Bay.

Gingerroot

This tropical plant can be grown outdoors during the frost-free season, or as an interesting houseplant. I've grown gingerroot purchased at the grocery with little trouble. Select a "hand" that is firm and plump, not shriveled or moldy. Enthusiastic pieces will even have growth buds emerging. If you have a large hand of ginger, break off a palm-sized section, and plant it an inch deep. After three or four weeks of watering, the leaves finally emerge (the roots have been growing, but you can't see those), and they will grow a couple feet tall, resembling a television antenna. In the fall, you pull up the plant. Young buds are pink instead of brown, and don't have as much flavor because the *gingerin* has not developed as much. Put a section with young buds into a pot if you want to keep it over the winter.

Lemongrass

Gingerroot.

Lemongrass

Lemongrass is used in Thai and Vietnamese cuisine. There is little information available on the cultivation of lemongrass because, as one book said, it's a tender plant suited to the hot, muggy climes of the tropical regions. I wasn't daunted. That sounds a lot like Kansas City summers! And in fact, the stuff grows like gangbusters.

You can get lemongrass through several mail-order firms, or from local Asian groceries. Select stalks with some roots or root buds at the base. Plunk the stalk into the dirt about 2 or 3 inches deep, and keep well watered. The leaves can get up to 6 feet long, but they arch over. This herb can get up to 3 feet wide, so give it room. Lemongrass spreads by making more clumps, and the single stalk you planted at the beginning of summer will have turned into a clump of several in a few months' time. Just the bottom 2–3 inches of the stalk are chopped and used in recipes. The rest of the leaves may be used for potpourris, or for sweetening the compost heap.

Rosemary

Rosemary is a popular Mediterranean herb that needs full sun. It can grow 2–6 feet tall. Prostrate rosemary is a creeping-hanging form especially suited to pots. You can prune off branches as needed, and even trim this into a topiary. The Arp cultivar is hardy to zone 7 (as far north as Oklahoma City); but here in the Heartland, we grow our rosemary in large pots, lugging them outside and inside twice a year. Overwintered rosemary needs bright light, so I trim mine back into a tidier shape and keep it under the plant-growing lights when it's indoors.

Rosemary.

French tarragon.

Tarragon

Always buy *French* tarragon; the so-called Russian tarragon has virtually no flavor. Never buy tarragon seeds, because these are always the Russian variety. French tarragon is propagated exclusively through cuttings. When picking a plant at the nursery, gently rub and sniff the leaves; there should be a licorice flavor if it's the real thing. Tarragon grows up to 2 feet tall, but is a half-hardy perennial. Tarragon is a favorite vinegar flavoring.

POPULAR ANNUAL AND BIENNIAL HERBS

You'll need to buy transplants of the following herbs, or seed them in every year. Annuals die at the first heavy frost. Biennials live for two years, seeding the second year. More on this when we discuss volunteer herbs.

Basil

You can go bonkers over basil—there are so many varieties! Basil is easy to grow from seed, either directly into the garden after the last frost, or indoors in early April. Sprinkle the seeds, just barely covering with a little potting soil, and press firmly. Keep well watered, and keep under fluorescent lights, 2–3 inches above the tops of the plants. Basils get 1–4 feet tall, depending on the variety.

When the young plants have three pairs of true leaves, pinch out the top buds to double the number of leaves and keep the plants bushy. Some basils are naturally neat and tidy, such as the mounded piccolo basil and bush basil. Others, like the plain sweet basil and dark opals, are taller and stragglier. Varieties include anise basil, bush basil, dark opal basil, lemon basil, purple ruffles basil, and so on. Basil is an absolute wimp, so get everyone else in the ground first, and plant it outside a couple weeks after your last frost date.

Basil.

Chamomile.

Chamomile

When Peter Rabbit ate way too many vegetables in Mr. McGregor's garden, his mum gave him chamomile tea to settle his tummy. This plant is grown for its tiny, daisy-like flowers, which are dried and used in teas. German chamomile is an 18-inch-tall annual. Roman chamomile is a 6- to 9-inch-tall perennial.

Marjora

See "Oregano" in the section "Popular Perennial Herbs."

VOLUNTEER HERBS

Volunteer herbs are the ones that, after you've planted them once, reseed themselves, coming back year after year. For some reason, the seeds that plant themselves often seem to grow better than the ones we seed. That's not terribly surprising when you think about it; it's how nature works. Simply thin out the spares or eat them.

So how can you make all this fecundity work for you? There are two ways. Collect the ripened seed heads before they scatter (they will be dry and brittle) and then break them open to sprinkle seeds where *you* want them. Or, gently bend (but don't break) the flower stem so it seeds back into the garden instead of over the lawn or garden pathway.

Of course, the next trick is to remember that you intended those seedlings to be there, and not weed them out.

Borage

Borage is a silvery-green annual that grows 2–3 feet tall. It has beautiful star-shaped, purply-blue blossoms. Baby borage leaves taste like cucumber, and you can drop them into salads and sandwiches just for this effect. The large leaves taste like cucumber, too, but are too hairy for most people. An 18-inch-tall tomato cage will keep borage from flopping over once it starts blooming.

Calendula

Often called "pot marigold" in English gardening books, calendula is not to be confused with regular marigolds. The orange or yellow flowers do look something like marigolds, but the foliage (leaves) is

Borage.

different and the flowers taste much better. (If you don't like the smell of marigold foliage, grow calendula instead.) Calendula petals are used for an inexpensive saffron replacement, giving the rice-cooking water a pretty color, though not the flavor of saffron. You can also pluck off the petals and sprinkle them into salads, like confetti. Calendula grows 1–2 feet tall.

Umbellifers: The Dill Family

Angelica, anise, caraway, chervil, coriander, cumin, dill, fennel, and parsley are all related to each other by virtue of their flower types. All have seed heads shaped like umbrellas, and the family is known botanically as *Umbelliferae*. Angelica, caraway, chervil, and parsley are biennials; fennel is a perennial. The others are annuals. Because the umbrella seed heads will shatter when completely ripe and dried, these herbs reseed themselves readily.

Angelica—The stems of this herb are candied for baking decorations. The seeds are used to flavor gin. Few home gardeners grow angelica.

Anise—Anise seeds have a licorice flavor, and the seeds are used in flavoring many of the less-expensive licorices and some liqueurs. Anise seeds are used mostly in baking. The plant grows 2 feet tall.

Caraway—Most of us are familiar with caraway seeds from their use as a flavoring in rye breads. The plants get 2 feet tall, and the leaves can be used to flavor salads and soups. Caraway is a biennial and won't produce seeds until its second year. Plant caraway two years in a row, and the two patches will take turns producing seeds for you. Let some of the seeds mature and fall for next year's plants.

Chervil—This herb is commonly used in French recipes. It prefers cool weather and grows 1–2 feet tall. Chervil retains little flavor when cooked, and is used in salads or with eggs. Reseed chervil every three weeks for a continuous harvest.

Cilantro/coriander.

Coriander, Cilantro—Same plant, two names. People use the name *coriander* for the seeds and *cilantro* for the leaves, but not always. Another name for the plant is Chinese parsley. Cilantro leaves are used

Dill.

dips. The seeds are used commonly in pickling. Fern Leaf (1992 AAS Winner and 18-inch dwarf), Dukat (also called Tetra), and Superdukat are less prone to bolting (going to seed), and are sold mainly for leaf cultivation. If seed heads are what you want, try Bouquet. Long Island and Mammoth are the standard cultivars, and they grow 3–4 feet tall.

Fennel—This is not the bulbous fennel or finnochio vegetable, but rather the source for fennel seeds, which are used to flavor Italian sausages. There are both green and purple variations; and both grow into tall, ferny plants. The purple fennel looks gorgeous with some orange-flowered nasturtiums or calendula in front of it. It would be wise to give the fennel some kind of support if your garden is prone to heavy weather. Fennels are an iffy perennial, but volunteer so easily that the patch is easily perennial, if not all the plants.

in Mexican and Asian cooking, and are added to recipes near the end of the cooking time. Coriander seeds are used in Indian recipes and Scandinavian baking. This multiple-personality plant has lower leaves that resemble Italian parsley, and its upper leaves resemble dill. Because cilantro is a short-lived plant, salsa fans should reseed new plants every two or three weeks for an ongoing harvest.

Cumin—Cumin grows 2 feet tall, and is grown for its seeds, which are used in Mexican and Indian cooking. Plant cumin in the summer after the soil has warmed, and let the plants mature into dried seed heads.

Dill—Like chervil, dill does best in cool weather. Plant dill in the spring and fall, reseeding every 3–4 weeks for an abundant harvest. The leaves, or dill weed, are used in flavoring breads and

Bronze fennel.

Curly parsley.

Parsley—Far from being just a garnish, parsley is chock-full of vitamins A and C. Parsley comes in the familiar curly variety as well as the flat Italian type, which many people think is better tasting. Sometimes flat Italian parsley is confused with cilantro, a different herb. Parsley seeds are notorious for taking a long time to sprout (an ancient saying holds that "parsley has to go to the devil nine times"). Otherwise, they're easy to start from seed, or you can just buy some seedlings. Parsley will return the next year and go to seed (it's not tasty once it bolts, though.)

Parsley is one of the few herbs that are bothered by any pests—in this case, the parsley "worm," which is actually a butterfly caterpillar (larva). This large yellow-and-black-striped caterpillar munches on the parsley stalks, and eventually makes a chrysalis and turns into the beautiful Black Swallowtail butterfly. My children and I so love watching this happen that we just plant extra parsley to share. (See

the section in Chapter 8 for the parsley worm and butterfly.)

Perilla

Perilla, a less commonly grown herb, is used in Mexican and Japanese cooking (for the latter, it's known as "shiso"). It's an annual that garden centers sometimes mislabel as Purple basil, and it also goes by the name Beefsteak plant. The stuff grows very easily and self-sows everywhere if you don't deadhead it! It is, however, quite a striking 2- to 3-foot addition to the herb bed, and always attracts interest. Sow directly outdoors after the last chance of frost.

THE GOURMET'S GARDEN
CHOOSING HERBS AND VEGETABLES FOR COOKING

One of the neatest things about the home garden is that it allows you to grow unusual vegetables and herbs that are either hard to find or ridiculously overpriced. In the following sections you'll find lists of appropriate herbs and vegetables to grow for cooking various popular cuisines.

Mexican Garden

- **Herbs**—Mexican oregano, cilantro, chile peppers, perilla
- **Cool-season vegetables**—onions, scallions, garlic, lettuce, radish
- **Warm-season vegetables**—corn, poblano (ancho) pepper, jalapeno pepper, pumpkin, squash, black bean, pinto bean, tomato, tomatillo (The tomatillo is only distantly related to the tomato but is grown in the same manner, and is used in salsas.)

Italian Garden

- **Annual herbs**—basils, marjoram, flat Italian parsley
- **Perennial herbs**—bay, chives, fennel, oregano, rosemary, thyme

- Cool-season vegetables—onion, garlic, broccoli rabe, broccoli romanesco, chioggia beet, roquette and raddicchio salad greens
- Warm-season vegetables—paste tomato, corno di toro and sweet peppers, artichoke and cardoon, romano bean, garbanzo bean, cannellini bean, finocchio, zucchetta rampicante (summer squash), cucumber

Chinese Garden

- Annual herbs—ginger, garlic, cayenne peppers, cilantro
- Cool-season vegetables—scallions, various greens and spinach, Chinese cabbage, pak choi, mung-bean sprouts, snow peas, carrots, turnips, long radishes
- Warm-season vegetables—eggplant, yard-long beans, hyacinth bean, bitter melon, winter melon, soybean, cucumber

Thai Garden (in addition to Chinese garden list)

- Annual herbs—lemongrass, Thai peppers, galangal

There are many types of leafy greens related to cabbages and mustards, which are loaded with vitamins. In Thai kitchens these greens are generally stir-fried until just limp. Scallions are grown like regular onions, but mature quicker from seed since the bulb does not get as large. Garlic (Chinese) chives can also be used in cooking instead of scallions.

Yard-long green bean and asparagus bean vines can grow 10 feet long, so grow them on tall or long trellises! Pick before the bean seeds get very swollen in the pods, around 12–15 inches long.

Galangal is grown just like gingerroot by planting fresh roots a couple inches deep in moist soil. Harvest at first frost or nine months later.

French Garden

- Annual herbs—basil, chervil, dill, marjoram, parsley
- Perennial herbs—bay, chives, oregano, rosemary, French tarragon, and thyme
- Cool-season vegetables—new potatoes, cabbage, kohlrabi, cauliflower, celeriac, chard, endive, chicory, escarole, mesclun mixed salad greens, petit pois (peas), turnips, Brussels sprouts, carrots, leeks, asparagus, shallots
- Warm-season vegetables—haricots vert, flageolet bean, aubergine (eggplant), Charentais melon, Rouge d'etampes pumpkin, tomato

The emphasis in French cooking is on seasonal foods, picked at the peak of ripeness and cooked that day. French vegetables are generally bred for flavor rather than for their shipping and storage qualities. French haricots vert (green beans) are picked when the pods are only pencil-thick.

HERB AND ETHNIC SEED AND PLANT CATALOGS

Papa Geno's Herb Farm
11125 South 14th Street
Roca, NE 68430
(Open to the public only during specified periods each year.)
phone 402-423-5051
fax 402-328-9766
www.papagenos.com
Excellent Heartland source for 300 kinds of herb plants, materials, 130 scented geraniums, and over 50 kinds of heirloom vegetable transplants!

Nichols Garden Nursery
1190 North Pacific Highway
Albany, OR 97321-4598

phone 541-928-9280
fax 800-231-5306
www.gardennursery.com
Vegetables and herbs

Richter's Herb Catalog
357 Highway 47
Goodwood, Ontario L0C 1A0 Canada
phone 905-640-6677
fax 905-640-6641
www.richters.com
Herb seeds, plants, and vegetables

Evergreen Y.H. Enterprises
P.O. Box 17538
Anaheim, CA 92817
phone 714-637-5769
e-mail EESeeds@aol.com
Oriental vegetables and herbs

The Cook's Garden
P.O. Box 535
Londonderry, VT 05148
phone 800-457-9703
www.cooksgarden.com
Kitchen garden seeds and supplies

The Gourmet Gardener
8650 College Boulevard
Overland Park, KS 66210
phone 913-451-2443
www.gourmetgardener.com
French and European vegetables and herbs

Le Jardin de Gourmet
P.O. Box 75
St. Johnsbury Center, VT 05863-0075
phone 800-659-1446
Shallots, herbs, and European vegetables

Kitazawa Seed Company
1111 Chapman Street
San Jose, CA 95126
phone 408-243-1330
Japanese vegetables and herbs

GATHERING, DRYING, AND USING YOUR HERB HARVEST

Whenever you need some herb for a recipe, go out and pick the amount required. Most recipes call for dried herbs; you'll need to gather twice the quantity of fresh herbs as dried; this is because herbs shrink when they dry. Remove no more than a fourth or a third of the plant at one time. If you find that one kind of herb is being overused, then you need to grow more of your favorite plant. Your perennial plants will be bigger next year to provide a greater harvest. For annual herbs, plant two or three times as much.

Growing tomatoes is easy; we all know what a ripe tomato looks like. When it's red (or whatever), you pick it. But when do you pick chives or basil or cumin? And how? Some herbs are used for their leaves (sage, basil, tarragon, etc.). Pluck or trim off larger, older leaves whenever you need some. You can pinch back annual herbs and harvest leaves at the same time. Some herbs are used for their seeds (cumin, fennel, dill). Wait until the herb flowers, then creates a seed head. When the seed-head stems become thin and yellow, but before they're tan and brittle, you can tie a small paper bag around the seed head to catch the seeds. The bag is important because ripe seeds will easily break off and scatter.

Drying herbs is quite simple. Gather your herb stems in the morning, after the dew has dried but before the sun dries out the essential oils. Most people hang their herbs to dry in upside-down bunches, to keep the flavor in the leaves. Tie them snug, and hang them out of direct sunlight, which can make them fade and lose flavor. I often use unflavored dental floss for tying up herbs, because it's strong, light, and no one ever "borrows" the dental floss and loses it. Herbs can also be dried in shallow layers on a dish some-

Oregano hung to dry.

can, and label them (one jar of dried green crumbs looks much like another jar of dried green crumbs!).

Many people like to keep their herbs and spices in a shelf right over the stove, for convenience. Unfortunately, this means that the heat bakes out the flavor of the stuff in short order. Herbs and spices keep best when stored someplace cool and dim. Dried herbs can keep for years; but frankly, if the stuff in the jar has lost its color, scent, or flavor, throw it out!

MAKING HERBAL OILS AND VINEGARS

Making up vinegars
Just how do we do it?
It's really quite simple,
There's nothing much to it.

You measure the vinegar,
Add half as much flavor,
Let it steep for two weeks,
Strain, and then savor.

You can add any favorite herb to a vinegar, or mix several herbs at once. If you're seasoning an Italian dish, focus on basil and oregano. If you want a general garden vinegar, try a blend of parsley, chives, basil, savory, and oregano in equal amounts. Tarragon vinegars are very popular for salads. Herb vinegars are more art than science. They're much easier than baking a cake and not nearly so fattening. Mix one part of flavored vinegar to two parts olive oil; add a pinch each of salt, pepper, and sugar; and you're ready to dress up a salad.

place safe (the top of the microwave or refrigerator, for instance).

Most herbs take a week or two to fully dry. The length of time is never exact, because it depends on the thickness of the herb (sage takes longer than thyme), the amount of moisture in the plant when picked, the atmospheric moisture content, and the size of the bundle. When the leaves are crispy-crunchy rather than flabby, they are dried. You can leave your bundles hung up for decoration as well as use, or keep them in jars. Lay a sheet of wax paper or a plate on the counter, and rub the branches or leaves between your hands to crumble them. Pour into a jar or

For each cup of cider vinegar, red- or white-wine vinegar, or rice-wine vinegar, mix in half that quantity of herbs. That is, for one cup of fresh herbs, use two cups of vinegar. Or for one-half cup of dried herbs, use two cups of vinegar. Crumble or bruise the herbs. Pour the vinegar over the herbs, and let it steep (like sun tea, although not in direct sunlight) for two weeks. If you want to heat the vinegar, then add the herbs and steep for three days, for the same effect.

Give the jar a shake now and then. When it's done, strain out the herbs, pour into a fancy bottle, and label. You can put in a fresh sprig of the seasoning herb if you wish. Most of the straining can be done using a colander, and cheesecloth or old linen/cotton toweling will strain out smaller sediments.

Volunteer Vinegar

Volunteer vinegar is made from herbs that reseed themselves readily: dill, lemon balm, and chives (or Chinese chives). Add 2 parts oil to 1 part volunteer vinegar, and you've an excellent salad dressing.

2   cups vinegar
1/3 cup chopped fresh dill
1/3 cup chopped fresh lemon balm
1/3 cup chopped fresh chives

Herb vinegars.

Three-Flavor Oil for Chinese Cooking

Three-flavor oil lets you skip the mincing of garlic, chives, and ginger, and get right to the heart of your dinner stir-frying:

2   cups peanut oil
2   inches of gingerroot, chopped
6   large scallions or 8 large Chinese chives, chopped (no roots, all of the white, 2 inches of the green)
6   large cloves of garlic, minced
2   cayenne peppers (optional)

Put oil in pan and sauté the seasonings over *low* heat. They will sizzle slightly as the water is cooked out. Cook for about 10 minutes. The oil will be-

come aromatic, with that "Yum! What's for dinner?" smell. Keep from browning or charring. Cool, then strain through a sieve. Keep in a sealed bottle in the refrigerator.

Peanut oil naturally becomes thick and cloudy when chilled, and will thin out again when heated. Next time you want to cook, simply heat up the oil in your wok and add your vegetables, meat, and/or tofu. (Daughter Anna says, "Just don't tell the kids about the tofu!")

Herb Vinegars Starring Single Herbs

Try these ideas for vinegars using just one herb:

- **Basil**—Lovely on tomatoes and other fresh veggies.
- **Mint**—The fresh blend makes a nice facial tonic for dabbing after yard work.
- **Tarragon**—an old salad standby.

Raspberry Vinegar

Any fruit can be used this way. Fruit vinegars are good in fruit salads, coleslaw, and as a base for mustards. They can also be sprinkled on strawberries.

4 cups raspberries fresh or frozen
3 cups white wine or rice vinegar

Crush the berries and stir them into the vinegar. Frozen berries will naturally burst upon defrosting and do not need crushing. Use cheesecloth or an old tea towel to thoroughly strain.

Spicy Vinegar

Use as a base for German and Scandinavian-style meat sauces, and in pilafs.

2 cups cider vinegar
2 teaspoons whole allspice
1 teaspoon whole mustard seed
1 teaspoon whole cloves
1 cinnamon stick, crumbled
1 bay leaf
1 teaspoon celery seeds
1 teaspoon black peppercorns
3 garlic cloves, minced
1 teaspoon dried rosemary

Olio de Provence

1 cup extra-virgin olive oil
6-inch sprig of fresh rosemary
several sprigs of fresh thyme
6-inch sprig of oregano
6-inch sprig of basil
2 cloves garlic, peeled and crushed
1 teaspoon peppercorns
thumb-size piece of dried orange peel (optional)

WARNING! Because of the potential for botulism, you must keep all herbal oils in the refrigerator and use them within 24 hours.

AWASH IN SQUASH AND OTHER BLESSINGS: VEGETABLE RECIPES

Notes on Canning and Pickling

Want to save some of this summer's treats? Homemade pickled things are easy to make. You can also create a batch of jars of unusual goodies for gift-giving later on. I've selected some things that are a bit out of the ordinary, since most people don't find anything useful in making what they can buy inexpensively at the market.

If you've never done any canning before, it's a good idea to read up on the basic procedures for keeping things safe and sterile. It's not difficult, but does require you to have your materials ready and clean before starting, and a familiarity with the procedure. Canning books such as *Balls' Blue Book* and equipment are available at many supermarkets and hardware stores. Extension offices often have how-to and recipe booklets, and sometimes classes as well.

Noniodized salt is used for canning because it doesn't make the solution cloudy. It's safer to use specially sold canning jars, rather than recycling nonstandard commercial mayonnaise jars, which are of thinner glass and not made to be reused.

If you blanch vegetables in boiling water before freezing them, it's helpful to know that most purple snap beans turn green when they're done blanching—a sort of built-in timer!

■ ASPARAGUS

Asparagus season is brief, but intense! When picking asparagus, just snap the stem off and it will naturally break at the point where the tender part meets the tough part. Do not cook asparagus until it's falling apart and stringy, just until it's fork-tender. Asparagus is also an excellent stir-fry vegetable.

Asparagus Toasts

    asparagus
    baguette
    blue cheese
    butter

1. Lightly steam asparagus until bright green and just barely limp.
2. Arrange spears atop a good, crusty baguette that has been lightly buttered.
3. Lay a slice of blue cheese atop the asparagus, and set it under the broiler (or in a toaster oven) until the cheese is just melted.

Swiss Asparagus Salad

2   big handsful of asparagus spears
2   oranges, peeled, seeded, and cut into
    bite-size pieces
about 1/2 cup of Swiss (Emmenthaler)
    cheese, julienned
about 1/2 cup of baked ham, julienned

Dressing:

3   tablespoons olive oil
3   tablespoons lemon juice

1/2 teaspoon salt
1/4 teaspoon pepper
1/4 teaspoon sugar

Toss salad with dressing and chill. Great for picnics.

■ BEANS, FRESH

Snappy Beans

Use string or snap beans; green, yellow, or purple beans.

2   tablespoons butter
1/2 onion, minced
4   cups fresh beans (remove strings),
    broken in half
about 1 teaspoon of savory, oregano,
    and/or thyme
1   clove garlic, minced

1. Sauté onion in butter until tender.
2. Add beans, herbs, garlic, and water, and cook with the lid on until the beans are tender, about 10 minutes.
3. Sprinkle with Parmesan cheese before serving.

■ BEANS, DRIED

It used to be that dried beans automatically meant navy beans, but with the interest in ethnic and regional cooking, dried beans of all sorts are becoming available. I'm especially fond of black beans, and substitute them for pintos in Tex-Mex recipes.

Black Bean Soup

The day before, soak a pound (about 2 cups) of dried beans in 3 quarts of water, or cook dried beans in a slow cooker on low overnight. Pour off the first water (to remove most of the burps), and put the beans into a soup pot with fresh water, covering them 2 inches deep. Add the following seasonings:

2   tomatoes, diced
2   large onions, peeled and diced
4   cloves of garlic, minced
2   bay leaves
2   teaspoons ground cumin seeds
1/2 teaspoon salt
1/4 teaspoon pepper

Optional for a spicy soup:

Mix 1 teaspoon mole sauce paste (found with Mexican foods at the market) with 1 cup of water and pour into the pot.

Simmer for 2 hours, and then remove the bay leaves. Use a potato masher to mash about half the beans and produce a thicker soup. Serve with sour cream or Parmesan cheese on the side.

Black Bean Wrap

When I was growing up, foods like salsa, tortillas, and even tacos were strange, exotic things I'd never tasted until visiting my uncle in Texas. Nowadays these foods are ubiquitous, and our local grocer stocks several brands of salsa and fresh tortillas. I like to buy tortillas made locally because they're fresher, and because I like to support local businesses. A wrap is simply a sandwich in a tortilla, folded up like a burrito. Canned black beans can be used; just drain and rinse them before using. Defrost frozen sweet corn; no cooking needed.

1 cup cooked and cooled black beans
1 cup sweet corn
1 sweet ripe pepper, diced small
salsa
pepper-jack cheese, grated
flour tortilla

Stir in just enough salsa to moisten the beans, corn, and sweet pepper. Fill a flour tortilla with this mixture, adding

grated pepper-jack cheese before folding the wrap.

Good Ol' Pot of Baked Beans

2   cups dried white beans (great northern, navy, etc.)
3/4 cup brown sugar
1   teaspoon mustard powder
1/2 onion (minced)
1/2 pound diced (raw) bacon

1. Soak the beans overnight, and drain off the remaining water.
2. Put the beans into a pot or slow cooker and simmer until tender. At this point the cooked beans may be kept in the fridge, or extras cooled and frozen in pint-size freezer boxes.
3. For baked beans, pour the beans in a baking dish with enough of the cooking liquid to just cover. Season to taste with salt and pepper. Stir in the brown sugar, mustard powder, onion, and bacon.
4. Bake at 350 °F until bubbly and browned on top, about 45 minutes.

■ BROCCOLI

Deanna's Broccoli

Deanna doesn't want to mess around in the kitchen any longer than she has to! Quick and wonderful.

broccoli
oil
minced garlic
minced black olives

Cut broccoli into florets, and sauté in a wok or skillet with some oil and minced garlic. Before serving, top with minced black olives. You can find small cans of minced black olives at the market; they're great for spiffing up pasta and other dishes.

■ BRUSSELS SPROUTS

Glazed Sproutniks

2 cups brussels sprouts
2 tablespoons molasses (or thereabouts)
2 tablespoons butter

Put sprouts in a microwave-safe dish with a lid, dot with butter, drizzle on molasses, and put the lid on. Zap on high for 5 minutes, stir and replace lid, and zap another 5 minutes. The sprouts should be tender enough to stab with a fork, but *not* mushy!

■ CABBAGE

This first recipe is really good when you've been reading too many January seed catalogs, and have the intense urge to head to your grocer's produce section and start grazing! It's especially fine with the light and lettuce-y Napa cabbage.

Garden Slaw

Feel free to substitute Miracle Whip for the mayonnaise (I am not going to get into that argument).

1 small red or green cabbage, cored and finely shredded
3 carrots, peeled and grated
2 tart apples, cored and sliced thin (Granny Smiths are good)
1 small onion, sliced thin

Mix dressing, pour onto mixed vegetables, and tumble well. Best prepared a few hours ahead of time to allow the dressing to soften up the cabbage.

Dressing:
2/3 cup mayonnaise
1/2 teaspoon salt
1/4 teaspoon pepper
1 tablespoon poppy seeds (or 1 teaspoon celery seeds)
2 tablespoons lemon juice
1 tablespoon sugar
3 tablespoons water, to thin mayonnaise

Andrea's Cabbage Rolls

Pick a green cabbage with most of the outer dark leaves still intact. Blanch in boiling water, stem side down, for several minutes, and then drain in a colander stem side up (this happens naturally when you dump the pot).

For the filling, mix:
2 cups cooked brown rice
1 diced onion
1 grated carrot
1/2 cup minced parsley
1 cup diced tomatoes
1/2 cup crushed or chopped walnuts or sunflower seeds
1/4 cup raisins or dried currants
1/2 cup feta cheese, crumbled
2 beaten eggs

Pull leaves off the cabbage. To make the cabbage rolls, orient the leaf so the stem is at the bottom and the narrowest part of the leaf is at the top. Put 1/4 cup of mixture in the center of a leaf and fold both sides of the leaf in; then bring up the stem bottom, and then fold the top over (just like a burrito). Lay seam-side down in a lasagna-baking dish, alternating the soft green bundles with the stiffer white bundles. Make about 9–12 cabbage rolls.

To a quart of your favorite spaghetti sauce, add 1 teaspoon cinnamon and 2 tablespoons lemon juice. Pour over the cabbage rolls to cover thoroughly, and reserve any extra to serve at the table (warm) in a pitcher or gravy boat.

Bake at 350 °F for 45 minutes. Can be frozen (assembled and uncooked).

> *Of course, you don't use all the cabbage up, so remember Cole's Law: slimy sliced cabbage (coleslaw), and cook the rest the next day.*

Braised Cabbage

4   strips bacon, diced
2   garlic cloves, minced
1   large yellow onion, peeled and sliced
1   small cabbage, cored and sliced
1/2 teaspoon caraway seeds
1/2 cup chicken or veggie stock
1/2 cup white wine (if you've some around)
salt and pepper to taste

In a large pot, sauté bacon until soft, and add the garlic and onion. Sauté until the onion is tender. Add the rest of the ingredients and a lid to the pot and cook for about 5 minutes (until the cabbage wilts). Remove the lid and cook for 10 minutes more, or until the cabbage is just tender. You can also stir in some sour cream after you're done cooking, yum!

■ CARAWAY

Caraway Soup

6   cups chicken (or beef) stock
2   tablespoons carraway seeds
2   tablespoons butter
2   tablespoons flour
1   cup sour cream
salt and pepper to taste

1. Bring 6 cups of chicken (or beef) stock to a boil, add 2 tablespoons car-

away seeds, cover, reduce heat, and simmer for 20 minutes.
2. Brown 2 tablespoons flour in 2 tablespoons butter, stir in 1 cup of broth; whisk until smooth and add to the pot of soup.
3. Simmer several minutes longer. Using a whisk, stir in 1 cup sour cream and salt and pepper to taste.

This can be served over egg noodles or dumplings if you like.

■ CARROTS

Carrots Anna

2 cups of peeled and grated carrots (approximately)

Dressing:

1/2 cup olive oil
1/3 cup balsamic vinegar
1/2 teaspoon salt
1/4 teaspoon pepper
1/4 teaspoon sugar

Mix dressing, pour on grated carrots, and toss. Great for picnics.

■ CAULIFLOWER

Cauliflower with Sunshine Sauce

I'm not generally a big fan of yellow ballpark mustard in recipes (OK, I normally loathe the stuff), but it's just the right thing to perk up this cauliflower sauce!

1   large or 2 small heads cauliflower
1/4 lemon or 1 tablespoon lemon juice

Sauce:

3/4 cup sour cream
1/2 teaspoon onion powder, or

2   teaspoons minced onion
1/2 teaspoon dill
squirt of yellow mustard

Cut cauliflower into florets, dump into microwave-safe dish, add 1/4 cup water, and squeeze lemon juice onto florets.
Toss lemon wedge in, and microwave-steam for 7 to 8 minutes on High. (The florets should be cooked but not mushy.)
Meanwhile, mix the remaining ingredients together for a sauce.
Pour off any remaining steaming water, and discard lemon wedge. Pour sauce onto florets and mix well. May be served hot or chilled.

■ CELERIAC

Warm Celeriac Salad

celeriac (julienned)
onion (minced)
bouillon or beef broth
vinegar
pinch of sugar

Sauté the julienned celeriac and minced onion in butter. Add a little beef broth (bouillon), a splash of vinegar, and a pinch of sugar, and simmer for a few minutes until tender but not mushy.

Celeriac Au Gratin

2   cups peeled and thinly sliced celeriac
2   tablespoons butter
2   tablespoons minced onion
1   teaspoon, total volume, of minced thyme and/or marjoram and/or lovage
1   cup dried breadcrumbs
1/2 cup grated Swiss cheese
salt and pepper, to taste

Sauté onion in butter until translu-

cent; add celeriac slices and a couple tablespoons of water. Cover the pan and braise the slices until they are hot. Then transfer to a wide, shallow casserole. Sprinkle with dried breadcrumbs and a layer of grated Emmenthaler (Swiss) cheese. Drizzle melted butter over the top, and bake until hot and toasty.

Cream of Celeriac Soup

1   onion, minced
4   tablespoons butter
3–4 celeriac roots, peeled and diced
1   potato or small rutabaga, peeled and diced
1/2 teaspoon marjoram
1/2 teaspoon thyme
1½ cups chicken or vegetable broth
1   cup cream or half-and-half
salt and pepper, to taste

Sauté the onion on low heat and cook, stirring frequently, until soft and browned.
Add the diced celeriac, potato, herbs, and broth, cook until the vegetables are soft enough to mash.
Puree in small batches in a blender, and then return to pot along with the cream and heat through.

■ EGGPLANT

Spicy Sautéed Eggplant

Eggplant has the unfortunate tendency to soak up oil, which can lead to calorie-laden recipes. In this case, try spritzing the pieces with an oil sprayer, or use a wok to sauté the eggplant, and add small doses of oil as needed to keep the pieces from sticking. Adding all the oil at the beginning leads to a few soggy pieces amongst the dry ones.

1–2 eggplants
1   teaspoon salt
1/2 teaspoon turmeric
1/8 teaspoon cayenne pepper
lemon wedges

Peel and slice an eggplant or two into half-inch (1 centimeter) thick slices, and then cut into quarters.

Mix salt, turmeric (yellow spice), and cayenne pepper together; sprinkle this spice mixture onto the eggplant pieces.

Sauté or stir-fry until the pieces are tender and reddish-gold.

Serve with lemon wedges.

■ LEEKS

Leek and Potato Soup

Leek and potato soup is one of my all-time favorites.

leeks
butter
flour
milk or cream
potatoes
salt and pepper to taste

Boil potatoes.
Sauté diced leeks in butter.
Add a little flour for a roux, some salt and pepper to taste.
Stir in milk or cream, and mashed, boiled potatoes.
Serve hot.

Three Alliums and a Pig Bread Pudding

stale bread slices (any non-sweet type); a
    leftover baguette is wonderful
4   eggs
1   cup of milk or a bit more
bacon, cooked and crumbled (or diced
    ham or Canadian bacon)
leeks, sliced lengthwise, cleaned, and
    chopped
couple cloves garlic, minced or pressed
handful of chives, minced
nice cheese, such as Gouda, Edam, or
    Swiss, grated

Mix the eggs and milk with a bit of salt and pepper.

Lay out the bread in a shallow baking dish. Scatter alliums and bacon atop.

Pour on egg-milk mixture until well covered. If the bread's really dry, mix up another batch (or half a batch) of egg-milk so the bread slices will be completely covered.

Sprinkle on grated cheese. Bake in moderate oven until brown on top.

Great leftovers for breakfast!

■ SALADS AND DRESSINGS

Greek Salad

Perfect for when the summer gets hot, and the lettuce has bolted.

1   cucumber, peeled and cut into bite-
    size chunks
1   tomato, cut into bite-size chunks
1   sweet pepper, seeded and cut into
    bite-size chunks
a few cubes of feta cheese (optional)
a few black olives (optional; Kalamata
    olives are really good)

Dressing:

1/3 cup olive oil
3   tablespoons lemon juice
1/2 teaspoon salt
1/8 teaspoon pepper
1   teaspoon fresh oregano or dill
    pinch of sugar

Mix well.

Green Tomato Dressing

1   large Aunt Ruby's German Green
    tomato, cored and quartered
3/4 cup mayonnaise
2   green onions, coarsely chopped
2   tablespoons chopped fresh tarragon
2   tablespoons cider vinegar or allium-
    lover's vinegar
1/4 teaspoon salt
1/8 teaspoon freshly ground black pepper

Place all ingredients in a blender or food processor and process until roughly chopped.

Japanese-Style Salad Dressing

1/2 cup minced onion
1/2 cup salad oil
1/3 cup rice vinegar
2   tablespoons water
2   tablespoons minced fresh gingerroot
    (peeled)
4   teaspoons soy sauce
2   teaspoons sugar
2   teaspoons lemon juice
1/2 teaspoon minced garlic (1 large or 2
    small cloves)
1/2 teaspoon salt
1/4 teaspoon black pepper

In a blender, mix all ingredients on high speed for half a minute until emulsified.
Makes 1³/₄ cups.

■ Peppers

Ortega Soup

Invented on Ortega Street, using Ortega New Mexican chilies. Good for what ails you!

1   quart chicken or vegetable broth
1/4 cup chopped green ortega or other New Mexican chilies (only mildly spicy)
4   diced tomatoes
2   ripe sweet peppers, diced
3   large cloves of garlic, minced
1   cup sweet corn
Several clumps of angel-hair pasta
    (crumbled before adding)

Put all ingredients in a saucepan and bring to a boil.
Simmer the soup for several minutes until the pasta is cooked.

Roasted Ripe Peppers

Roasting peppers is a Southwestern tradition that's spreading like salsa around the country. You can roast either chili or sweet peppers; just keep straight which is which (one charred pepper looks much like another). When handling hot peppers, beware of the capsaicin oils: use gloves and tongs, keep your hands far away from your eyes and face, and wash up well afterward. You have several options for roasting your peppers. Invite friends over for an orgy of grill-roasted peppers out on the patio, or roast your peppers indoors, under the oven broiler.

Simply wash the peppers, leaving the stem on or off. Place your peppers near the heat source, letting them char gently (avoiding the "flambé marshmallow" effect). You'll need to turn them several times to char the pepper over most of the surface. Keep a close eye on peppers when broiling; you know how quickly things go from raw to burnt under a broiler.

After the pepper skins are soft, black, and blistery, pop the hot things into a brown paper bag and roll the top closed for about 10 minutes. This lets the skin steam loose from the peppers. You'll need several paper bags if you have dozens of peppers.

Next, peel the charred skin off each

pepper. Use rubber gloves when handling hot chili peppers. Some folks swear by peeling under a running faucet (I'm fond of this method); others swear that flavor is lost this way. Take your pick. Don't worry, it's neither possible nor necessary to remove every last shred of skin from the peppers.

Eat your roasted peppers now, or freeze them in a single layer on a sheet, then store loose-packed in a freezer container or zipper bag. Roasted peppers are wonderful for cream of roasted-pepper soup, on sandwiches and pizzas, or in pasta dishes.

Ripe Pepper Pickles

Makes 2 quarts or 4 pints

2½ pounds of ripe peppers (red, orange, yellow)
3   large cloves of garlic, sliced thin
2   teaspoons noniodized salt
3¾ cups white or rice-wine vinegar
1¾ cups water
4   small leaves fresh basil

1. Prepare the peppers by washing, drying, and cutting out the seed core, stem, and pithy membranes. Slice into evenly sized strips from top to bottom.

2. Divide the garlic slices and basil leaves evenly among the jars. Stuff each jar with pepper slices. If you have more than one color, alternate the colors. Be sure to leave a half-inch of headspace at the top of the jar (above the pepper slices).

3. Sprinkle 1 teaspoon of noniodized salt into each jar.

4. Bring vinegar and water to a rolling boil in a saucepan, and then pour the solution into each jar, leaving a half-inch headspace.

5. Submerge each jar into a boiling-water bath, bring back to a rolling boil,

and process for 15 minutes (either quart or pint jars). Cool and label.

The pickles have the best flavor after mellowing for a month.

◼ POTATOES

Russet-type potatoes are baking potatoes that have large starch molecules, allowing the potato to bake fluffy. Russets also make good french fries. Boiling or new potatoes are the waxy type that have small starch molecules, making them a good choice for salads and soups.

Potato Kugel

A wonderful casserole, especially nice for breakfast.

4   potatoes, peeled and shredded
1   onion, peeled and diced
3   eggs
1   teaspoon salt
1/2 teaspoon pepper
1/3 cup flour
1/2 cup milk
1/4 cup melted butter (half a stick) or oil

Mix everything well and pour into a 9-by-13-inch pan.

Bake 1 hour at 350 °F.

Bluejacket Potato Salad

This is my family's recipe, now in its third generation of tweaking. Diced here means a small dice. Mix ahead of time for the flavors to marry. Precise quantities are not given to allow for variable levels of potatoes and your particular fondness for various ingredients.

red, yellow, or blue potatoes, boiled until tender, then peeled and diced
couple celery stalks, diced

1   small onion, minced
cheddar cheese, diced small
couple hard-boiled eggs, diced
generous amount of green olives with
    pimentos, sliced (salad olives are
    already sliced)
mayonnaise (or Miracle Whip)
small squirt mustard
1 or 2 tablespoons sweet pickle relish

■ RUTABAGAS AND SUNROOTS

Turnips can be substituted for rutabagas, but aren't as sweet. Be sure to harvest turnips at golf-ball size or not much larger. Rutabagas can get larger without getting bad-tasting. Rutabagas take about 50 percent longer to cook than potatoes do, because they are so incredibly dense. Cut into smaller chunks before boiling.

Mashed Rutabagas

A classically rich Scandinavian recipe that's hard to improve upon!

1   large or 2 medium-size rutabagas, cut
    into chunks and peeled
1 or 2 carrots, peeled
2 or 3 potatoes, peeled

Boil roots until soft; the rutabagas will take about twice as long as the carrots and potatoes, so start them first and add the other two later.
Drain off the water and add:

1   cup or so of half-and-half
1   teaspoon of sugar
1/2 teaspoon salt
1/4 teaspoon (white) pepper
pinch of nutmeg

Mash together until fluffy.

Winter Roots Soup

This is an upscale variation on the old-fashioned cheese and potato soup.

2   tablespoons butter or oil
1   small diced onion
3   leeks, diced—include only the white
    parts
3   cups of chicken or vegetable stock
3   sunroots, peeled and diced
1   carrot, peeled and diced
4   yellow potatoes, peeled and diced
1   rutabaga, peeled and diced
1   pint of whole milk
1   cup of grated smoked Gouda cheese

1. In a large pot, sauté together the butter or oil with the diced onion and leeks. Cook until tender, and add the chicken or vegetable stock.
2. Add the sunroots, carrot, potatoes, and rutabaga. Let simmer for 30 minutes until the rutabagas are soft.
3. Mash the vegetables into the stock (or puree in small batches in the blender), and add the milk and the Gouda cheese. Stir until the cheese has melted. Salt and pepper to taste.

■ SUMMER SQUASHES

Pattypan Patties (low-fat squash fritters)

1   cup dried breadcrumbs
2   tablespoons chopped chives
4   tablespoons mayonnaise
2   eggs, beaten
1   tablespoon Dijon mustard
1   teaspoon Worcestershire sauce
1/4 teaspoon cayenne pepper
1/4 teaspoon dill (or 1/2 teaspoon if using
    fresh)
1/4 teaspoon nutmeg
1/2 teaspoon salt

1   cup seeded and grated pattypan
    squash (I find that a serving spoon is
    handy for "gutting" pattypans. No
    peeling is necessary if picked young.)

1. Preheat oven to 450 °F; coat baking
sheet with no-stick spray.
2. Mix all the ingredients together, divide mixture into halves, and then divide
each half into thirds. Gently shape into
six patties, each as thick as a finger.
3. Place onto baking sheet and bake 4
minutes. Turn patties over and bake 4
minutes on the other side.
Serve with lemon wedges, if desired.

Zucchini "Soufflé"

Cube, steam (microwave works great),
drain, and mash or puree 4 cups of zucchini. Add:

1   cup fresh breadcrumbs
1   small onion, grated
1   teaspoon salt
1/8 teaspoon pepper
1   beaten egg
3   tablespoons milk
2   tablespoons butter or bacon drippings
1   teaspoon Worcestershire sauce

Pour in buttered baking dish. Bake for
35 minutes at 350 °F, uncovered.

Butterstick Cake

*This cake was named for an abundance of
straight-necked yellow squashes called
"Butterstick," and for the stick of butter in
the cake. It's a wonderfully moist snacking
cake that doesn't need frosting! Use any
kind of summer squash.*

Cream together:

1¹/2 cups brown sugar

1/2 cup (1 stick) butter

Add and mix well:

3   eggs
1   teaspoon vanilla
1/2 cup buttermilk
2¹/2 cups flour
1/2 cup unsweetened baking cocoa
1/2 teaspoon cinnamon
1/2 teaspoon salt
2   teaspoons baking soda
1/2 cup salty Spanish peanuts
1   cup vanilla chips
3   6-inch-long summer squashes, peeled,
    seeded and grated

Grease a 9-by-13-inch baking pan,
scoop the batter in, and bake at 325 °F for
45 minutes.

■ WINTER SQUASHES

Spaghetti Squash

*This hard-shelled squash has the curious
habit of breaking into long spaghetti-like
strands when cooked. You can then butter
the strands, or use any favorite pasta sauce
on them; pesto is especially yummy.*

To bake:

Pierce the squash deeply several times,
and bake at 350 °F for 1 1/2 hours.
Cut in half, scoop out the seeds, and
use a fork to fluff out the strands.

To microwave:

Cut the squash in half lengthwise and
scoop out the seeds. Cover with cling-
wrap and microwave on High for 10 minutes. Then use a fork to fluff out the
strands.

Pesto Sauce for Spaghetti Squash

I freeze rather than dry all my basils. So in the freezer is this gallon zipper baggie of herbs. Pesto made from dried basil is blech tasting, in addition to the unlovely Army olive drab color. But frozen basil, aah!

1   cup (firmly packed volume) of fresh or frozen basil leaves, any type(s)
1/4 cup walnuts or pine nuts
2   large cloves garlic, minced with garlic press
1/3 cup olive oil (I prefer extra-virgin)
1/2 cup grated Parmesan cheese

Just grab a handful of frozen leaves, and crumble them into the blender with the olive oil, garlic, and nuts.

Remove to mixing bowl and stir in the Parmesan after the nuts quit clanking around.

Scoop out of bowl and toss thoroughly with spaghetti squash.

■ SWEET POTATOES

Jewel Sweet Potatoes

A nice change of pace from the oversweetened dish served at Thanksgiving.

2   sweetpotatoes, baked and peeled, and cut into chunks
1   large can of juice-pack pineapple chunks
4   tablespoons butter
1   cup raisins
a pinch each of ginger, clove, cinnamon, and nutmeg

Mix well and bake or microwave until thoroughly heated.

Sweetpotato Soufflé

Who would have thought that anything so heavy could bake into something so light? Remember, soufflés don't wait; serve immediately before it deflates.

1   cup milk, scalded (microwave on High for about 1 minute)
1   tablespoon butter
1/2 teaspoon salt
2   tablespoons honey
2   cups cooked, peeled, and mashed sweetpotatoes
1/2 teaspoon nutmeg
1/2 teaspoon cinnamon
2   eggs, separated

Mix the milk, butter, salt, honey, spices, and egg yolks with the sweetpotatoes, blending until smooth.

Beat the egg whites until stiff peaks form, then gently fold the sweetpotato mixture into the whites.

Scoop into a buttered baking dish and bake at 350 °F for 20–30 minutes until lightly browned.

■ TOMATOES

People who grow tomatoes often end up with *lots* of tomatoes! We share them with grateful neighbors and coworkers and still have more. There's nothing so heartwarming as having a pantry shelf lined with jars of homemade sauces to get you through the cold winter.

Traditional saucing methods for processing tomatoes required dropping the fruits into boiling water until the skins cracked, fishing them out and peeling them, and then pressing the pulp through a sieve to remove the seeds. Very labor- and time-intensive, and steamingly hot during the hottest part of the summer!

Well, mess no more. For about $25 you can get the greatest machine since

Tomato press.

Disassembling the tomato press for cleaning.

the invention of the blender: an Italian tomato press, sold by Gardener's Supply Company. Theirs is no ordinary tomato press. The plastic gizmo allows you to drop in whole ripe tomatoes (cut the big ones into chunks, or else they'll squirt you in the eye), and turn the crank. Seeds and skins come out one chute, sauce out the other. I can run through a bushel of ripe tomatoes in just 15 minutes, and then get on with my sauce making!

Tip: Run the seeds and skins through a second squeezing, to get more of the good-tasting part of the sauce.

Another tip: Do *not* put the seeds and skins into the compost heap; you'll have thousands of volunteer tomatoes next year!

Picante Salsa by the Pint

1 1/2 cups chopped tomatoes
1   cup water
1/3 cup chopped yellow onion
1/4 cup chopped fresh jalapeno peppers, with seeds (about 3–4 peppers)
2   tablespoons white vinegar
1/4 teaspoon salt
1   large clove of garlic, minced

1. Combine all ingredients in a saucepan over medium/high heat.
2. Bring to a boil; then reduce heat and simmer for 30 minutes or until thick.
3. Pour into sterilized 1-pint jar and process 20 minutes in boiling water bath.

For mild salsa, use 2 tablespoons (2–3) jalapenos. For hot, use 1/3 cup (4–5) jalapenos.

Salsa for a Crowd

7   pounds tomatoes
8   Anaheim chili peppers, seeded and chopped
3   jalapeno peppers, seeded and chopped
2   cups diced onion
5   cloves garlic

1/2 cup vinegar
1   tablespoon sugar
1   teaspoon salt
1/2 teaspoon pepper
1   small can tomato paste
2   tablespoons minced cilantro, if desired

1. Peel, seed, and dice tomatoes. Place in large colander to drain for half an hour.

2. Dump into a very large pot (not iron). Bring to boil and simmer (uncovered) for 45 minutes, or until as thick as you like it.

3. Add the remaining ingredients. Return to a boil, then remove from heat.

4. Ladle into hot pint jars. Leave a half-inch headspace in jars.

5. Process in boiling-water bath for 35 minutes.

Chili

Take a can of chili beans, a pound of cooked hamburger (I precook mine and keep it in freezer boxes) or 1 1/2 cups veggie crumbles, and a jar of this chili sauce, and stir them together in the Crock-Pot for those busy winter days! Makes about 6–8 pints.

Chili sauce:
4   quarts tomato puree (no seeds or skins)
2   cups chopped onions (about 2 medium)
2   cups chopped sweet peppers (any color, about 4 small)
1   cup sugar
3   tablespoons salt
4   tablespoons oregano (dried, or double amount for fresh)
2   tablespoons cinnamon (yes)
3   tablespoons ground cumin
1   level cup chili powder
2 1/2 cups vinegar (added later)

1. Measure spices into a bowl before adding them to the pot, to avoid accidentally putting in too much spice.

2. Bring everything but the vinegar to a simmer and cook for about half an hour, until somewhat thickened. Add vinegar and bring to a boil.

3. Ladle hot sauce into sterilized pint jars, leaving a quarter-inch headspace. Adjust caps.

4. Process for 15 minutes in boiling-water bath (1 inch water above tops of jars, with kettle lid on).

We like to eat our chili with grated Colby cheese and oyster crackers (family tradition; don't ask why).

Tomato Soup

There's nothing like having jars of soup lining the shelf, canned summer sunshine ready to be opened and heated up! Yields about 7 pints

4   quarts tomato puree (any type and color of tomatoes, without skins and seeds)
1   cup chopped celery or lovage
1/2 cup chopped onion (1 small)
3   cloves garlic, minced
1/4 teaspoon black pepper
1   tablespoon sugar
2   teaspoons salt

In blender, puree 1 cup of tomato sauce with the celery and onion, until smooth.

Then mix all the ingredients in a pot and bring to a rapid boil.

Ladle into sterilized pint jars, leaving a half-inch headspace. Adjust caps.

Process in boiling-water bath for 15 minutes.

Roasted Tomato Sauce

A fragrant recipe with no peeling or seeding required! Any shape or color of tomatoes may be used. Cut large Beefsteak types into fourths instead of halves.

10	pounds tomatoes
3	tablespoons of olive oil
2	teaspoons dried mixed Italian herbs or
4	teaspoons chopped fresh herbs (basil, oregano and/or rosemary)
1	tablespoon salt
1	teaspoon sugar
1	teaspoon black pepper and/or
1/2	teaspoon crushed red pepper flakes
3	cloves garlic (minced)
1	tablespoon lemon juice or
1	tablespoon vinegar

1. Place top oven rack high in the oven and preheat to 425 °F.

2. Cut tomatoes into halves and spread in a single layer, skin-side down in a shallow baking pan.

4. Drizzle on olive oil. Sprinkle with herbs, salt, sugar, black pepper and/or crushed red pepper flakes. Scatter on minced garlic.

5. Roast for about 90 minutes, until the slices have cooked down and the edges are slightly charred.

6. Scoop mixture into blender or food processor (you may need to do this in batches) and process until somewhat smooth.

More grows in the garden than what comes by a seed.

7. Add lemon juice or vinegar to mixture and reheat if necessary.

8. Pour into hot (sterilized) pint canning jars, being sure to leave a quarter-inch headspace. Adjust lids and rings.

9. Process in boiling water bath for 35 minutes.

Makes about 2 pints.

Sun- or Oven-Dried Tomatoes

The weather is ornery sometimes; you need several days of full sun for drying tomatoes, and suddenly it's overcast. Fortunately, you can dry tomatoes in your oven as well. Any kind of tomato will do, but paste tomatoes (such as San Marzano or Italian Gold) or cherry tomatoes are well suited. For giant Beefsteak-type tomatoes, slice into thin slabs. The oven method takes most of one day; the sun method takes about three sunny days.

5 1/2	pounds tomatoes (8 pints)
	olive oil

1. Preheat the oven to 200 °F. Take tomatoes, washed, stemmed, and cut in half lengthwise (from stem to tip).

2. Lay the halves out on a tray, inside up. Sprinkle lightly with salt.

3. Bake in the oven for 7 to 8 hours, until they are no longer juicy, but are leathery. It helps to turn the pans and sometimes shift the halves a bit so they don't stick, and so they are fully dried. This means they should look like large, ruby-colored raisins, not soft and flabby.

Or you may want to lay your tomatoes on a clean nonmetallic screen, then set them outdoors in full sun for 3 sunny or 5 cloudy days. Bring them in at night so they don't get damp from dew.

Layer the dried slices in a jar, cover with olive oil, and keep in the refrigerator for up to six months.

■ WATERMELONS

Watermelon-Rind Pickles

4	quarts cubed watermelon rind
1	gallon cold water
1	cup noniodized salt
2	cups vinegar
7	cups sugar
1	lemon, sliced and seeded
3	cinnamon sticks, broken into 1-inch lengths
1	teaspoon whole cloves
1	teaspoon allspice

1. Prepare the watermelon rind by paring off the green skin and pink flesh. Slice into evenly sized 1-inch cubes.

2. Dissolve salt in water, add the rind pieces, and let sit overnight (or 6 hours).

3. Later, drain and cover the cubes with cold water in a large cooking pot. Simmer for 20 minutes until tender and drain.

4. Tie the spices into a cheesecloth bag, or put them into a large tea ball. Put them into a saucepan with the vinegar and sugar. Bring to a boil for 10 minutes to season. Add the rind and simmer until it is transparent. Remove the spice bag. Save the solution!

5. Stuff the rind pieces into your jars, being sure to leave a half-inch headspace at the top of the jar where no rind cubes are.

6. Bring vinegar-sugar solution to a rolling boil again. Then pour the solution into each jar, leaving a half-inch headspace.

7. Submerge the jars into a boiling-water bath; bring back to a rolling boil, and process for 10 minutes. Cool and label.

The pickles have the best flavor after mellowing for a month. Makes 6 pints.

CHAPTER EIGHT

Bugs, Slugs, and Four-Legged Thugs

IPM AND ORGANIC PEST CONTROL

IPM, or **integrated pest management**, is simply a new name for an old practice. It considers all available methods of pest control, rather than relying on pesticides alone. IPM consists of using a variety of measures to manage insects and weeds in your garden and cut down on their presence and impact. There are several principles to IPM.

- Avoid bad gardening habits that encourage pests, such as overwatering, overfertilizing, or poor pruning.
- Select plants that will thrive in your yard/garden's conditions (sun or shade, wet or dry, etc.) and will resist pests. Just as you can select plants, flowers, trees, and shrubs based upon how much water they require or how much maintenance they demand, you can also choose vegetation for its ability to withstand insects. Some trees and plants are hardier and are not attractive to pests. Or they may be better able to withstand the damage caused by insects.

- Watch your plants for infestation. This is one of the most important parts of IPM. If you work to identify insects and diseases when they first appear, you will have a head start on knowing which ones are not harmful and which should be controlled. Your garden center or extension service professionals can help you identify insects and diseases.
- Introduce a pest's natural predators. If pests are widespread in your site, you may be able to eliminate many of them by encouraging natural predators. Natural predators are other insects that will feed on the pests you are seeking to eliminate. Insects like ladybugs and praying mantises can devour hundreds of unwanted aphids or other pests.
- Learn to identify beneficial insects. If you have beneficial insects, avoid spraying pesticides that may kill them. Consider purchasing and introducing more predators into your garden and greenhouse.
- Properly prune your plants and pick off any insects you find. Despite taking all these precautions,

probably at some point you will encounter pests in your garden. With an IPM approach, that doesn't mean to spray at the first sign of insects. If there are only a few, you can just pick the insects off the plants. If you are able to destroy all of the harmful insects that you see, you can keep them from multiplying and infesting the rest of your garden. Another easy way to avoid spraying at the first sign of some insect and disease problems is to prune out the affected parts of the individual plant or tree, rather than using pesticides on the entire lawn or garden site. Don't compost affected material; seal it off in a trash bag, or burn it.

- **Use an appropriate pesticide when necessary.** IPM involves the judicious use of pesticides to eliminate those harmful pests that cannot be destroyed any other way. Be sure to follow label directions! Even pesticides considered "organic" are still poisons meant to kill other things.

Whenever you purchase a pesticide, buy the smallest quantity possible, and only what you need. The safest way to dispose of a pesticide, herbicide, or miticide is to use it for the purpose it was intended. If you must dispose of excess, be very sure to read and follow the directions on the label. Doing otherwise is against the law! Some pesticides require or recommend rinsing the container three times, putting the rinse water in the spray tank, *before* disposing of the container. Many civic landfills will not knowingly accept any pesticide containers, so call the trash company or city dump and ask them about their rules for toxic wastes (batteries and paints are often included in "toxic wastes"). Often, special pesticide collection days are held by the county extension office, waste removal companies,

or state department of agriculture.

Some kinds of pesticides will deteriorate with age and containers may leak, so early disposal of unused chemicals is a good idea. Do not mix different kinds of pesticides together unless the labeling says the mixture is OK; bad chemical reactions can occur.

Be sure of your insect ID before using a pesticide. Remember, the goal is *not* to "Kill all bugs!" Rather, we just want to reduce the number of pests. Many bugs are benign, or even beneficial.

GALLERY OF GARDEN PESTS

Aphids are small, squishable insects that may be green, yellow, pink, or black. They suck the juices from plants, and multiply something fierce. Organic controls include ladybeetles and lacewings, or Safer's or M-Pede brand soaps. Neem oil helps against aphids, as well as white flies and mealy bugs, often found on plants indoors. *Be sure* to spray the undersides of leaves, which is where aphids often hide! Like the Tribbles of "Star Trek" fame, aphids multiply rapidly. This is because they can reproduce several generations without mating. Monitoring your crops becomes very important, because it's easy to clean up a few aphids, but a full-blown infestation takes much more work.

Asparagus beetles are a quarter-inch long, with red bodies and blue wing covers with yellow spots. They lay their eggs on the foliage, after asparagus cutting season. Organic controls include cleaning up the bed after the plants die back, to prevent eggs from wintering over. You can also blast the pests off with a high-pressure garden hose. Pyrethrin or rotenone helps bad infestations.

Bean beetles are red to yellow, with black spots. There are one or two generations per year. Only the first generation causes problems. The Mexican bean beetle is a rounder bug with pale yellow to coppery brown color and eight spots on each wing. They can be controlled with insecticidal soap (such as Safer's brand) or Neem oil.

Potato beetles have black and yellow stripes, and you'll find these beetles chewing on leaves and stem ends of potatoes, tomatoes, peppers, and eggplants. Use row covers, or *Bacillus thuringiensis v. san diego* (one brand name is M-Trak) kills the larvae.

Cabbage moths bother all members of the cruciferous family (cabbage, broccoli, cauliflower, etc.). If you see white butterflies fluttering around your garden, nab them! Their eggs will hatch into *cabbage worms*, which are easily sprinkled with salt, picked off and squished, or just picked off and tossed into the lawn. Growing reddish-purple plants makes these bright green inchworms as easy to spot as a snowball in a coalmine. Of course, they also hide on the undersides of leaves. Fabric covers, such as Reemay, are very effective for growing picture-perfect crops, as is *Bacillus thuringiensis*, also known as Bt, and Neem.

Corn-ear worms are large, 2-inch-long green or brown caterpillars with light brown stripes up and down their bodies. They feed on the silks and then on the corn ear. An organic control is to apply a half-dropper of mineral oil to the silk just inside the tip of each ear. Wait to do this until *after* the silk has wilted and begun to turn brown at the tip, so the corn can be pollinated.

Cucumber beetles come in both striped or spotted varieties, yellow or green with black markings. If you see "yellow ladybugs," they are *not* beneficial ladybugs! Cucumber beetles ("cukerbeetles") affect all members of the cucurbit family, including melons, summer and winter squashes, and pumpkins. Worse than the mere chewing, they also

spread bacterial wilt disease. Organic controls include interplanting with radishes; covering with Reemay (remove at flowering time); or applying Neem, a 5-percent pyrethrum-rotenone mixture, or sabadilla.

Cutworms feed by eating the stems of vegetable and flower seedlings, cutting them right off at ground level. They can clear-cut a patch of freshly transplanted veggies like loggers in a forest. Don't bother with making "cutworm collars" out of paper or cardboard; the little beasties crawl out of the soil into the arena and eat stuff down anyway. Instead, put a stick right next to the plant stem, and it can't wrap itself around to eat through the stem. If you have cutworm damage, dig around the base of the damaged plants and kill the fat larva you see there.

Flea beetles bother all sorts of vegetables. They look like jumping punctuation marks that bounce away when you try to catch them. They afflict potatoes, eggplants, beets, and radishes. The easiest method for dealing with flea beetles is to lay down thin insect-barrier row covers for your crops.

Hornworms are giant, three- to four-inch-long green caterpillars appearing in July and August. They chew on the leaves and fruits of peppers, potatoes, and eggplants. Organic controls include Bt or handpicking. Do *not* mess with the caterpillar if it has small white cocoons on its back. These are from the braconid wasp, whose larvae will hatch and kill the hornworm, so you don't have to.

Leaf miners come in different types, for flowers, trees, and leafy vegetables. These insects make tunnels between the upper and lower surfaces of the leaves. Use Reemay for vegetables, and remove and destroy affected leaves on flowering plants. You can also spray heavily invested ornamentals with Neem oil.

Mildew, also known as powdery mildew, is a fungal problem. Mildew is best treated in a prevention program of spraying weekly with a combination of one tablespoon each baking soda and summer-weight horticultural oil (for a spreader-sticker) per one gallon of water. Make it up fresh each time, and coat the plants. Do *not* use this mixture on hairy plants, such as tomatoes.

Milkweed caterpillar A black-, yellow-, and white-banded caterpillar with antennae at each end is a familiar sight on your milkweed. *Don't* squish these guys—they're baby monarch butterflies! The butterflies love the nectar in milkweed or butterfly weed (*Asclepias* family) flowers, and the caterpillars eat the leaves. So plant extra milkweed and provide a habitat for these living gems.

Parsley worm is actually the caterpillar of the black swallowtail butterfly (they're also found on dill, anise, fennel, and Queen Anne's lace). We plant extra parsley to share, because how much parsley do you eat in a week? We also love to watch them hatch into butterflies.

Slug controls usually involve a barrier, such as a copper strip, rough sand, or rough wood slats; an attractant, such as beer (it's the yeast that draws them, not the alcohol); or removal, by sticking, squishing, stomping, melting them with salt, and so on. Avoid messy gardens that give them places to hide. Lime or diatomaceous earth applied on the surface also discourages them. To remove slug slime from your skin, scrub off with salt and/or vinegar.

Spider mites are arachnids related to ticks, scorpions, and spiders. They are very small, best viewed either with a hand lens or by tapping the leaf over white paper, where the mites may be seen. Ladybugs and lacewings both will gobble these up. You can also use insecticidal soap, Neem, and spray fruit trees with dormant oil (before they leaf out).

Squash bugs are flat gray bugs with a single black teardrop marking. Mature adults are a dark slate gray; nymphs are a lighter ash gray with less distinct markings. They are visible swarming around the plants, sucking the sap and injecting a toxin that causes wilting. Watch out for clusters of small copper eggs on the undersides of leaves.

Organic controls include trellising or applying a 5-percent pyrethrum-rotenone mixture.

Squash vine borers also cause wilt. The white worm chews into the stem at the base, leaving behind a pile of yellow-green excrement called *frass*. ("Frass" also makes an excellent cuss word, "Oh frass! My pumpkins have vine borers!") Organic controls include wrapping old nylon stockings around the stems to discourage egg laying by adults, putting on Reemay covers until flowering time, or applying a 5-percent pyrethrum-rotenone mixture or sabadilla. You can also slit the squash stem lengthwise to extract the worms, and then bury the stems to encourage healing and rooting.

PESTICIDE AND HERBICIDE SAFETY

When it comes to insect control, the organic farmers and gardeners often butt heads with the chemical users. And then the organic crowd splits into several subgroups: those who never use pesticides, those who use a few chosen "organic" pesticides, and those who use pesticides only as a last resort and in small quantities.

As you know, the goal of pest control is not to *get rid of all the bugs in the garden*. Many of those insects and bugs and spiders are beneficial. They are the "good guys." The goal, rather, is to remove the pest bugs from your garden plants without excessive use of poisons.

A poison is simply a chemical designed to kill something. Weed killers don't actually kill "weeds." Weed killers for your lawn simply kill the broadleaf plants but not the grass. If any of this type of herbicide drifts or washes onto your fruit, vegetable, or flower gardens, it can kill those plants. Pesticides kill bugs and insects. Butterflies and bees are also insects. Pesticides kill butterflies and bees.

I garden organically to avoid those chemicals that damage the environment beyond temporarily eliminating the creatures it was designed against. Remember DDT? It stayed in the food chain all the way up to the eagles, and caused mortal damage to their eggshell structure. It also killed the predators of mites, but not the mites themselves, so levels of mites actually went up after spraying DDT. *"But we don't have chemicals like that anymore. The government checks them."*

Well, we like to think so, but the government agencies are not omniscient. Periodically another chemical is banned for home use. Concerns about groundwater and aquifer contamination are increasing. Besides, we really don't know everything we should about the hundreds of ways that thousands of chemicals can interact with the environment.

So when in doubt, play it safe. I use soap washes on my tomato aphids. I pour hot water on the weeds growing in my walks. It kills them every time (and does a number on the ants, too) without my having to worry about children or a cat coming in contact with the product later. If the squash beetles get above my squishing level, pyrethrin-rotenone dust can be used on them. Pyrethrin-rotenone dust, although considered an organic pesticide, is not completely safe to humans and other life-forms, though. You have to read the labels!

Read Every Label

When the can tells you not to let this concoction run into streams and ponds and groundwater sinks, do you want to use it? If so, try using it in smaller quantities, and be careful where it's going to wash off to.

Poisons have specific titles according to their toxicity. When a label mentions the material's "LD50," this means that the dosage mentioned is a lethal dose for 50 percent of the animals it was tested on. I don't mention these "enough to kill an adult" levels for the benefit of potential murderers, but to make you aware of how dangerous some chemicals can be.

- **Highly toxic** poisons are marked **DANGER**; a few drops to a teaspoonful is enough to kill an adult. If the substance has a skull and crossbones or "poison" marked in red, then it's acutely toxic not only through oral contact but also by inhaling or skin contact. If just the word *DANGER* is used, the toxicity is for skin and eye irritation.
- **Moderately toxic** poisons are marked **WARNING**; a teaspoon to an ounce can kill an adult.
- **Slightly toxic** poisons are marked **CAUTION**; an ounce to a pint/pound would have to be ingested to kill someone.
- **Relatively nontoxic** poisons are also marked **CAUTION**; over a pint/pound would have to be ingested.

Remember, children and pets would be hurt by even a fraction of these dosages.

Wear Protective Clothing

I shudder to think of how many times I've seen people spraying roses. These women are wearing shorts and halter-tops. Did you know many labels say to wear long-sleeve shirts, long pants, a hair covering, a pollen mask, safety goggles, and gloves? To wash these garments separate from the other laundry afterward? Not to spray on windy days because you shouldn't inhale the fungicide? Inciden-

SAFETY TIPS

- Pesticides should *always* be kept in their original containers.
- Store pesticides (as well as herbicides, miticides, fungicides, etc.) in a location that does not freeze or get excessively hot. The materials should be stored (and locked) where children and pets cannot get into them.
- Read labels to determine how close to harvest time the product can be used, and to follow proper washing instructions for produce harvested.
- Do not use kitchen measuring tools for poisons; keep special measuring tools with the poisons, not to be used anywhere else.
- Do not spray on windy days or before rains.
- Do not use granular pesticides near crops that are bee-pollinated; the bees can pick up the poisons and take them home to the hive along with the pollen grains they collect. Spray in the evening, after the bees have gone home. Bees are legally protected.

tally, this same warning is on some of my organic pesticides, as well!

To get unbiased, current, scientific information about the safety and toxicity of many pesticides, written for nonscientists, go to ExToxNet, the Extension Toxicology Network at http://ace.orst.edu/info/extoxnet. ExToxNet is a cooperative effort of the University of California-Davis, Oregon State University, Michigan State University, Cornell University, and the University of Idaho.

Gardeners sure are picky folks; we want butterflies, but only certain kinds. We want birds, but only certain kinds. We want cute wildlife as long as it isn't munching down on our landscaping.

What to do about the unwanted critters has kept people occupied for millennia. Nowadays we can't go posting our young children out in the fields to keep the crows and rabbits out of our vegetable gardens; modern law wants them in school instead. So we fall back on the other three methods: barriers, deterrents, and traps.

Avoid using mothballs containing napthalene or paradichlorobenzene, which are poisonous.

Cats

Cats aren't generally a problem except when they can't resist using some freshly tilled earth for a litter box. Barriers work best in this case. People turn grating-bottomed seed-starting flats over the ground, or liberally sprinkle around pinecones or sweet-gum balls. Another deterrent is to plant stakes throughout the area and weave a webbing of string a few inches above the ground. This not only keeps the cats out but also helps support your plants. Some cats are deterred by the scent of orange peels. Others can be kept out of an area by setting several mousetraps *upside-down* and then covering the mousetraps with a tarp or newspapers. The whole area is mined with snapping, harmless mousetraps and scares the cat into avoidance.

Personally, I use a piece of slightly arched wire fencing to lay over the freshly turned or seeded ground. This works well to keep our three cats out.

Arching wire over newly planted ground keeps cats out.

Deer

If you live out in the country—or in a new subdivision that was countryside until recently—and are beset by deer, enclose the garden with an 8- to 10-foot fence. Folks in the burbs find this tricky, not only because of the cost but also because of zoning laws. Instead, invest in an electric fence at 30 inches aboveground (sink posts 15 inches deep), and tag it about every three feet with strips of masking tape spread with peanut butter. Why the peanut butter? The deer nibble it and get zapped. The charge won't hurt them, but it's unfriendly.

They also don't like to walk across uncertain ground; a four-foot-wide stretch of chicken wire held a few inches above the ground will provide a barrier they don't want to cross.

A truly starving deer will eat nearly anything, but under normal circumstances there are plants that deer don't like—generally those that are fuzzy, strongly flavored, or poisonous.

Overenthusiastic ("Weedy") Dogs

Some previous neighbors of ours had a Brittany spaniel and a rottweiler. Although at opposite ends of the temperament spectrum, both dogs had a singular disregard for the fine distinction between yard and garden. Their master finally invested in some electric fencing outlining the beds. This worked great: The dogs were surprised, but unharmed. The neighbors' garden was then made into a showcase for their son's graduation party. The rottweiler learned where the fence was, so they turned it off. But it turned out the Brittany conveniently forgot, so they had to turn the juice back on.

When I was a child, there was a giant white dog in our neighborhood with a passion for dumpster diving. Every trash day we'd find the street strewn with wrappers. So my mother filled one of our squirt guns with green food coloring and turned the dog into a four-footed Jackson Pollock painting. The food coloring wasn't harmful to the dog, but its owners sure knew that someone was unhappy with its behavior. We never saw the dog again.

If you're out in the yard, you can apply some negative reinforcement by hollering "No!" and throwing a can filled with twenty or so pennies in the general direction of the dog. Please don't actually hit the dog; scaring it will be enough.

Rabbits and Squirrels

At garden centers you can buy a powder to mix with birdseed to help repel squirrels. The stuff is essentially a hot chili pepper essence. I've been using black or red (cayenne) pepper sprinkled on my plants for years to keep the rabbits and squirrels out of them. Contrary to Warner Brothers' cartoons, the rabbit doesn't want my carrots. It wants my beet greens, young sprouting peas, cabbage transplants, lettuce, strawberries, and green coleus. So I sprinkled pepper on the leaves and that kept the rabbit away. Unfortunately, the stuff washed off every time it rained. Nowadays there's a product on the market that is a hot pepper wax spray, and the stuff works great.

If you choose to fence out the rabbits with rabbit fencing, be sure to install it twelve inches down into the soil so they don't slip underneath. Snow fencing will not substitute; rabbits can apparently turn boneless at will and slip between the slats.

Raccoons

Raccoons are another kettle of fish. Clever and handy, they can get into anything that's not bungee-corded or locked down. Coons also have the annoying habit of picking the sweet corn the very

Chicken wire stapled to the fence and planted 12 inches deep keeps out rabbits.

night it's ripe. (If only the bottom cornstalks are bent down and eaten, you may have skunks instead.)

Use electric fence with a pair of wires at six inches and twelve inches above the ground. Be sure to use fiberglass posts, because those coons can climb the wooden ones.

The presence of dogs helps keep coons away if the pet's left out all night, free to roam the garden. Some folks find that raccoons are deterred by the sound of a radio rock station or Rush Limbaugh. Apparently urban raccoons are used to this; not everyone reports success with the radio trick.

Woodchucks, Gophers, and Moles

Woodchucks climb as well as burrow. Buy some 1-by-1-foot or 1-by-2-foot fencing and bury the bottom 2 feet deep. The aboveground section should be 18 inches high, with the top 6 inches folded at a right angle on the outside side of the fence. The overhang keeps the woodchucks from simply climbing over the fence. This fence will keep out the rabbits, too.

Folks have reported success with putting a few unwrapped sticks of mint chewing gum or marshmallows down the mole holes. My neighbor (he of the weedy dogs) was able to watch a mole dive into its run and then trap it between two shovels quickly jammed into the ground, one on each side of the animal. He then removed the mole from our street. Traps are a conundrum: What farmer wants a critter *delivered* to their field?

Moles dig vertical holes for their nests and horizontal "runs" or tunnels for finding the worms and grubs they like to eat. A popular formula you can spray on your lawn to deter the moles from tunneling in your yard is 6 tablespoons castor oil plus 3 tablespoons liquid detergent. Add half a cup of water and blend well. Using a 15-gallon hose-end sprayer, add one cup of the mixture and fill the remainder with water. Then attach the sprayer to your hose and spray the entire lawn. Do not spray too quickly; walk slowly to get a good saturation. Spray before a rain, or run the sprinkler for twenty minutes after spraying, to water the solution into the soil. Repeat if you observe new mole activity.

GOOD GUYS DON'T WEAR WHITE HATS

Garden spiders, or Argiope. The zigzag (or stabilimentum) in the spider's web warns birds not to fly into the web. This saves the spider from expending extra protein to remake the web. Spiders catch lots of insect pests, but can be killed by insecticides.

Garter snakes are sometimes called garden snakes. Like the spiders, their garden name indicates that they're friends, and belong in the garden. They eat many pests, including grasshoppers, slugs, and even mice, moles, and voles.

Lacewings eat a variety of soft-bodied insects, including aphids, mealy bugs, thrips, smaller caterpillars, mites, moth eggs and some types of scales.

Ladybugs, or **ladybird beetles,** are hard to release in the outdoors and keep resident. They're much easier to use in greenhouse operations. They eat aphids, mealy bugs, soft scales, and spider mites. Their offspring are much larger, purple, bumpy things. Learn what they look like so you don't kill them accidentally.

Praying mantises are indiscriminate eaters. They'll eat any bug they catch, even beneficial ones and other praying mantises!

Toads are like snakes, but with legs for those of you who mistrust legless critters. You can attract toads and other beneficial critters by having ground-level water basins, and by leaving logs or rocks piled loosely for shelter.

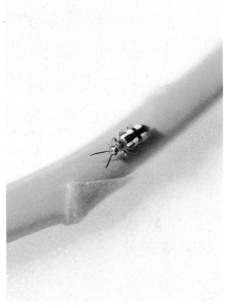

Aphids.

Asparagus beetle.

Bean beetle.

Cabbage white moth.

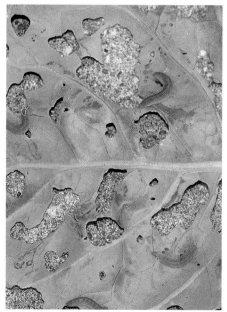

Cabbage "worms" (caterpillars).

Cutworm.

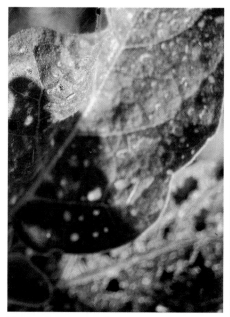

Flea beetles on an eggplant.

"Parsley worm"—the Black Swallowtail caterpillar's egg, larvae, and chrysalis.

Black Swallowtail butterfly, hatching.

Sand piles and slug traps protect lettuces.

Slugs on lettuce.

Spider mites and damage.

Squash bugs—adults and nymphs.

Squash bug eggs on the underside of a squash leaf.

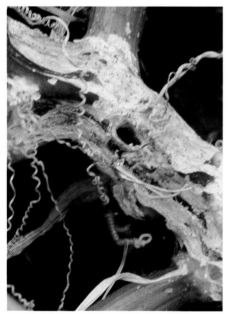

Evidence of the squash vine borer.

The squash vine borer revealed.

Tomato hornworm caterpillar.

Argiope garden spider.

Convergent ladybug/ladybird beetle.

Ladybug larvae.

Praying mantis.

Friendly garden toad.

Blossom-end rot.

COMMON PLANT DISEASES AND QUESTIONS

TOMATO TRIAGE

Q.: *My hubby fertilizes the tomato plants every week, just like he's supposed to. Our problem is that there aren't any flowers on any of our plants. They just keep growing taller and taller!*

A.: Too much fertilizer is probably your problem. Tomato plants are not heavy feeders. Excess fertilizer (especially high-nitrogen fertilizers like lawn fertilizer or houseplant fertilizer) can lead to lots of lush leaf growth and no fruit. Please tell your hubby to stop fertilizing and let the plant move out of its adolescent growth cycle and into its adult reproductive cycle of bearing fruits.

Q.: *Gross! The bottoms of my tomatoes are getting black and mushy. What's wrong, and what do I need to spray on them?*

A.: Blossom-end rot (BER) is usually seen during the early part of the harvest season. Some types of tomatoes get it worse than others. It is *not* caused by insects or diseases. BER happens during uneven rainfall or watering, too much rain, too much nitrogen fertilizer, and rapid plant growth during the early part of the season.

BER is *not* due to insufficient calcium. In fact, clay soils with underlying limestone generally have sufficient calcium. So burying TUMS, eggshells, and so on is not necessary. What happens is that during the periods of fast growth in the young tomato plant, the calcium the plant has moves from the fruit into the stems of the plant. This means there's less calcium in the fruits, and this lowered

Longitudinal cracking.

Q.: *How can I keep my tomatoes from cracking?*

A.: Tomato cracks that run from top to bottom are generally caused by heavy rains. Some varieties of tomatoes are more prone to post-rain cracking than others. Consistent watering will help prevent this problem, as will picking ripe tomatoes before a heavy storm comes through.

Concentric ring cracks around the stem end are common with some tomato cultivars, and are generally not a problem unless continued rains create conditions for mold.

Q.: *My tomatoes aren't ripening all the way; the tops by the stems are still green!*

A.: Green-shouldered tomatoes are not really a health or cultivation problem. Some types of tomatoes simply ripen this way because they don't have a "uniform ripening gene." Supermarket tomatoes are bred to contain this gene for perfect red color. Then again, they're also bred for bouncy strength to ship well, rather than for flavor. Worrying about having picture-perfect tomatoes should not be a concern for the home gardener; we want flavor! Again, some varieties ripen this way, and some don't. Don't worry about it.

Q.: *The flowers are falling off my tomato plants!*

A.: This problem occurs when it's too cool or way too hot. The weather will change and the plant will start setting fruit again. Don't worry about it. No need to fertilize.

Q.: *The leaves on the bottom halves of my tomato plants are getting spots, turning yellow, and dying! What kind of insecticide should I use?*

A.: Don't bother with insecticide. This is a fungus problem, either septoria leaf

amount is what causes BER. High transpiration rates during hot weather or drought (not unlike sweating in people) also has this effect. What you end up with is a plant that is *not* calcium deficient, just calcium displaced. University studies show that adding extra calcium does not prevent BER. Calcium sprays do not help either, because the calcium cannot enter the skin of the fruits. Maturing of the plant itself will correct the problem, just as teenagers outgrow pimples. Just pick off affected fruits.

Concentric cracking.

spot or early blight. Both are common problems, especially during rainy, humid weather, and they're often seen after the blossoms have set fruit. The fungus over-winters on plant debris, so cleaning up in the fall helps. If you have plants with either fungus problem, at the end of the growing season, do not compost them, but set them out in the trash.

A weekly fungicide spray program will help prevent the problem. Around here, once we hit the "hot and doesn't rain" part of our summer weather, the fungus is less of a problem. Don't plant your tomatoes too close together; give them three feet or more for better air circulation. If you have spotted lower yellow leaves from septoria leaf spot or early blight, then removing those affected leaves can help, just to reduce the level of contagion. Personally, I think this is a good reason *not* to remove suckers; more branches means there's more foliage remaining for the plant to work with. Granted, after snapping off those affected lower branches the plants do look a little "leggy," but they also look cleaner.

Septoria blight.

Tomato wilt.

just one side is affected. The wilting and dying continues to creep up the plant, and eventually the whole thing dies. To tell which wilt you had, cut the stem at an angle; a browning of the vascular (water pipe) system of the stem means it died of fusarium wilt.

Verticillium wilt is more common in cooler spring weather and sometimes does not kill the plant completely, but it severely stunts the plant's productive ability. Both wilts are caused by fungi, and can overwinter in the soil. A five-year crop rotation can help (Crop rotation is discussed in the next section).

Root-knot nematodes also cause stunting and wilting, with stunted or pale green leaves. Wormlike nematodes infect the roots, and the injury makes it difficult for the plants to take up nutrients. Cultivars listed with V, F, or N have resistance to these problems, and the plants will last longer before succumbing, allowing you to get in more harvest. Unfortunately, that's not the same thing as being "bullet-proof." Some heirlooms are prone to these fungi, which is why VFN hybrids became popular. Some of the heirloom cultivars also have these same resistance genes; but because testing is an expensive procedure, and no one owns exclusive rights to the genes, plants aren't tested and labeled accordingly.

Q.: *My tomato plants just up and died; they're an awful mess! I even bought one labelled "VFN"; I thought it wasn't supposed to get diseases.*

A.: Verticillium wilt (V) and fusarium wilt (F) are the two major wilt diseases that can take down tomato plants. Nematodes (N) cause problems, but don't usually kill the plants outright.

We usually see fusarium wilt in midsummer, when it gets really hot. The lower leaves turn yellow, and sometimes

Other Vegetables' Problems

Q.: *The leaves on my cabbages are turning yellow and wilting, but I don't see any bugs.*

A.: The pests that cause this problem live underground. Cabbage maggots riddle the roots as they eat tunnels through the roots. Root-knot nematodes can also cause these symptoms. Pull up the plant. The maggots will be visible, or the roots will have the nodules and galls that signify nematodes. Remove all diseased plants. Adding lime to bring your soil up to a pH of 7.0–7.2 will also help.

Q.: *I have trouble getting my carrots to sprout!*

A.: Consistent moisture is essential. Some people lay a board on the seeded area to keep the moisture in, and check daily. Once the seeds start sprouting, immediately remove the board. You can also sprinkle the area on days it doesn't rain. Making sure the ground has adequate moisture *before* seeding also helps.

Q.: *When I dug up my carrots, the roots were all twisted and forked, not straight.*

A.: Lumpy, rocky, or compacted soil makes it hard for the carrot roots to grow easily. Deep loosening of the soil and removing hard lumps and rocks will enable you to grow straight carrots. Raised beds make this easier.

Q.: *I can't get pretty-looking cauliflower; the heads turn purply-brown or green.*

A.: Cauliflower needs "blanching"—or covering up the developing flower head—to prevent sun exposure. Wait until the head is about 3 inches in diameter, then tie or rubber-band the innermost leaves to shade the head. "Self-blanching" cultivars are also available; look for those in the catalogs. Freezing of growing plants will also cause injury to the flower heads.

Q.: *Eeuw! My melons are rotting on the bottom!*

A.: This rot is caused by dampness. Growing melons on a trellis helps, or propping them up on the hole-side of bricks, or on tuna cans with the ends removed.

Q.: *The onions aren't growing well, and the leaves are turning yellow. Do they need fertilizer?*

A.: Yes, they do. Onions are heavy feeders, and nitrogen is the nutrient shortage causing the yellowing on older leaves. Digging in compost before planting, mulching with (untreated) grass clippings, or adding blood meal or fish emulsion can alleviate the problem.

Q.: *My radishes are tops and no bottoms! What went wrong?*

A.: Sometimes weather will change the maturity time so your radishes won't be ready to pick in "just 35 days," or whatever the packet said. This is especially true if dry weather slowed down germination considerably. Another problem is that root crops cannot grow well if crowded. Stunted, small, twisted, or thin roots are symptoms not only of poor soil texture but also of a gardener who sowed too thickly or didn't have the heart to thin properly. Be sure to allow 3–4 inches between each plant.

Q.: *I have a problem with zucchini: The squash gets about 4 inches long, looks great, and then starts to yellow and shrivel. What's happening?*

A.: More like what's not happening: sufficient pollination. Pollen must be transferred from the male flowers to the female flowers, and there must be enough pollen delivered (in one or more trips) for the fruit to develop properly. Honeybees, bumblebees, and squash bees are the primary pollinators for squashes. However, both domestic and wild bee populations have been decimated by two kinds of mites, and the number of pollinators available has fallen dramatically. Improper use of pesticides (such as powdered Sevin) also kills bees.

If you're getting both kinds of blossoms and two weeks later there still aren't any good zucchinis, the problem may be lack of insect pollinators. You can take over the bee's job by transferring the pollen manually. Take a cotton swab and collect the dusty yellow pollen from the male blossom (the one with the plain stem) and dab it into the center of the female blossom (the one with the little zuke behind the flower).

CROP ROTATION

To minimize pest and disease problems and nutrient depletion as well, avoid planting the same annual crops in the same place each year. So when you plan your next year's layout, check back to last year's notes or map to see where you grew plants last year. This technique is known as crop rotation.

Pests and diseases tend to be family-specific. For example, tomatoes, peppers, and eggplants are in the same botanical family. So it's best not to plant tomatoes where peppers or eggplants grew last year. The most common vegetable families are

- **Beet family**—beet, chard, spinach
- **Cabbage/cole/cruciferous family**—broccoli, Brussels sprouts, cabbage, cauliflower, collard, kale, kohlrabi, radish, turnip
- **Dill/umbellifer family**—carrot, celery, chervil, cilantro, dill, parsley, parsnip
- **Grass family**—corn
- **Lettuce family**—artichoke, chicory, endive, lettuce
- **Lily/allium family**— chives, garlic, leek, onion
- **Pea/legume family**—bean, cowpea, pea, peanut
- **Squash/cucurbit family**—cucumber, melon, pumpkin, squash

- **Tomato/solanacious family**—eggplant, pepper, potato, tomato

Of course, this crop-rotation technique works best in larger gardens. In small gardens it's difficult to move the crop far enough away from last year's location.

SOIL SOLARIZATION

Cleaning up your soil does not require dumping lots of chemicals on it. What the solarization process can do is to remove a great deal of the weed seeds, nematodes, fungi, and other pathogens. The beneficial worms will move out, but they will return once you add organic matter again.

Solarization is not difficult; but it does remove part of the garden ground from growing use, because it requires two months during the hot part of the year. If you have several beds and a large population of weeds, you might consider rotating which bed is treated. You can also put in a fall crop after the ground has been solarized.

Buy a large sheet or two of 4-mil clear plastic, both wider and longer than the size of the bed. You will need enough plastic to cover the bed in two layers. Some plastics have UV inhibitors to keep them from degrading as quickly, and they can be reused.

Add any amendments you feel the soil needs, and mix them in well. Smooth the bed with the back of a garden rake for an even surface. Run a sprinkler long enough that the soil is moistened to a 1-foot depth (stick a deep spade in and do a visual check). This watering encourages weed seeds to germinate, and germinated seeds will die better than dormant ones. Dig a trench a few inches deep around the edge of the bed.

Lay on one sheet of plastic, smoothing

it flat to the soil surface, and tuck the edges into the trench. Scatter empty soda cans or bottles two feet apart into a grid pattern, to separate the two layers of plastic sheeting. Lay the second sheet of plastic atop the cans/bottles, and tuck it into the trench as well. Close the trench well on all sides for a snug seal.

Depending on the amount of daily sunlight and ambient temperature, the soil can take a month or two to heat up fully. You can check the soil temperature by sliding a soil thermometer under the bottom layer of plastic (reseal afterward). Once the soil reaches 120 °F, it's cooking out the bad stuff. Leave the plastic on for most of a week at that point. Then remove the sheets, rinse and dry them, and store them for use another year.

The earthworms will tunnel deeper, or away from the site. Beneficial soil microorganisms will also be killed, so digging in fresh compost afterward is helpful. Don't dig more than a few inches down, or you will bring up old weed seeds that the heat cannot penetrate.

"WHAT IS THAT?" GETTING HELP FROM YOUR EXTENSION OFFICE

Each of the land-grant agricultural universities has a system of extension offices, one per county in the state. Being blessed with living in an agricultural part of the United States, all or nearly all of us have one of these offices within our own counties. The extension offices provide information and services from the universities, ranging from agricultural (farming) to horticultural (gardening) to family information (home economics) and 4-H clubs.

If you have questions about any aspect of gardening, the offices can answer them, and they often have brochures and other handouts. They can also take samples for soil testing by state labs. Offices in counties with larger populations frequently have extension master gardener programs, where you can learn more about horticulture and become a volunteer to help spread gardening information throughout the populace. (I received training through Kansas State University's Master Gardener program.)

Due to the staggering number of counties within each state of the Heartland, I'm simply listing the university website that provides the information for county extension offices in your state. You can also call or write the university in question. The county extension offices are usually listed under County Offices in the blue pages of the phone book.

- Listing of County Extension Offices with University of Illinois: http://web.aces.uiuc.edu/ve/
- Listing of County Extension Offices with Purdue University (Indiana): http://www.agriculture.purdue.edu/agis/extension/counties.html
- Listing of County Extension Offices with Iowa State University: http://www.hort.iastate.edu/pages/conshort/c_frame.html
- Listing of County Extension Offices with Kansas State University: http://www.oznet.ksu.edu/root/units.htm
- Listing of County Extension Offices with University of Kentucky: http://www.ca.uky.edu/county/
- Listing of County Extension Offices with Michigan State University: http://www.msue.msu.edu/msue/ctyentpg/
- Listing of County Extension Offices with University of Minnesota: http://www.extension.umn.edu/offices/

- Listing of County Extension Offices with University of Nebraska Extension: http://ianrwww.unl.edu/ianr/coopext/countyoffices.html
- Listing of County Extension Offices with Ohio State University: http://www.ag.ohio-state.edu/distcoun.html
- Listing of County Extension Offices with Oklahoma State University: http://countyext.okstate.edu/

- Listing of County Extension Offices with South Dakota State University: http://www.abs.sdstate.edu/county/
- Listing of County Extension Offices with University of Wisconsin: http://www.hort.iastate.edu/pages/conshort/c_frame.html

CHAPTER NINE

Tool Selection—or Whoever Dies with the Most Toys, Wins!

SIMPLE PLEASURES: WHAT YOU REALLY NEED

The only tools you absolutely need are a shovel and a bucket. Everything else is gravy. However, this is like saying you only need a knife and a pot to cook. Some frugal Asian housewives may manage with just a knife and a wok, but it's a known fact that gardeners are a growing market for nifty gadgets.

And luckily, once you make it known that you are A Gardener, gift giving is simplified. The only reason I even own a pair of genuine Wellies (those knee-high, green Wellington gardener's boots) is that my dad lives near a Smith & Hawken store in California. I put them to extended use, and as my husband Andy points out, will be the best dressed next time we have a flood.

Most beginning gardeners pick up some inexpensive **trowels** and weeders at the local discount department store, or garden shop, and then spend the next two years wondering what they're doing wrong. Cute little trowels with pink plastic handles are fine for serving up potting soil; but after you've bent two or three,

you know that they're useless for digging in clay soil. I would recommend instead an aluminum version that's cast as a solid piece.

Of course, all gardeners have stuff to lug around: bags of composted manure, weeds we've pulled, piles of dead stuff when the season is over. A tool I use every time I'm out gardening is the **burden cloth**, a specially reinforced canvas tarp with loop handles at each corner. I grab a handle and drag it around the yard, or grab all the handles and "Ho, ho, ho," like Santa Claus, haul my bag of goodies over to the compost heap. Burden cloths are produced as a small cottage industry, and when yours eventually wears out, you can send it back for a discount on a new one! They come in different sizes. (Children also find them useful for play tents or play mats—Legos are easy to pick up and pour back into the bin.)

Timeless Enterprises
P.O. Box 824
Eugene, OR 97440
phone 541-689-2123
e-mail timelesent@aol.com

A baffling variety of **weeders** awaits the novice gardener. Most of us are familiar with the three-prong type, which is popular because it's popular—that is, it's sold most everywhere, so it's bought most everywhere. In various parts of the country, particular affections for specific designs will reign. Many of these have to do with ethnic influence. The ho-mi is popular among many Asian populations. It's shaped like a heavy deck-of-cards spade, and has a sharp handle. The heavy-duty Japanese weeding knife is useful for grubbing out annoying weeds and opening up ground for transplants.

Another heavy hoe has a rectangular blade sharpened on the end, and the handle affixed at a 90-degree angle. It's the grape hoe, which Italian vineyard workers brought over to this country.

Why would anybody want a heavy hoe? For the same reason that we use sledgehammers. You let the mass of the tool work *with* gravity, allowing for a controlled fall to slice through the weeds. Styles of hoes are seemingly endless: round, flat, wide blades, thin blades, winged blades, scuffling blades, pull blades, push blades, and so on. Hoes are designed to be used when you are standing up, *not* bent over. Happy hoeing means the handle is long enough for you to stand without straining your back, and that the cutting edge is actually sharp enough to slice off the weeds just below soil level. Hoes were never meant for bludgeoning the ground.

HOW TO PICK THE WEEDER FOR YOU

1. Do you want to weed standing up (or from a chair)? Choose a long-handled weeder, like a hoe. If you'd rather weed close to the ground, get a short-handled weeder.

2. Do you want to cut off the weeds? Get a hoe. If you want to pull them out, choose a cultivator.

3. Do you need a narrow weeder (for planting a wide block)? Use a finger weeder, Cape Cod weeder, Japanese weeding knife, etc. If you need a wide one (for single rows), go for the ho-mi.

4. Are you right- or left-handed? There are both nonspecific and hand-specific tools available.

The Shovel

If you own a shovel (chances are that you do), you'll also need to own a file. I don't say this out of horticultural snobbery. Keeping your shovel sharpened ranks right up there with keeping your tires inflated and your oil clean and topped off. Too bad garden centers don't offer shovel sharpening the way fabric stores offer scissors sharpening! An emery cloth is handy for pruners, and a file will restore the cutting edge to shovels and hoes. Shovels are sharpened on the inside of the curve (concave side), while hoes are sharpened on the underside (generally you pull them toward you to cut; some are push-hoes).

Most casual gardeners have never experienced a sharp shovel, so they don't know what they're missing. The general thought on shoveling is that it requires large amounts of upper-body strength and mulish endurance. I would say that this is a load of manure, but being a gardener, I know the value of a load of manure. This concept is, in fact, stuff-and-nonsense.

When a shovel has been sharpened, it will slice into the soil with just a bit of foot pressure. Yes, I know that we often have soil that's not only clay, but also gravel-laden and compacted as well. In that case, you stab the shovel into the ground straight down (sometimes by jumping onto it—you are wearing heavy work shoes with arch supports, rather than sneakers, are you not?). Once it's bit into the soil, lean back onto the shovel, remembering that a fulcrum is most effective at the further end, rather than the nearer one. If the handle feels like it's straining to keep from snapping, pull up and take a smaller bite.

When lifting soil, don't strain your back. The trick is to keep your back straight and your knees bent. Locking your knees and pulling with your lower back will send you to the physical therapist. Remember all those roasted or fried chicken dinners? No one ever exclaims at the dinner table, "Ooh, gimme the back! I want the back!" Of course not—there's no meat on the back! The thighs are meatier than the backs, and your thigh muscles are larger and stronger than your back muscles.

It's actually smarter to take medium-size slices of ground when digging up. Great big slices are as hard on the shovel as you, and little nips will drive you to impatience. Take one chomp out of the middle of the hole, then carve out bites around the edge.

When shovel shopping, be aware that there are different kinds of shovels. A round-pointed shovel is for general hole digging (post-hole diggers are an entirely separate tool). The point at the apex of the rounded cutting end forces all of the work energy into a small area, letting you cut with ease. Some shovels have cuts like shark teeth along the edge, for biting into really obnoxious soil. They work well, but of course their blades require more time to resharpen.

If you find your soil is full of obstructions, like rocks and tree roots, then you may wish to take out the square-pointed shovel. This looks like a round-pointed shovel before the manicure. Because the digging edge is flat, it can slice through most problems, rather than twisting. It is also better for general earth moving, because of the wider surface. Construction workers use these all the time, especially when clearing junk off a flat piece of pavement.

Always use shovels with l-o-n-g handles. A longer handle means you don't have to bend over as far, and gives you greater leverage.

The third kind of shovel is a **spade**. With its shorter handle (sometimes with a T- or D-shaped handle), this is the favored tool for gardeners across the ocean. The difference between a spade and a shovel is that shovels are scoop-faced for carrying soil or sand or concrete or whatever, while spades are flat-bladed. Spades are great for cutting deeper, straight slices into the sod. They are superb for digging straight-edged trenches.

Other Tools

An **edging tool**, a half-moon-shaped device, can slice sod, but doesn't dig. It's great for reclaiming the edges on your garden beds, and for reclaiming the sidewalk or drive from encroaching turf. It should also be sharpened before use.

Whenever you do any digging, stop every five heaves or so and stand up straight, stretching. Otherwise you'll seize up before realizing so, and two days later, will regret any gardening plans.

Spading forks are the things that look like great big forks. You step them into the ground, then pull back. The point of this tool is to bring up, loosen, and mix the soil. When you dig a hole to plant something, always be sure to loosen the soil below the hole, for its roots to wiggle into. The spading fork will do this, without making you dig halfway to Perth, Australia.

After you're done with all your digging work, be sure to clean off the shovel right

Brass quick-disconnects.

away. Like lasagna on last night's dinner dishes, the dirt will harden on, making your job three times as hard. A plain old bristle scrubbing brush or a spinning wire brush attachment for your power drill will remove really stubborn petrified junk. Once the tool is thoroughly cleaned, sharpen its cutting edge and then lube down.

Some folks keep a bucket of oily sand, giving the shovel a few slips in and out. In a pinch, I've rubbed in shortening for winter storage. That can of WD-40 that lost its handy little straw for keyholes will still do just great for shovels, saws, and pruners. Linseed oil will keep wood handles from drying out and splitting.

Essential Tools

Yes, but what tools do you *have* to have? I would recommend the following:

A shovel. Get a brush and a file to maintain it.

A bucket. Get one built for carrying heavy stuff, not just a little kitchen pail. There should be a handle, not just a wire bail that will cut into your hand; water weighs eight pounds per gallon, and earth even more! Bigger is better.

A burden cloth. Some people are "born to shop," but I seem to be "born to schlep." Just one burden cloth holds as much plant stuff as four buckets, but won't bang against your shins the way buckets do.

A trowel. Avoid the cheap kind that are stamped from a single piece of metal, and then bent to slip into a plastic handle. If you already have one of these, explain to the household budgeter that it's a "transplanter," and that you need a "small digging tool." Aluminum trowels never rust, even when lost under the leaves for a year! I know this personally. Some have inch markings on the blade to determine hole depth, and some have cushioned red foam handles.

A hose. Avoid the bottom-price vinyl hoses that wear out so quickly (short, $5 vinyl hoses are good only for apartment dwellers with waterbeds). Get a hose with reinforcing, and sturdy connectors. Unless you garden in a townhome lot, get a really long hose. The fewer the connections, the fewer the breakdowns. Some modern hoses are made out of *food-grade* plastics; this means they are better to drink from than recycled-rubber hoses.

Brass quick-disconnects. No one loves screwing and unscrewing hoses! My friend George turned me on to these, and at first they seemed like a gimmick. But I tried a pair. The female end goes on your faucet; the male end goes onto the faucet end of the hose. Click! Attach the hose. Click! Detach the hose with just one hand. Hmm, I bought some more male ends for all of my sprinklers and watering wands. Then I bought another male and female set to hook the second hose onto the first hose. Click! Click! You have better things to do with your life than fiddle around with hose connections. Buy the brass kind; they'll outlast the plastic by years.

A hoe or your favorite weeding implement. Square-foot and intensive gardens do better with smaller hand-weeders.

Gloves. This is another item whose price is money well spent. Cheap cotton gloves are washable, but they also shrink and wear out in a few months. Buy several pairs; you'll be more able to find a complete pair of clean, hole-free gloves. Leather gloves are an investment, but will outlast cotton gloves—uh, hand over fist. I'm very fond of the gloves made by Womans-Work. Most gloves are cut and sewn flat, as though we gardeners have nothing better to do than the "queen wave." WomansWork gloves are cut and sewn to be worn by a hand curved around a tool (what a concept!). The company makes gloves out of different types of leathers (including washable ones), different lengths, Thinsulate lined gloves, and gloves for children and men as well. Womans-Work also makes work boots. And they have women's size 9, extra-large, which is what I wear (men's size medium gloves fit my palms, but I don't have bratwurst-size fingers).

WomansWork Gloves
Little Big Farm
P.O. Box 543
York, ME 03909-0543
phone 800-639-2709
www.womansworkgloves.com

Wall O' Waters. An option for those impatient folks, or anyone who doesn't trust the weather. (Gee, I guess that's most of us.)
Kneeling pad
Old sneakers, raggedy jeans, stupid hat
Rain gauge

By the way, a cracked old kneeling pad and slightly worn gloves are great to keep in the car for tire changes or checking your oil. (One is rarely dressed for these activities.)

HANDY TOOLS FOR ADVANCED GARDENERS

The next time you're out to buy more advanced tools, here's your shopping list:

- **Garden rake.** Different from a leaf rake, the garden rake has heavy tines at a right angle to the spine. Garden rakes gather up and smooth down soil, and are invaluable if your raised bed doesn't have any boards. Whenever you add compost and turn over the soil, you'll want to smooth it back down for planting. This is the tool.
- **Pruners** are not just for thin trees and shrubs. They're also for harvesting fragile peppers and tough eggplants and okra.
- **Loppers** are long-handled pruners for tree and bush branches that are thicker than your thumb. Branches thicker than shovel handles should be sawn off.
- **Garden cart or wheelbarrow.** My neighbor had the wheelbarrow and I had the spreader. This worked out very well, until one of us moved. Garden carts are easier to wheel around heavy things; wheelbarrows are easier in tight spaces, and you can mix concrete in 'em, too.
- **Soaker hoses** that live in the garden through the whole growing season. Put brass quick-disconnects on them!
- **Mulching mower and/or leaf shredder**
- **Tool rack** to get other residents off your back about that "mess of tools."
- **Handsome shade hat, instead of "that thing."** If you have skin sensitivity due to illness, medication, bad burns, or fair-skin genes, consider buying some shirts with an SPF 30 weave to them. Ordinary T-shirts have an SPF factor of only 5–9, wet ones even less (not to mention that exquisite "farmer's tan" you get on

half your arms). L.L. Bean sells SPF 30 T-shirts in its travel clothes section, and other retailers will probably follow suit. Sun Precautions is a company that specializes in Solumbra brand sun-protective clothing (hats, shirts, jackets, pants, skirts, water gear, sports gear):

Sun Precautions
2815 Wetmore Avenue
Everett, WA 98201
phone 800-882-7860
www.sunprecautions.com

- **Rubber garden clogs.** Several different companies make these. Most have removable inner soles. Rubber garden clogs not only keep your feet dry, but they also provide more support to your insole when digging. Best of all, they're easy to slip on and off, making it easier to run inside for the phone, the bathroom, or even to stroll outside and fetch the morning paper.
- **Designer compost bin or tumbler**

TOOLS FOR THE MANIACAL GARDENER

No, even I don't own all of these. Yet.

- **Cold frame**
- **Cloches and Reemay hoops**
- **Seed-starting supplies** (fluorescent lamps and warming mat)
- **Advanced models of plant supports and cages**
- **Potting table**
- **Chipper-shredder.** To turn limbs into mulch. *Don't forget your safety goggles and ear plugs!*
- Special **gardening pants** with pockets to insert kneeling pads
- **Wellington boots**
- **Worm-composting bin** for kitchen scraps
- **Weather-recording station** (rain

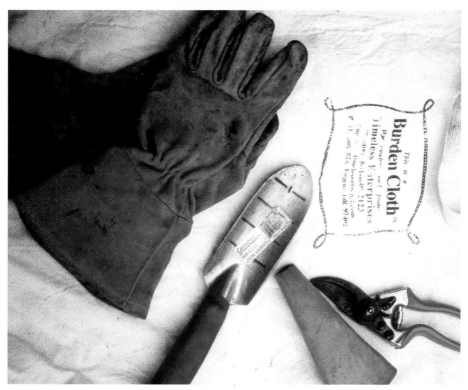

Favorite tools: A burden cloth, Felco pruners, and WomensWork gloves.

gauge, minimum-maximum thermometer, wind gauge)
- **Fancy hose winders and keepers**

HOMEMADE TOOLS FOR EASIER GARDENING

Here are some homemade tools you may want to consider using.

A **dibble** is nothing more than a sharpened stick. In ancient times, people used an animal's horn. Most of us don't use a dibble regularly, unless we're transplanting 100 leeks or a whole flat of annuals, and then it's mighty handy. Select a branch 1 inch thick when pruning trees. Or salvage the end of a broken tool or broom handle. Your dibble should be 8–12 inches long, with one end carved to a blunt tip.

If you still like to garden in long, straight rows, then a **row marker** is quite useful. Get two stakes, each 2 feet long. Take one stake, and attach (with a nail) a crossbar 6 inches from the bottom. Slip a spool of kite string onto the stake. Use waterproof marker to mark inches on the second stake, and then tie the end of the kite string to it. To mark your row, stick the first stake with the ball of string at the beginning of your row. Unwind the string and stick in the other stake at the end of the row. Draw your hoe or planting stick along the string to make an even, shallow furrow for dropping in the seeds. The inch markings on the second stake can be used to space your rows apart more evenly. You can use rows in a modified block system by planting several rows (of peas, lettuces, root crops, beans) closer to-

Raised bed for wheelchair use.

gether instead of putting pathways between each row.

To **carry seed packets** around easily, nab a free promotional cloth apron from the local hardware store. Army surplus pants are also useful; they have pockets galore, reinforced sections, and a good price.

To **prick out seedlings** for putting up into individual pots, get a butter knife from the thrift store. Also pick up some stainless steel kitchen knives, which you can sharpen and keep for **small machetes** for chopping things in the com-

post pile, or harvesting tough veggies like eggplants.

Many gardeners find that they need their tools out by the garden, not lingering in the garage or inside the back door. A small **mailbox** can be posted by the garden for storing short-handled tools. But don't keep seeds out in the mailbox, where their viability will go downhill from heat and humidity.

Make a **seed spacer** with a long block of wood. It's used for punching dimples into the soil, and you then drop a seed or two into each depression. You will need:

- 24-inch-long block of wood, 2 inches high and 1 inch thick
- Galvanized roofing nails
- Drawer knob and screw
- Stain or paint (optional), paintbrush
- Ruler
- Pencil
- Hammer

Turn the wooden block so the 1-inch-wide side is up; this is the bottom. (Optional: Stain or paint the block before continuing.)

1. Mark the centerline down the length of the bottom.
2. Measure from the center of the bottom, and mark Xs every 4 inches along the length.
3. Turn the block over and mark the center of the top.
4. Hammer in a roofing nail at each X; leave each nail sticking out half an inch.
5. Turn the block over and screw in the drawer knob for a handle.

A SEED BOOK FOR KEEPING ORGANIZED IN THE FIELD

When you're out planting in the garden, it's awfully easy for those seed packets to get muddy, crumpled, or damp. And of course, none of these conditions are good for maintaining your seeds' viability for future plantings.

Another problem is trying to remember everything you've done and wanted to keep note of: where you planted the new variety of marigolds, what needs pruning later on, or something that needs harvesting. It would also be helpful if you could remember just where you meant to put the lettuces and broccoli!

To solve this, I put together a Seed Book. Fairly waterproof, it takes me and my seeds out to the garden and back, neatly organized, clean and dry. To put one together for yourself, you need to stop by the office supply store, not the garden center. If you want to use one of the novelty garden fabrics for a cover, you'll also need to make a stop by the fabric store, or go digging through your fabric piles. You will need:

- 1-inch wide vinyl three-ring binder with a clear overlay cover (office supply stores call these presentation binders)
- 10-by-12-inch piece of charming garden calico, or an illustration to decorate the cover
- 10-by-12-inch piece of shirt board (light cardboard)
- Rubber cement
- Several sheets of 4-by-6-inch photograph pocket-pages, fitted for three-ring binders, not photo albums (4-by-6-inch pockets hold even the largest bean or corn seed packets)
- A few page-protector sheets for your garden plan maps
- Several sheets of notebook paper
- Plastic pen pouch to clip inside the binder for pens

To get that cute but flimsy piece of calico or magazine illustration down into the cover of your Seed Book, use rubber cement to glue it to the piece of shirt board. Let it dry before slipping in.

I like to print out a schedule for seed starting and garden plans to keep in my Seed Book. Nothing is so brilliant I can't have forgotten it in short order!

MAKING GARDENING EASIER

Although the number of gardeners nationwide increases, the population is also aging. Even younger people with various disabilities are finding gardening to be a soothing therapy. But there has to be an easier way to grow goodies without standing out in your field with a hoe. Thankfully, there are many ways of making gardening easier.

One of the most noticeable trends is the design and sale of ergonomic tools—those designed to be used with less stress to the body. Even fit gardeners are finding that these tools are easier to use than many of the old-fashioned ones!

Ergonomic tools come in a wide variety of forms: those with squishy handle grips; those with bent handles; those with arm brackets on longer handles to reduce wrist stress; pruners and loppers with ratchet action for more results from less squeezing; and hand tools with extension handles for people who are not close to the ground. Brass quick-disconnects make connecting hoses and attachments much easier.

You can make gardening easier in several other ways that involve redesigning your garden layout:

- Make higher raised beds. I've seen them 30 inches tall, for use by people in wheelchairs. Large containers, such as halves of whiskey barrels, also work well.
- Use trellises for vining crops to have the harvest right in front of you.
- Use hard pathways for wheelchairs, including a turn-around area at least five feet in diameter. Have ramps installed, with a slope of no more than 1:12.
- Locate the garden near the house to shorten the trip.
- Have a faucet extension set up next to the garden, so you can turn the water off and on without climbing behind bushes.
- Have a tool caddy or mailbox next to the garden to save trips.
- Use a kneeling bench, the sort with arms on it so you can get back up after you've knelt down.
- Carry a wrapping-paper tube to drop seeds into a shallow trench.
- Buy seed tapes if you have trouble handing small carrot or lettuce seeds.
- Use long-handled tools to avoid bending over.
- Get your tools sharpened so they're easier to use.

CHAPTER TEN

How to Get Brilliant

WHY WE BOTHER WITH RECORD KEEPING

Record keeping probably sounds like a compilation of statistics by some really Type-A anal-retentive gardener. It can be, if that's what you want. What record keeping does for the common, laid-back gardener is simply to jog the overstuffed brain.

You *think* that you'll remember all the kinds of things next year: That the OG50 tomatoes did better than the Beefsteaks. That you need to get the lettuces in earlier, but plant only half as many. When the lilacs bloomed down the street, and the name of that shorter variety you want to plant next fall. When the potato beetles hit your own patch. The name of that incredible rose you'd like to plant as a family memorial. When it really *was* warm enough to put out the peppers.

Unfortunately, few gardeners have computer-like memories, especially those of us who've gardened for more than a single year.

There are several ways to keep records, depending on your temperament.

Calendar Method

Some folks just jot notes on the calendar: "Seeded carrots," "Hailstorm," "Carrots sprouting." If your calendar is like mine and full of appointments, then you'll need another one just for the garden, perhaps something like the Farmer's Almanac calendar, which lists moon cycles, seeding times, and other hints. When you seeded, the variety, and the sprouting and harvesting times are important to note here. This might be easier kept next to your tool rack in the garage (with the pen on a string), rather than in some kitchen drawer.

Varietal Method

Some folks prefer to staple or glue the seed packet (if it's empty) to a sheet of notebook paper, and keep tabs on each variety: When it was planted, how it grew, how much was harvested. This kind of notebook keeping allows you to track the performance of different varieties. You can also clip in maps of your garden, brochures and fliers with growing information, those little picture labels that came with plants, and so on.

Stay on top of your garden journal!

Notebook Method

A simple spiral-bound notebook has a particular appeal for the casual gardener who doesn't take notes every day, because in addition to the same kind of information put on the calendar, it allows you to put in other miscellaneous, but real information, such as when the toddler first said, "Pea!" after munching down on a sugar snap. Charts or graph paper are handy for marking where something was planted, so you can rotate crops and prevent disease problems and nutrient deficiencies.

Trials of Record Keeping, or Vice Versa

For trial variety testing, we take notes on

- The planting date and method
- Germination and seedling observations
- Insect and/or disease observations
- Weather factors (like floods, which swamped my previous garden for 2 days, or the hailstorms that broke off the tomato leaders, those topmost stems)
- First and last maturity dates
- Taste, appearance, fragrance, and yield
- Comparisons to similar varieties
- What we might have done differently

For instance, one year I got to trial a quicker-maturing cultivar of sweet corn (Kandy Kwik). For happy coincidence, I had grown the original version the year before, and still had seeds (Kandy Korn). So I grew a block of each variety, and got to compare the old and new versions. What I discovered was that the quicker-maturing variety had but one ear per stalk instead of two, so it was lower-yielding. This was because it only grew $5^1/_2$ feet tall, instead of $7^1/_2$ feet tall. It also yielded sooner—all of 10 days sooner. With this dramatic loss of production, I did not feel that this was worth 10 fewer days of maturity time.

Comparisons like this are more effective than growing Roma paste tomatoes one year and then San Marzano the next. And in the case of these tomatoes, the comparison is not quite accurate. Differences in weather conditions make non-concurrent comparisons tricky. Also, Roma is a determinate (bush) tomato, while San Marzano is indeterminate (pole). Roma was developed for a single canning spree, but San Marzano keeps on producing.

A more productive comparison was San Marzano red paste tomato to an Italian Gold paste tomato. The golden tomato proved to have larger, meatier fruits, although a bit milder in flavor. The plant itself was more upright, strong, and decorative than the red paste variety, but succumbed sooner to septoria blight. In this case, there's no clear-cut winner. However, the yellow-tomato ketchup is exquisitely tangy and spicy!

When you're testing flowers, the requirements are different. In addition to disease resistance and how floriferous the plant is, I also look for how well it holds up during inclement weather, how long the flowers last, whether they fade, and their tolerance to part shade. When you have a dozen kinds of petunias, it's easy to get a good grasp on the habits of petunias in general.

In sum, half the benefit of conducting trials is comparing the plant to similar varieties at the same time. You can do this, too, in your own garden. Your ex-tension office has lists of vegetable varieties that have been tested across the state and done well. These are helpful if you're staring at catalogs for the first time, or are shopping around the garden centers and want something beyond the usual Big Boy or Beefmaster. All of these different record-keeping methods have their benefits and drawbacks. You can also incorporate several of them, having seed packets, charts, and a general journal all in one notebook.

Things You May Want to Keep Records Of

- *When* you planted things
- What *varieties* they were
- When they *sprouted*
- How much you *harvested*
- The quality of the *flavor*
- The *color, quality,* and *length* of bloom season
- *Temperature* highs and lows (from the newspaper or your own min-max thermometer)
- *Rainfall* levels (gardens need 1 inch per week—more in sandy soil—but the average shower delivers only 0.2 inches of rain)
- Weather weirdnesses
- Observations about flowering times, insects, birds, and other factors of the natural world around you
- Tips to yourself for a better garden next year (this is *very* important!)
- Funny things the children said or did
- Article clippings, brochures, handouts, and so on

SKY-WATCHING FOR GARDENERS

It's all too easy for gardeners to turn into weather fanatics, because the weather rules our lives all during the growing season.

We live in a semiarid zone, getting an average of 35 inches of rain a year (the

Cirrus clouds.

Altocumulus undulatus.

Mackerel sky.

October and November 1999 7-inch rains were quite unusual). That's not as dry as Denver, which gets an average of 15 inches annually. But when you consider that there are 52 weeks in a year, and most lawns, vegetable, and flower gardens need an inch of rain a week, we soon run into a shortage. Generally there's little rain to be had during the months of July and August, and what little falls only adds to the humidity.

Sometimes Mother Nature will look at her weather desk and exclaim, "Oh! I forgot to give them their month's rain!" and then *whoosh!* We get four inches overnight. There's little consistency.

A rain gauge (specially marked plastic or glass, or even a can set outside) will tell you just how much rain you had from that last shower. Generally, the average sprinkle gives little more than a quarter-inch, not enough to satisfy a thirsty bed of tomatoes, and only enough to get the lawn wet. But if you're looking to the heavens for rain, you'll want to learn what the signs are before you start dragging out the hoses. Or, you'll want to learn what the signs are to get out and cover things up before hail falls.

Here is a short version of a cloud chart.

Cirrus fibratus are good-weather clouds when the wind is from the dry west or north. **Cirrus** clouds are the highest ice-crystal clouds (altitude 20,000–40,000 feet), and they appear in wisps, bands, ripples, or sheets. Generally they forecast good weather when the wind is from the west and north, but can be an indicator for further cloud development if the wind is coming from the moist Gulf of Mexico.

Altocumulus undulates—Like alto singers, **alto** clouds are in the middle (altitude 6,500–20,000 feet). When these clouds cover only part of the sky, they may not last. But if they are lower and heavier, the rippled storm clouds can cover much of the sky and linger, signaling weather coming in or passing through.

Mackerel sky, sometimes seen in the morning. These **altocumulus** clouds are middle-level clouds, generally formed from southern moisture heading northward. Mackerel sky can turn into more organized, denser clouds that indicate incoming precipitation. Or they may appear in only a part of the sky and dissipate.

Cumulus humilis—Small **cumulus** clouds have flat bottoms and rounded tops. **Cumulus humilis** are wider than they are tall, and too small to make rain. Winds can shred them into **cumulus humilis fractus**, little torn pieces without flat bottoms. When these clouds are seen in the afternoon, there's no rain in the immediate forecast. If seen in the morning or early afternoon, they can clump together into larger rain clouds.

Cumulus congestus are what humble little **cumulus humilis** clouds can join up into. **Cumulus congestus** are recognizable not only for their mounded shapes but also because they are taller than they are wide. They often have flat bases and start out as separate clouds. When seen in the morning, they frequently don't develop into rain clouds. Afternoon clouds can gather up enough mass to turn into **cumulonimbus** (clouds with dark bases and rain falling from the bottom).

Cumulonimbus clouds can produce rains, sleet, hail and/or snow. **Cumulonimbus incus** or "anvil" clouds, with wedge or saucerlike projections near the top, signal thunderstorms and possibly other severe weather.

Nimbostratus clouds are those dense, flat layers of rain clouds that move in and unpack their bags for several hours' stay.

Cumulonimbus mammatus have rounded, pouch- or udderlike protrusions from the bottoms of **cumulonimbus**

Cumulus humilis.

Cumulus congestus.

Cumulonimbus incus.

Nimbostratus clouds.

Cumulonimbus mammatus.

clouds, and are a bad sign for gardeners and everyone else. They signal unstable and moisture-laden conditions inside the cloud, and likely hail and/or tornadoes. Sometimes these skies have that sickly greenish-gray color that looks like the sky is going to barf—hail or tornadoes!

YIKES! COPING WITH STORM DAMAGE

Floods are a bane to people everywhere. Because floodwaters pick up not only mud, but also backed-up water and effluents from sewers and storm drains, you should *never* eat any crops that have been flooded. You can probably eat root crops, if you thoroughly wash, peel, and cook them completely (don't bother with radishes). Avoid eating any plants that have split, torn, or cracked. Produce grown from flowers that appear after the flooding should be OK (tomatoes, peppers, eggplants, sweet corn, cucumbers, and squashes).

Another problem with flooding is compaction. Water is quite heavy, and the longer it takes the waters to recede, the more compacted the ground will be. Do *not* do any digging or rototilling until the ground has dried out to a normal moisture level to several inches deep.

Hail is often not the problem we fear it is. Although large hailstones can flatten a garden, many crops will recover. Smaller hailstones only puncture the leaves a bit, and they will recover.

The gardener's first impulse is to drop a tarp over the garden. Unfortunately, both water and hailstones are heavy, and gallons of precipitation weighing down a tarp will flatten a garden far worse than if it were left alone. Small, young plants can be covered with a motley collection of large plastic pots and buckets.

Clean up any smashed produce to avoid rot problems and fungus. Wait a week before deciding which plants have "bought it" and which will survive. Plants often surprise us; asparagus looks messy, but does fine. If the storm is before August, you can generally replant for a new crop. Be sure to select quick-maturing varieties of corn and beans.

If the leaders (top of the main stem) of your young tomato plants have gotten

The flood of '93.

broken off, don't despair. You can create a new leader with a sucker (you didn't pinch off the suckers, did you?). Choose the undamaged branch closest to the top of the tomato plant. Carefully set in a stake next to the main stem, and gently tie this good branch to the stake so it is pointing upward. Whichever branch is highest on the plant is the one that will receive the most growth hormones, and it will become the new leader.

You can also root suckers or broken-off tomato branches to create new plants! This is especially helpful if really big hailstones went through. Make a clean cut, remove any leaves on the bottom 6–10 inches of the stem, and remove any flowers, buds, or baby tomatoes. Plant the stem into either the ground or a pot. Water daily as the plant grows its roots. The leaves will be wilted until the plant is able to draw in enough moisture, but as long as they're just soft and not actually

Hail damage.

OK, I'll admit it: I'm a weather junkie. I like to leave the Weather Channel on after I've heard "My Local Forecast" (they have nice background music.) With the advent of the home computer and the Internet, we can not only request catalogs and order from catalogs, we can also view radar pages of our own state, check the weekly forecast for where we're vacationing, or monitor a worsening drought.

- Dew-point map for the Midwest: http://www.wunderground.com/US/Region/Midwest/Dewpoint.html
- Drought monitor: http://enso.unl.edu/monitor/monitor.html
- Lightning Map for the north central United States: http://www.intellicast.com/LocalWeather/World/UnitedStates/NorthCentralLightning/
- Radar Images (for the United States, then go to your local area): http://www.intellicast.com/LocalWeather/World/UnitedStates/Radar/
- Sun/Moon Rise/Set/Phase US Naval Observatory, Astronomical Appl. Dept.: http://aa.usno.navy.mil/AA/data/
- How to build an indoor tornado shelter: http://www.wind.ttu.edu/inshelter/inshelte.htm
- General tornado website (commercial): http://www.tornadoproject.com/

flat on the ground or crispy, the plant will be OK. After a couple of weeks you should start seeing new growth. Aren't tomatoes amazing?

Drought of course presents different problems. The annoying thing is when you have drought following floods and the compacted soil starts to crack, and everyone starts muttering about Mother Nature's really lousy distribution system. To combat drought, you need not only efficient watering but also moisture preservation. Use soaker hoses or drip hoses instead of sprinklers (there's nothing so stupid as expensive sprinkler water flying off into the hot wind). Water in the morning or evening, so the moisture can soak into the soil to the plant's benefit.

- Use mulches to cool the soil and slow down evaporation.
- To water single plants (such as thirsty cucumbers), rinse out an empty plastic milk jug, poke a few small holes in the bottom, and set it next to the main stem. The water will slowly soak into the ground, sparing you from having to stand there with a hose. Be sure to either stake the jug so it doesn't blow away, or collect them after watering.
- Wind fencing, specially sold semipermeable fencing, is sold at hardware stores. Solid fences simply lift the wind, but wind fencing will slow it down.
- A Southwestern gardener's trick is the waffle bed. By building up earthen walls around the planting blocks, you slow down the wind (and some evaporation), and concentrate moisture to where the seeds and plants are. And during a downburst, the walls keep the rain from running sideways across the hot, baked earth.

Building waffle beds for salad crops.

Salad crops growing in waffle beds.

THUNDERSTORM AND TORNADO SAFETY

Severe Weather Myths

Some of these we learned as gospel truth in school, but they aren't true at all (nor will ducking under a school desk will protect you from nuclear fallout). You may be surprised. (*False statements are in italics.*)

- *Lightning never strikes the same place twice.* Not!
- *Your car tires protect you from lightning strikes, because they're rubber.* Rubber from tires and shoes offers no protection. The steel frame of your hard-topped vehicle does, as long as you're not touching metal.
- *Heat lightning on hot summer days isn't dangerous.* The so-called heat lightning is simply lightning from a storm that's too far away to hear. But that storm can be headed toward you, so take cover. Don't keep on working out of doors with those long-handled, metal garden tools!
- *Lightning is dangerous only where it's raining.* Not!
- *You're safe from a tornado when you're parked underneath a highway overpass.* You may have seen a video of someone hiding under a highway bridge, but that person was a very lucky exception. In truth, flying debris can easily hit you; you can get pulled out from under the bridge; the bridge might collapse; other vehicles may be blinded and run into you. Instead, lie flat, facedown, in a ditch and cover your head.
- *You should open up your house windows to equalize pressure so it doesn't implode.* Wrong. Don't waste time messing with windows—head for the basement!

- *Big cities are immune from tornadoes.* History proves otherwise.
- *You should take cover in the southwest corner of the basement.* There is no proof that this is safer. You should actually take cover underneath something strong (such as a workbench), away from windows, or in a closet. You want the greatest number of walls and closed doors between you and the outdoors.

Emergency Supplies for a Tornado Shelter

Remember, a *watch* means that the weather is likely to produce tornadoes. A *warning* means that one has been sighted and you should head for cover immediately!

NOAA (National Oceanic and Atmospheric Administration) weather-band radio or regular radio, wind-up type or with batteries
First-aid kit
Flashlight with extra batteries
Bottled drinking water, one gallon per person for three days
Three-day supply of nonperishable food (plus a can opener)
Spare clothes and shoes
Pet carrier
Pillow and blanket

ELEMENTARY SEED SAVING

Gardeners save seeds for a variety of reasons. It's frugal and saves considerably on that overwhelming seed order in the winter. It's the only way to perpetuate your favorite family heirlooms. It prevents the shock of discovering that a seed company has discontinued your favorite cultivar. Sometimes it's just the whimsical, "Oh look, seeds!" that prompts a person to grab some and drop them into an envelope.

Note: A "cultivar" is a CUL-tivated VAR-iety, a named breed of plant. Some cultivars are hybrid and some aren't. Growing a cultivar usually means that the plant will be smaller, faster, stronger, more floriferous, more productive—or whatever—compared to the generic, wild version of the plant.

Before we discuss how to save seeds, you need to understand the problems of hybrids and cross-pollination.

Hybrids occur when the pollen from one cultivar is used to fertilize the ovary of another cultivar. The two parents are genetically dissimilar (in fact, all humans are "hybrids"). Although you can physically save the seeds from hybrid flowers and vegetables, the next year you'll end up with a whole motley array of genes being expressed, and only a few will resemble the original hybrid source. Seed companies value hybrids because it gives them the ability to have exclusive sales on a particular cultivar.

Cross-pollination happens when a natural force (bees, insects, birds, or wind) transfers pollen from one cultivar to another. Some kinds of plants will self-pollinate, and you have little chance of cross-pollination. Others will cross-pollinate with their relatives. You won't notice the difference in the fruits, but you will if you eat the seeds (think of sweet corn) or plant out the seeds the next year. Special measure needs to be taken to prevent this with some types of plants, as mentioned later.

To store your seeds, you can use film canisters, snack-size zipper baggies, clean peanut butter or canning jars (useful for large bean seeds), glassine envelopes, or paper envelopes. Be sure to label each container with the cultivar and harvest date.

The better the storage conditions, the longer the seeds will keep. Some seeds like beans and corn will last for years. But parsnip and parsley seeds last only one year, and onion seed germination drops after the first year. To test how well old seeds will grow, roll ten seeds up in a moist paper towel and tuck that inside a baggie. Check the seeds several days later; the number of seeds that sprouted is your germination percentage.

Once they're bagged, you can keep your seed packets in boxes. I like to use a sealable plastic box, and toss in some of those antidesiccant packets I get with new shoes, to keep down moisture. Then I keep that box in the spare fridge. But really, anyplace cool and out of direct light and moisture will be good.

Of course, save only seeds from healthy plants! It also helps to trim your fingernails short before saving seeds, so you don't mix things up.

Legumes: beans and peas—These are self-pollinating, and among the easiest of seeds to save. Near the end of your harvesting season, let the best bean and pea pods ripen until they are completely tan and dried out. Shell out the seeds, and put them in the freezer for a couple of days to kill any bugs that might try to be hiding there.

Brassicas: broccoli, Brussels sprouts, cabbage, Chinese cabbages, cauliflower, collards, kale, kohlrabi, rutabaga, turnip—All of these plants can cross-pollinate each other via insects. Many of them need to be pollinated by another plant, and some are biennials, not producing flowers until the second year (for example, cabbages). You need half a mile's distance from other brassicas, and screen cages covering all but the one cultivar you want pollinated that day. With these inherent problems, few gardeners save their own brassica seeds.

Beets, carrots, parsnips, radishes, Swiss chard—Beets and Swiss chard can cross-pollinate, and both bees and wind can transfer the pollen. Save six roots of

Parsnips going to seed.

and discard the rest. Radishes planted early in the spring will produce pods that summer; let the pods mature until dry and collect the seeds. Chard also over-winters nicely, and you can collect the seeds in midsummer the next year.

Corn will cross-pollinate, and is wind-pollinated. Fortunately, the pollen is heavy and won't blow far. The easiest way to prevent your sweet corn from crossing with your popping and flour corns is to separate the tasseling times, by staggering plantings or by planting early and late types. Let some sweet-corn ears ripen all the way to the hard, dry stage when the whole plant withers up, and shuck as you would for popcorn.

Cucurbits: cucumbers, melons, summer and winter squashes—Slicing and pickling cukes can cross with each other, but not with melons and squashes. There are several families among squashes, and Hubbards can cross with jack-o'-lantern or crookneck can cross with zucchini.

You'll need to hand-pollinate to keep pollination pure. The evening before, select male flowers (longer stem) and female flowers (shorter stem with micro-cuke or micro-melon behind it) that haven't opened yet. Tape the petals shut (any old kind of tape, such as the ubiquitous duct tape) so no bees can access them. The next morning, pluck the male flower, remove the petals from the male flower, and rub the pollen from the male flower onto the sticky stigma (pole) of the female flower. Some recommend using the pollen from several males on a female. Tape to seal the female flower shut to prevent further pollination. Do this to several female flowers, and tag these fruits as seed sources. Let cucumbers and summer squashes get over-ripened, turning color and getting hard-shelled before picking. You'll want to save seed from only a single vine, since seed production causes the plant to "shut down" much future production. After the

your best beets, with 2 inches of stem, and keep them in the fridge or root cellar, for replanting out in the spring. Carrots can cross-pollinate with Queen Anne's lace, so you'll need to have no other carrot or wildflowers within 200 feet to prevent cross-pollination. Overwinter carrots as you do the beet roots, and replant in the spring. Parsnips are easier, because they will overwinter outside in the garden. Both carrots and parsnips make umbrella-shaped seed heads; select seeds from the largest head, fruit is mature, then scoop out and dry the seeds.

Leeks are biennials, producing seeds the second year (avoid seeds from plants that bolted the first year.) Leeks are—thankfully—self-pollinating, and won't cross with each other. Collect seeds once the heads are dry and the black crystal-shaped seeds are ready to be released.

Lettuce seed is one of the easiest, right after beans and peas. Lettuces are self-pollinated, and quickly "bolt" once warm weather hits. The stem stretches out, blooms briefly, and turns into a cluster of fluffy seeds. Clip off the seed heads and bring them inside to dry in a vase where they won't blow everywhere. Just crumble off the dried seeds and store.

Okra is self-pollinated. Simply let the pods mature and go to seed in late summer. Remove the dry, brown pods before they split and drop the seeds everywhere.

Onions can cross-pollinate; you'll need one mile's distance between onion types, or screen cages to prevent insects from cross-pollinating onion types (see brassicas). Save seed as for leeks.

Peppers are usually self-pollinating. Insect-barrier fabrics or a distance of 50 feet will prevent any insect pollination. Sweet and hot peppers are grown the same. Let the fruits mature on the plant until they've changed color (purple, yellow, orange, red, brown) and turn hard. Then crack them open and retrieve the seeds; watch out for those membranes, where the spicy-hot capsaicin oil is!

Potatoes We don't save true seed from potatoes, because it's so genetically variable. Instead, we save golf-ball-sized tubers (the taters themselves). Planting these smaller tubers the next spring instead of cuttings reduces rot problems. I just stick them in a paper bag marked with "Seed potatoes" and the cultivar name, and chuck them into the crisper drawer for the winter.

Tomato seed saving will be the messi-

Lettuce plant going to seed.

est kind you do, but is otherwise quite easy. Tomato flowers are self-pollinating. Simply select two or three good-looking and very ripe tomatoes. If you grow several plants of the same cultivar, select a tomato from each plant inside the row. For each cultivar of tomato, you'll need a separate glass or plastic cup (label them!). Cut them in half, squish the seed pulp into the glass (or cup), and set it someplace out of the way for five days. Meanwhile, it'll get moldy on top and smelly. Don't panic, and don't stir. This fermentation is removing diseases and the goo from around the seeds. Take them to the sink, and begin filling the cups with water, one at a time. The moldy mat will float off, as will most of the junk. The bad seeds are floaters; let them go. The good seeds are sinkers. When the water's clear, spread the good seeds in a single layer on a (plain, cheap) paper plate (label the plates), and let dry for a week. Then package the seeds.

Remember, if you're saving the only source of a particular cultivar of seed, *never* plant out your entire supply; one bad storm and the crop can be lost forever.

For in-depth information about saving seeds, see *From Seed to Seed* by Susan Ashworth (Seed Savers Exchange, 1991). *The New Seed-Starter's Handbook* by Nancy Bubel (Rodale Press, 1988) gives some seed-saving information, along with how to grow a variety of flowers, herbs, and vegetables from seed.

HOW LONG DO SEEDS LAST?

Seed germination is an interesting topic. When you hear "the experts" say that seeds are "only good for" a certain number of years, they are really saying, "are good for an acceptable germination rate" for that number of years. Which rate is variable, but in a high-grade range—about 85–100 percent of the seeds will sprout.

Someone who says her three-year-old parsley seeds germinated "just fine—about half of them grew" is giving evidence that yes, you'll get seeds to sprout. But with some types, the percent germination just plummets after a year or so. Farmers and commercial growers would *not* be happy with a 50 percent germinate rate! On the other hand, the average home grower is always excited when anything sprouts—and frequently lacks the guts to do their own thinning. Hence the

Scottish phrase about "having your neighbor thin your turnips."

How Long Do Seeds Last?

These dates are given for optimum germination rates. Of course, many of the seeds will still sprout even after the times given, with good storage techniques.

Plant	Years
Asparagus	3
Bean	3
Beet	4
Cole crops	5
Carrot	3
Chives	2
Corn	2
Cucurbits	5
Eggplant	5
Kale and greens	5
Lettuces	5
Okra	2
Onion	1–2
Parsley	1–2
Parsnip	1–2
Peas	3
Peppers	4
Radishes	5
Rutabagas	5
Tomato	4
Turnip	5

Cool/cold, dry storage helps germination rates quite a bit. And if you're sprouting older seeds, patience helps! They've been asleep a long time.

HOW MUCH YIELD CAN YOU EXPECT?

Yield depends on a wide variety of factors: the type of vegetables you grow (pole-type beans and tomatoes yield much more than bush type), how you grow them, the weather that year, the health of your soil, and so on.

The following potential yields give the number of ounces of seed needed to plant 100 square feet. The average yield, in pounds of vegetable per 100 square feet, is listed second.

Plant	Oz. seed needed	Yield (in pounds)
Asparagus	159	5
Pole beans	8.3	8–9
Bush beans	7.8	8–9
Beets (ball)	1.35	30
Broccoli	0.01	18 heads
Brussels sprouts	0.01	25
Chinese cabbage	0.03	45
Regular cabbage	0.01	45
Carrots	0.2	60
Cauliflower	0.01	23
Swiss chard	0.76	25
Sweet corn	1.1–0.35	16
Cucumbers	0.2	22
Eggplants	0.015	36
Garlic	19.5 lb. (cloves)	32
Kale	0.01	16
Kohlrabi	0.22	50
Leeks	0.1	150
Head lettuce	0.007	50
Leaf lettuce	0.016–0.012	50
Melons	0.09	20 cantaloupe or 36 honeydew
Mustard	0.055	16
Okra	0.64	20
Onion	0.39	75
Parsnips	1.9	50
Peas	3.9 (bush type)– 13.7 lb. (tall vining type)	8
Peppers	0.064	20
Potatoes	23.25–31 lb.	60
Pumpkin	0.44–0.16	varies by size
Radishes	3.9	40
Rutabagas	0.07	60
Shallots	14.8	50
Spinach	0.35	15
Pattypan squash	0.37	45
Winter squash	0.53	50
Zucchini squash	0.24	140
Sweet potatoes	12 lb.	45
Tomatoes	0.003–0.006	50
Turnips	0.13	60
Watermelon	1.0–0.12	25

KEEPING THE GARDENER IN TOP SHAPE

Getting—and keeping—your soil and plants in top shape makes for a great garden. But what's rarely addressed is keeping the gardener in top shape. Gardening exposes people to a range of environmental factors they don't find elsewhere: pesticides and herbicides, sunburn, aching backs, grungy hands second only to a coal miner's, and blisters. Granted, you can get those from other activities, too. But gardeners, unlike joggers, are less inclined to remember to stretch (gently and slowly, without bouncing) before diving into a strenuous workout.

Digit Care for Gardeners

Gardeners are sometimes called "green thumbs," but "dirty nails" would probably be more accurate. Doubtless there are a few genteel lady gardeners who can daintily pull on those pretty little "ladies' gloves," and then plant petunias without grinding clay under their nails and into their knuckles. I am not one of them.

I was going to title this section "Hand Care for Gardeners," but that would probably turn off half my audience, since the men would assume I'm discussing nail lacquer. I'm not. The goal here is how to look socially acceptable during the rest of the week.

Keeping Dirt Off

Not all the dirt, mind you. For that, you need Martha Stewart's grounds crew to do everything *for* you. But you can reduce the amount of dirt with the following tricks:

Wear gloves. Granted, some tasks (like seeding) are impossible to do with gloves on. But wearing gloves whenever you do tool-wielding jobs will keep your hands from drying out and getting abraded and blistered. "But my hands still get dirty!" Yes, but not *as* dirty.

Wear glove liners under leather gloves. Usually the most favorite pair of gloves are the oldest ones, those with dirt ground between the loosening seams. Thin cotton gloves (the type sold in pharmacies) underneath will add another layer of protection. So does putting on your favorite hand lotion before the glove liners. You can also wear hand lotion and (another, cleaner) pair of cotton gloves at bedtime to help heal hands, but I guarantee it doesn't look very sexy (unless your mate has a secret passion for Minnie Mouse or Mickey Mouse).

Before gardening, scrape soap (the bar kind, not the pump kind) underneath your fingernails. Its presence will deny room for dirt, and it washes out more easily. This of course presumes you have longish nails in the first place.

Venturing into the World of Non-Gardeners

On occasion we'll need to leave our private Edens and venture out to go shopping, go to work, or (gasp!) attend a social function. You need to not only smooth your nails and cuticles, but find some way to remove the clay and chlorophyll stains. I keep asking nurses (who must wash their hands several dozen times a day) what their favorite hand lotion is. Apparently it's a trade secret, because they all answer obliquely, "An expensive one." *Humph.*

The prime ingredient in most hand lotions is water. When your cuticles are cracking and your palms resemble museum-age saddles, you don't want watered-down stuff. Here are some salves I swear by.

My favorite hand lotion, reduced. I pour some on a flat plate and let it sit out for a week. Once it's thick and waxy, I use a plastic spatula to scrape it off and then store it in a small, sealed container. This is much less expensive than tiny $15 jars of "cuticle cream." I keep mine next to where I usually sit, so I can apply it often to my nails, cuticles, and knuckles. Works wonders!

Udder balm (also called bag balm). Yeah, it has a disclaimer saying it's for veterinary use, but you'll notice it's sold on the same pharmacy shelf as the other first-aid salves. The mild antibiotic helps prevent infections. Smells like plastic bandages though, so save it for bedtime, not dinner occasions (the larger tin is considerably cheaper than the tiny purse-size tin). Plain old petroleum jelly (Vaseline) also works, but is a tad sticky.

For the truly grungy and desperate, I'll pass along this method recommended by a gardening friend: Soak your fingertips in fizzing denture solution. Yes, it's another "not marketed for that use" product, but some people swear by it.

As for myself, I either use a washcloth and some nonabrasive cleanser (such as Bon Ami) or give "Miss Kenmore" a break and hand-wash a bunch of dishes. A long soak in soapy water does the trick. Sorry, Madge—I must do the dishes while I soften my hands.

■ GARDENER'S SOAP

The advent of liquid pump soap is something of a sad thing. Yes, it means there's a lot less gummy mess to scrub off the dish; but it also means that you have fewer slivers of soap bars hanging around.

"And why," you ask, "would anyone want slivers of leftover soap bars?"

Why, because they're perfect for recycling into larger, new bars of fancy soaps. You can use any sort of soap to recycle. However, avoid using highly scented soaps or transparent glycerin soaps, which require different handling. Odds and ends of soap bars, including those little ones accumulated from hotel stays, or worn "fancy dish" novelties are perfect. Color doesn't matter; they'll blend to-

gether. For the mold, you can buy soap molds, or use any rubber or soft-plastic mold, such as the sort sold in festive holiday shapes for wiggly gelatin snacks.
You will need:

- Leftover soaps
- Molds, or two tablespoons and waxed paper
- Grater
- Double-boiler pot
- Instant (unflavored) oatmeal or finely chopped fresh rosemary
- Heat-resistant spatula

1. Grate the soaps.
2. Put grated soap into double-boiler pan and melt with a little water on low heat until melted. It's better to start out with just a little water, and add a few drops as needed, just enough to keep the soap flakes from sticking to the pan. The melted soap should have a thick, pasty texture. There may be some lumps in the mass if the bars were not grated evenly.
3. When soap is thoroughly melted, add oatmeal or rosemary, about 1 tablespoon per each half-cup of melted soap. Stir in well.
4. Quickly scrape into molds, and press well to firm the mixture into a tight mass. Lacking molds, you can use two tablespoons. Scoop up some soap mass with one, and transfer it to the other spoon, back and forth, until it's a nice ball shape. After the soap ball has cooled enough to handle, roll the balls between two sheets of waxed paper to even the shape.
5. Let the soap set for several days, up to a week. It will progressively harden, and can be removed from the mold after a day or two.

■ GARDENER'S SALVES: HOMEMADE HAND CREAMS

Between finishing up the garden and the dry winter weather, hands can lose moisture quickly, drying out and cracking. To remedy this, here are a couple of recipes for easy homemade salves.

Before you make these, be sure to find a suitable container to pour the hot mixture into. Once it sets, it's not easily transferred into another container. Small pots can be found at import and antique stores, or you can recycle other small containers for the purpose.

Lanolin, cocoa butter, and essential oils can be found in pharmacies and health-food stores.

Scented Hand Cream

8   ounces anhydrous lanolin
1/4 cup coconut oil
1/2 teaspoon sweet almond or rose
     essential oil

Use a nonreactive saucepan, such as glass, stainless steel, or Teflon. On low heat, melt lanolin and coconut oil together, mixing well.

Remove from heat, let cool for 5–10 minutes, then stir in the essential oil for scent.

Mix well, and pour into container(s).
Makes 1 cup.

Chamomile Hand Cream

1   tablespoon cocoa butter
1   tablespoon sweet almond oil
1   tablespoon beeswax
1   packet chamomile tea (1 tablespoon-
     quantity teabag)

1. Make an infusion of chamomile by bringing ___ cup water to boil, and let the teabag steep for five minutes. (*Infusion* means "flavoring liquid"; when you make

tea or coffee, you're making an infusion.)

2. Meanwhile, melt together on low heat: cocoa butter, sweet almond oil, and beeswax.

3. Pour off 2 teaspoons of chamomile infusion and mix with the other ingredients. Stir together well, and then pour into container(s).

Makes 1/3 cup.

TIME TO KICK BACK? NEVER!

Ah, winter! Must say, I look forward to it. Winter gives me a chance to kick back, and take a break from weeding and mowing. Time to make new plans, let the garden rest, let the soil recover its proper texture, let the bugs die, let the annual weeds turn into compost—all those wonderful things.

But while the garden is resting, often the gardener is, too. Granted, the break from sunburns and blisters is nice. On the other hand, many of us are turning into TV-tube tubers.

Well, set that Way-Back Machine for last March—remember the sore muscles? The aching back? It's *not* inevitable! It's time to take an active part in off-season fitness. OK, I don't need to tell you that exercise is good. But I may need to motivate you.

Even when you are doing nothing more strenuous than watching a landscape makeover on HGTV, your muscle cells burn more energy than your fat cells. So changing your muscle-to-fat ratio (your body mass composition) will not only make you look better, but will keep you from gradually enlarging as you become more "seasoned."

Speaking of age, after 30 your metabolism slows down. You probably know this. But did you know that many of the "signs of aging" are *not* inevitable? Most of the things we used to assume are a part of being middle-aged or old are actually symptoms of reduced activity, a change from an active life to one behind a desk. These include

- Weight gain
- Potbellies
- "Wings" on the undersides of your upper arms
- Osteoporosis
- Loss of flexibility
- Weakening of the muscles

The definition of "regular stretching and exercise" is constantly changing, but the consensus is that it means aerobic exercise for half an hour, three times a week. Be it brisk walking, running, biking, using a treadmill, or whatever strikes your fancy! This *also* includes working out with weights. Keeping your muscles in good shape will help you:

- Live longer
- Live with fewer disabilities and diseases
- Build stronger bones (calcium supplements alone aren't enough)
- Increase muscle mass instead of fat mass
- Sleep better
- Halt that metabolic slowdown
- Be less stressed
- Have time to think
- Be a good role model for other family members, friends and garden club members

Come to think of it, all those benefits are the same as gardening! Weight training is becoming common for both women and older people. Scrawny and helpless is out. Fit and able are in, and will never go out of style!

CALENDAR OF GENERAL GARDEN ACTIVITIES BY MONTH

January

Place orders for seeds and plants early, to avoid "out of stock" disappointments and substitutions. Make garden plans for rotating crop families, putting cole crops, cucurbits, tomatoes, roots, and so on in places they haven't been for several years. Get a garden journal or notebook to keep track of information (and photographs!) throughout the year.

Organize supply of pots. Buy short labels to mark pots, and later, garden transplants. Start parsley seedlings. Root cuttings of scented geraniums, rosemary, and other tender herbs you wish to propagate.

On the one nice day of weather, check for frost heaving and rodent damage.

February

Buy new fluorescent bulbs for seed starting. Start earliest tomato seedlings early in month, and other tomatoes, peppers, and eggplants late in month, along with parsley and onions. Revive dormant geraniums.

Get a sealable can, jar, or box to store seeds in your fridge so they don't lose viability.

Clean, sharpen, and oil tools if you've not already done so. Get mower tuned up and sharpened if you've not already done so.

Turn over compost pile if it's defrosted.

March

Zones 4A, 4B, and 5A—Start cruciferous transplants late in month. Start second batch in two weeks, if desired.

Zones 5B, 6A, and 6B—Start cruciferous transplants early in month. Start second batch in two weeks, if desired. Start tender tubers and summer bulbs. Transplant out hardy spring crops, seed hardy root crops, and seed or sod bare areas in the lawn.

After the ground thaws and the soil is like cake instead of Play-Doh, plant asparagus crowns, rhubarb, and horseradish roots.

Before the rains start, clean out the gutters and downspouts! After a heavy 1-inch rain, go out and pull weeds, roots and all.

April

Zones 4A, 4B, and 5A—Transplant out hardy spring crops, seed hardy root crops, and seed or sod bare areas in the lawn. Start tender tubers and summer bulbs.

Zones 5B, 6A, and 6B—Watch for asparagus beetles, potato beetles, and striped flea beetles.

Mowing season begins; try to cut no more than a third of total grass height, rain permitting. Mix grass clippings with last year's leaves to make compost piles. Use 25 percent grass clippings/green stuff and 75 percent leaves/brown stuff.

Remove winter mulch as the ground thaws and leaves begin to peek out. Collect windfall sticks for "pea brush" to support short pea vines. Install any extra trellises you need.

Thin direct-seeded salad and root crops before the plants suffer; pinch out extras, instead of disturbing the soil by pulling.

Get those weeds *now*! Enjoy the asparagus season; quit harvesting when stems are pencil thin, 6–8 weeks. Start cucurbit transplants two weeks before the last frost date. You can lay on clear plastic to warm soil and pre-germinate any weeds to be removed, or use black plastic for just warming.

May

Zones 4A, 4B, and 5A—Watch for asparagus beetles, potato beetles, and striped flea beetles.

Zones 5B, 6A, and 6B—Watch for flea beetles, spotted and striped cucumber beetles, and cabbage worms. Plant heat-loving winter squashes and lima beans.

Plant out beans and other summer crops once the soil has warmed up to 60 °F. Thin those direct-seeded crops if you haven't already! Remove rhubarb flower stalks.

Don't let water stand around for mosquito larvae; dump all containers. Keep after those weeds to prevent them seeding. Smother them to death with (no more than) three inches of grass clippings. (Do not use Zoysia or Bermuda grass stems or roots for mulching.) If your area is prone to drought and water rationing, be sure to mulch to conserve moisture.

June

Zones 4A, 4B, and 5A—Watch for flea beetles, spotted and striped cucumber beetles and cabbage worms. Plant heat-loving winter squashes and lima beans.

Zones 5B, 6A, and 6B—Watch for webworms, squashvine borers, squash bugs, corn earworm, and parsley worm. Aerate Zoysia and Bermuda grass lawns.

Start harvesting salad crops; compost those that are bolting. Tomatoes and raspberries ripen. Don't let veggies get overripe; the plant will go against you and try to make seeds. Keep summer squashes, cucumbers, and tomatoes picked.

Watch out for hoses sitting out in the sun; the water inside can get really *hot*! Don't let brush and areas around buildings and fences get messy; grasshoppers breed there.

July

Zones 4A, 4B, and 5A—Watch for webworms, squash vine borers, squash bugs, corn earworm, and parsley worm.

Start transplants of cruciferous and salad autumn crops; select quick-maturing varieties. Gooseberries, garlic, shallots, onions, and potatoes ripen. Watch for tomato hornworm.

Water as needed; one inch per week. Morning is the best time. It's also time to set the lawnmower blade up to three inches high for cool-season grasses (bluegrass, fescue, etc.). The added height will help shade the ground to keep it cooler and moister.

Beware of thunderstorms and hailstorms; keep tarps or blankets on hand to toss on the garden at a moment's notice.

August

Don't forget to add more organic mulches as the previous applications compost. Don't you dare let weeds get the upper hand; it's a great time of year for seeding! Keep flowers deadheaded. Prune berry canes that have fruited down to the ground.

Keep picking okra, summer squashes, cucumbers, and tomatoes. Do not can overripe tomatoes! Transplant or seed in autumn crops, including a new set of dill. Melons and sweet corn ripen. Cut down cornstalks and create a decorative shock for Halloween.

Visit county fair; pick up a copy of flower and vegetable competition rules booklet if you're keen to try your hand next year.

September

Zones 4A, 4B, and 5A—Dig up tender tubers and bulbs for winter storage. Wait until a couple of frosts to harvest parsnips and Brussels sprouts, for best flavor.

Cover salad crops and overwintering vegetables with row covers when frost threatens. Sweet potatoes, sunflowers and apples are ripe; so are some pumpkins. Pick before frost and store in cool, dim place.

Plant cover crops where you're not building compost barrows. Time to bring in the houseplants and tender herbs; keep them in isolation for three weeks to watch for insect pests.

October

Zones 4A, 4B, and 5A—Dig up horseradish roots after a few frosts. Sunchokes can also be harvested while the ground's not frozen.

Zones 5B, 6A, and 6B—Plant evergreens. Dig up tender tubers and bulbs for winter storage. Wait until a couple of frosts to harvest parsnips and Brussels sprouts, for best flavor.

Gather neighborhood leaves (if needed) to build compost barrows, or till into the soil. Before ground freezes, plant (golf-ball-size) potatoes, garlic, and shallots for next year's crops.

Water perennial veggies and flowers if it's been a dry year. Drain hoses and put them away!

You can start a new pepper plant from seed for a few winter fruits and some entertainment; "ornamental" peppers are edible, though very hot!

November

Zones 5B, 6A, and 6B—Dig up horseradish roots after a few frosts. Sunchokes can also be harvested while the ground's not frozen.

Keep on raking; leaves left will smother the lawn. Clean up garage/tool shed. Leave the leaves on woodland plants; they're used to it and need the coverage.

Clean, sharpen, and oil tools. Consider painting the handles a bright color. Get mower tuned up and sharpened. Take a break and sit down to make a list of all the things you want to remember next year: what varieties to get or avoid, special chores that need to be done, additions you want in the way of plants or structural elements, and so on. Send off for seed catalogs you don't currently get, and bulletins from the extension office.

December

Catalogs begin arriving; find someplace to store them until after the holidays. Beware of the "hyper-Kodachrome" syndrome. If it's a dry year, water evergreens and any new fruit trees and bushes once a month. Research the new varieties for the next year in the garden magazines. Make a list of what you want or need in the way of seeds and other goodies. Allow yourself a couple of new things not on the list.

APPENDIX A

Tables of Measures

TABLES OF AMERICAN MEASURES, SOME PRETTY DARN OBSCURE

These measures do not include variations in Great Britain.

Linear and Square Measures (or "Why the world went metric!")

12 inches (in.) = 1 foot (ft.)
36 inches = 3 feet = 1 yard (yd.)
43,500 square feet = about 69.5 yards each side = 1 acre
16.5 feet = 5.5 yards = 1 rod (or pole or perch)
40 rods = 1 furlong
5,280 feet = 1,760 yards = 320 rods = 8 furlongs = 1 mile
3 miles = 1 land league

144 square inches = 1 square foot
9 square feet = 1 square yard
30.25 square yards = 1 square rod (or sq. pole or sq. perch)
43,560 sq. feet = 4,840 sq. yards = 160 sq. rods = 1 acre
33 feet x 66 feet = 1/20 acre
50 feet x 100 feet = 1/8 acre
640 acres = 1 square mile (mi.)

Liquid Measures

3 teaspoons (t. or teasp.) = 1 tablespoon (T. or tblsp.)
2 tablespoons = 1 ounce (oz.)
4 ounces = 1 gill
16 tablespoons = 8 ounces = 2 gills = 1 cup (c.)
16 ounces = 4 gills = 2 cups = 1 pint (pt.)
32 ounces = 4 cups = 2 pints = 1 quart (qt.)
128 ounces = 16 cups = 8 pints = 1 gallon (gal.)
32 quarts = 8 gallons = 1 bushel (bu.)

Precipitation Measures

1 gallon water = 10 pounds
10 inches snow = 1 inch rain
23,332 gallons = 1 inch water for 1 acre
3,000 gallons = 1 inch water for 5,000 feet

Dry Measures

16 ounces = 1 pound (lb.)
8 quarts = 1 peck
4 pecks = 1 bushel
1.25 cubic feet = 1 bushel
2,000 pounds = 1 ton

Variable by density:
1/4 pound powder = 1 cup
1/2 pound powder = 1 pint
1 pound powder = 1 quart
16 cubic feet = 1 cord-foot
128 cubic feet = 8 cord-feet = 1 cord wood

Larger to Smaller Equivalencies

From 100 gallons liquid quantity	To 1 gallon liquid quantity
1/4 pint	1/4 teaspoon
1 pint	1 teaspoon
1 quart	2 teaspoons
3 pints	3 teaspoons
1 gallon	2 1/2 tablespoons

From 100 gallons dry quantity	To 1 gallon dry quantity
1/2 pound	1/2 teaspoon
1 pound	1 teaspoon
3 pounds	1 tablespoon

TABLE OF U.S. AND METRIC VOLUME EQUIVALENCIES

These are approximations useful for everyday work; few people use 1/100th decimals when measuring! As our chemistry teacher said, "It's about the same as a quart, but a liter is a 'leetle' larger!"

1 teaspoon = 5 milliliters (mL)
1 tablespoon = 15 milliliters (mL)
1 ounce = 30 milliliters (mL)
1 cup = 250 milliliters (mL) = 1/4 liter (L)
1 pint = 500 milliliters (mL) = 1/2 liter (L)
1 pint + 5 teaspoons = 1/2 liter (L)
1 quart = 1,000 milliliters (mL) = 1 liter (L)
1 quart + 10 teaspoons = 1 liter

Converting Fahrenheit and Celsius

Fahrenheit (F°) to Celsius (C°):
    C = 5/9 times (F° – 32)
Celsius (C°) to Fahrenheit (F°):
    C = 9/5 times (C° + 32)

TABLE OF METRIC MEASURES

Everything is 10-based—very simple!

Linear and Square Measures

10 millimeters (mm) = 1 centimeter (cm)
1 inch = 2.54 cm.
10 centimeters = 1 decimeter (dm)
10 decimeters = 1 meter (M)
1 meter = 3.28 feet
10 meters = 1 decameter
10 decameters = hectometer
10 hectometers = 1 kilometer (km)
1 kilometer = 0.621 mile
10 kilometers = 1 myriameter

100 square millimeters = 1 square centimeter
100 square centimeters = 1 square decimeter
100 square decimeters = 1 square meter = 1 centiare of land
100 square meters/ centiares = 1 square decameter/ 1 are of land
100 square decameters/ ares = 1 square hectometer/ hectare
1 hectare = 2.471 acres
100 square hectometers/ hectares = 1 square kilometer
1 square kilometer = 0.386 square miles

Liquid Measures

10 milliliters (mL) = 1 centiliter (cL)
10 centiliters = 1 deciliter (dL)
10 deciliters = 1 liter (L) = 1.0567 quarts
10 liters = 1 decaliter = 2.64 gallons or 0.284 bushel
10 decaliter = 1 hectoliter
10 hectoliters = 1 kiloliter

Dry Measures

1,000 cubic millimeters = 1 cubic centimeter
1,000 cubic centimeters = 1 cubic decimeter
1,000 cubic decimeters = 1 cubic meter
1 cubic meter = 35.314 cubic feet

Weights

10 milligrams = 1 centigram
10 centigrams = 1 decigram
10 decigrams = 1 gram
10 grams = 1 decagram
1 decagram = 0.3527 ounce
10 decagrams = 1 hectogram
10 hectograms = 1 kilogram
1 kilogram = 2.2046 pounds
10 kilograms = 1 myriagram
10 myriagrams = 1 quintal
10 quintals = 1 metric ton
1 metric ton = 2,204.6 pounds

CIRCLE MATH

Fiddle dee dum
Fiddle dee dee
A ring around the moon is pi times d

But if a hole you must repair
the formula is pi r squared

Grade-school rhyme (thanks, Anita!) Remember that pi = 3.14.

My Mnemonics

Radius: radiates from the center of the circle.
Diameter is twice as far (di = two)

Circle Math

- Area inside of a circle = pi times r^2
- Circumference (perimeter around a circle) = 2-pi-r (2 times pi times r)
- Surface area of a sphere/ball = 4 times pi times r^2
- Interior volume of a sphere/ball = 4/3 times pi times r^3
- Surface area of a cylinder (i.e., tomato cage) = 2 times pi times r^2 plus 2 times pi times r times h.

  h is the height, so multiply 2 times pi times radius times height and add 2 times pi times r^2.

- Interior volume of a cylinder = pi times r^2 times h
- Area of a triangle: height times base divided by two

HOW TO CALCULATE THE HEIGHT OF A TREE WITHOUT USING TRIGONOMETRY

This is one of those things that's really quite simple, once you understand it. The only trick is that you need to measure the tree's shadow, so you'll need a sunny day and a tree with a shadow that's not obscured by other shadows.

You will need a really long tape measure, foot-long ruler, paper, pencil, and perhaps a calculator. This involves a little simple algebra, which you may have forgotten through disuse, so I'll explain.

Go outside about mid-afternoon or mid-morning, when the tree is casting a medium-size shadow. Measure the length of the tree's shadow (ts) in inches from the trunk to the tip of the shadow. Write this down. (If it's a big trunk, estimate the thickness of the trunk, divide by half, and add that onto your shadow figure.) It's also more accurate if you can measure the shadow along flat ground, rather than uphill or downhill. Measure perpendicular to the slope of a hill, if you can.

In a sunny spot and mostly easily done on hard pavement, stand the foot-long ruler on end (nice and straight), and measure its shadow (rs) in inches with the tape measure. You already know the height of the ruler (rh) is 12 inches.

The only missing length in this equation is the tree height (th). So we set up an equation. The ruler height and ruler shadow lengths go on one side of the equal sign, and the tree height and tree shadow go on the other side. A fraction is used not just to explain a piece of something (like a pizza slice), but also as a relationship comparing two things. The equation will look like this:

$$rh/rs = th/ts$$

Put your numbers into the equation. Use *th* or *x* for the unknown tree height. Of course, we want to solve for *th* (tree height). We need *th* (tree height) all by itself in the equation. So to get rid of ts in the denominator (bottom of fraction), multiply the ts number by both sides.

Now the equation looks like this:

$$ts \text{ times } rh/rs = th$$

Go ahead and multiply the tree's shadow length by the ruler's height. Then divide that product by the ruler's shadow length. The result is the (fairly accurate) height of the tree, in inches. Divide by 12 for feet.

Now you know how tall the tree is today. A month later it will have grown.

APPENDIX B

Addresses for State Extension Offices

Cooperative Extension Service
University of Illinois
College of Agriculture
Urbana, IL 61801

Cooperative Extension Service
Purdue University
West Lafayette, IN 47907

Cooperative Extension Service
Iowa State University
Ames, IA 50010

Cooperative Extension Service
Kansas State University
College of Agriculture
Manhattan, KS 66502

Cooperative Extension Service
University of Kentucky
College of Agriculture
Lexington, KY 40506

Cooperative Extension Service
Michigan State University
College of Agriculture
East Lansing, MI 48823

Cooperative Extension Service
University of Missouri
College of Agriculture
Columbia, MO 65201

Cooperative Extension Service
University of Nebraska
College of Agriculture & Home
   Economics
Lincoln, NE 68583

Cooperative Extension Service
Ohio State University
Agriculture Administration Building
2120 Fyffe Road
Columbus, OH 43210

Cooperative Extension Service
South Dakota State University
College of Agriculture
Brookings, SD 57006

Cooperative Extension Service
University of Wisconsin
College of Agriculture
432 North Lake Street
Madison, WI 53706

Glossary

AAS (All-America Selections) A not-for-profit organization that trials new flowers and vegetables around the country to evaluate them and promote superior plants.

acid Having a pH below 7.0.

activator Any material that is said to "speed up" compost workings (decomposition) of leaf piles. Actually, anything that provides nitrogen (like grass clippings or lawn fertilizer) will do this.

aeration Loosening up the soil to allow the roots to grow more easily and air to enter in.

alkaline Having a pH above 7.0.

annual A plant that lives its life cycle in one year; it sprouts, grows, seeds, and dies in one growing season. Some plants we treat like annuals (geraniums and peppers) are actually perennials, but are not winter-hardy in the Heartland. Annual flowers provide color all season long.

anther The part of the flower that produces the pollen.

antrachnose A fungus disease that causes sunken dark spots or black blisters.

aubergine English name for eggplant.

axil The shoulder between a leaf and the stalk it's growing from.

Bt (bacillus thuringiensis) A special bacteria that's parasitic to caterpillars and the larvae of sawflies. Used by gardeners to keep cabbage loopers and similar annoyances at bay.

biennial Like an annual, but these plants flower and set seed the second year. Biennials that are started very early in the winter may react like annuals. Many vegetables we grow as annuals are really biennials (carrots, etc.). Leave them in the ground and they'll go to seed the next year.

biological control Naturally occurring parasites, predators, and pathogens (bugs, insects, arachnids, diseases, and other organisms) that can be used to restrain your pest population.

blanch (1) In the garden, to shade a vegetable to lighten its color and flavor; asparagus, celery, and cauliflower can all be blanched. Blanched asparagus and celery are more common in European cooking. Asparagus is blanched with soil; celery blanched with a collar, and cauliflower blanched by tying the inside leaves atop the head. (2) In the kitchen, to drop in boiling water until no longer raw, but not cooked. Frozen foods are first blanched to preserve their color and texture (blanching also reduces cooking time later). (3) To lose facial color due to shock; gardeners blanch when they add up how much they spent this year on garden stuff.

bolt When a plant goes to seed. Unless you're keeping the fruits for eating or seeds for planting, the plant is overdue for the compost pile.

bonemeal Animal bones that have been dried and powdered as a source of phosphorus-rich fertilizer.

broadcast (1) To evenly scatter seed or other dried material (fertilizer, pesticide) over an area. (2) To scatter a pile of garden catalogs atop the television.

Bt. *See* **bacillus thuringiensis**.

bunching onion An onion that does not form large bulbs, but rather multiplies itself into more onions, a permanent form of scallion. Used in Chinese cooking.

bush (bean, squash) Bush plants are those that have been dwarfed or shrunken through breeding, or those with a natural size limit. Bush beans do not need to be staked, and will produce their crop all at once. They were developed for the canning trade. Bush squash plants still get about 5 feet across, but do not "run" everywhere.

butterhead (lettuce) A loosely headed kind of lettuce, very tasty.

cage A device, usually of wire, built to contain a plant (tomato, pepper, eggplant, bush squash). Cages can be round, square, hexagonal, and so on. Choose wire with at least 4-inch-square openings, so you can get your hand in and your produce out!

capsaicin The pungent oil in hot peppers. Don't try to remove this oil from your mouth with water—water and oil don't mix. Eat bread or starches (rice, beans) instead.

carbon materials In composting, the stuff that is usually brown and dry (straw, leaves, sawdust, paper).

chitting Another name for **presprouting**.

chlorosis When green parts of plants turn yellow; caused by nutrient or light deficiency, too much water, not enough water, or disease.

clay Soil particles of such minute size (less than 0.002 millimeters) that they can pack together tightly, which causes drainage and aeration problems. However, clay soils are usually rich in nutrients. These are Baby Bear soil grains. (*See* **silt** and **sand**.)

clone, cloning Done to humans only in science fiction novels, but a regular practice in botany. Cloning means to make an exact genetic replica of the parent from some other part instead of from a seed. Taking a cutting of a potato eye is cloning; so is rooting a raspberry branch.

cold frame An insulated, sheltering box with a top window for growing seedlings and crops.

cole crops Also called *cruciferous* crops because their flowers have four petals in the shape of a cross. Cole crops include broccoli, Brussels sprouts, cabbage, cauliflower, kohlrabi, and many Asian cabbage variations such as bok choy.

companion planting A theory suggesting that some plants will grow better in each other's proximity by repelling pests or by being a "trap crop" to draw the insects away from the intended crop. There is no scientific basis for companion planting. However, planting dill near cucumbers or basil near tomatoes does simplify harvest.

complete flower A flower with both male (stamen) and female (pistil) parts that is self-fertile and doesn't need pollination. Tomato flowers are self-fertile; they need only wind to complete the act.

compost The product of accelerated or slow decomposition of organic materials. Composting is a natural process that replenishes the necessary nutrients and micronutrients to the soil and improves water-retaining ability, drainage, aeration, and soil structure. You can hardly add too much compost to a garden. A minimum of 2 inches is best. Humus is natural compost.

cotyledon The first, baby leaves of a seedling, which store nutrients to feed the seedling in the beginning growth days. They rarely look anything like the regular leaves, with the exception of corn or other monocots (one-leaved seedlings) and nasturtiums.

cover crop A planting of winter wheat, rye, clover, or other field planting that is turned back under (dug into the soil) before going to seed. Cover crops increase local nutrients, prevent erosion, and smother out weeds. A cover crop is the gardener's equivalent of letting a field go fallow.

crop rotation Planting different species of vegetables (cole crops, alliums, solanaceous, etc.) in succession in the same area, to reduce the risk of plant diseases in the soil.

cross-pollination When pollen is transferred from a male flower to a female flower of the same plant, but a different variety. Vexing for seed-saving purposes. You will not get weird squashes unless you grow the seeds of cross-pollinated fruits. "Cukermelons" and "melocumbers" are just old gardeners' tales. However, you *will* get weird or icky-tasting corn if your sweet corn and field or popcorns cross-pollinate. This is because you eat the seeds!

cultivar Short for CULTI-vated VAR-iety. A name for a species subgroup that's notable for distinctive characteristics. Cultivars are noted for being improvements upon the wilder species varieties.

damping off A fungal disease found in unsterile soil or seed-starting mixes that causes the seedlings to fall over and die.

determinate (tomato) A "bush" form of tomato that grows only to X size, and produces only X amount of fruits. Many determinate tomatoes die after having done their thing. Useful to the home canner who desires to put up tomatoes only once. Also useful to gardeners who don't need lots of tomatoes, or don't want to cope with 6- to 7-foot-tall plants. You can leave the suckers on bush tomatoes for maximum cropping.

dicot; dicotyledon A plant whose seeds have two cotyledons (baby leaves). Most vegetables are dicots.

dioecious (di-EE-shus) Plants that have just male flowers on one plant and just female flowers on another plant (for example, holly).

dormant Seeds are living things, and while being kept, they are dormant (hibernating). If kept cool, dry, and in the dark (sealed, and in the fridge), they will stay dormant. Exposure to water, light, and warmth breaks dormancy.

English pea What Southerners call green peas, to distinguish them from cowpeas and black-eyed peas (both of which are actually beans—go figure).

eye The growth bud of a plant, like the sprouts on potatoes.

F1 hybrid The seed or plant that comes from the controlled cross-fertilization of different species or varieties. Hybrids usually have any of these features: better blooming/fruiting habits, better vigor, better color, fancier flower structure, larger size, and so on. F1 hybrid seeds cannot be saved, for they will not have the same features. *F1* means the first generation from the cross.

fertilization When pollen is transferred from a male flower to a female flower. This is necessary for fruit to form.

field pea These are cowpeas, black-eyed peas, crowder peas, and cream peas commonly found in Southern gardens. Actually, they are all beans.

flat A shallow box used for sprouting or growing seedlings.

fluorescent lamp An inexpensive necessity for growing plants indoors. Plants that take only 2–4 weeks may do OK in a windowsill; but for longer transplants, you need the longer exposure and higher intensity that fluorescent lights provide. Regular shop lights are fine. Use a timer to ensure 14 hours of light. A "warm white" paired with a "cool white" bulb works best. Keep the plant tops 2 to 4 inches from the lights to avoid legginess.

fruit The part of a plant containing the seeds. Tomatoes, squashes, and cucumbers are botanically fruits. Only cooking custom and Congress declare tomatoes to be vegetables.

fungicide Substance that kills fungi.

germination The sprouting of a seed.

gourd Gourds are used in crafts, bird houses, and for Thanksgiving decorations. Loofah gourds have their skins and seeds removed for loofah "sponges."

green manure *See* **cover crop.**

gynoecious (guy-no-EE-shus) A plant with all female flowers—cucumbers can have this characteristic. Such cucumber plants then need another cucumber plant around with some male flowers, in order to be pollinated and produce cukes.

harden off To gradually get a plant used to outdoor conditions of wind, temperature, and sunlight intensity. (Gardeners must go through hardening off every autumn and spring, too.)

hardpan A layer of clay or silt beneath the cultivated layer of the soil which is tougher and acts as a barrier to drainage and root growth.

hardy Able to stand cold conditions without special protection. Does not generally refer to summer heat-hardiness.

heavy soil (1) Soil with a high level of clay. (2) How the last shovelful of soil feels.

heirloom An old-fashioned variety that is not hybridized. Or, any old variety that has been handed down through friends and family. Or, a variety from "the old country." Or, a cultivar predating the 1940s, when hybrid vegetables first appeared.

herb (culinary) Herbs are the leaves of plants, which we use to flavor foods. Spices are the roots, stems, bark, and seeds of plants and are used for the same purpose. Not all herbs are culinary (cooking) herbs. Some herbs are used medicinally, for dyeing, for making potpourri, and other uses.

herbicide Substance that kills certain plants.

hill A small mound of soil used for planting watermelons, cucumbers, and so on.

hill up To mound soil around plants (like rose bushes) for winter protection, or to mound soil around the stems of vegetables.

hot bed A cold frame with a heat source, such as buried, rotting manure or electric heating cables; a miniature greenhouse.

hybrid A plant that was artificially pollinated to produce a cross whose seeds you buy. A plant with two genetically different parents (you and I are animal hybrids). Hybrid plants will not grow true to form if you save the seeds. Hybrids are bred for better disease resistance, flavor, form, color, and so forth.

indeterminate (tomato) The tall, vining tomatoes that keep on growing until the frost hits them. These are the kind that require trellises or stakes for best results, or you can let them sprawl everywhere. For staking, you will want to remove the suckers or your plant will have too many stems.

insecticide Substance that kills insects, and not always just the ones you were aiming for.

intensive planting Used in wide-row gardening, intensive planting means to cover the ground with plants laid out in such a way that the *mature* size will carpet the ground, thus smothering out competing weeds, retaining moisture by shading the ground, and ensuring the most production from the given space.

interplanting This method mingles different plants according to their maturation schedule, growing heights, and root-space requirements. Deep-rooted carrots can be interplanted with shallower lettuces, making sure that each has sufficient space to grow and is not crowded. As the lettuces mature and are harvested, the carrots will then have more room.

larva (plural *larvae*) Immature insects between egg and adult stages, frequently grublike or wormy in appearance. Caterpillars are butterfly larvae.

leach To rinse out chemicals in the soil by excess watering.

leggy When plants get too tall in the stem because of insufficient light and/or crowding.

legume A member of the pea and bean family (clover is also a legume). The fruits are pods that split in half, and the seeds inside are attached to the bottom seam.

loam That ideal soil mixture of clay, silt, sand, and organic matter.

loose-leaf; loose-head (lettuce) A non-heading lettuce, useful for gardeners who want to continuously harvest a few leaves from each plant, or employ the cut-and-come-again method of mowing part of a lettuce patch with scissors.

manure tea Steep a quantity of livestock manure in water for a day (use five times as much water). The resultant liquid is used as a mild fertilizer.

miticide Substance that kills mites.

monocot, monocotyledon A plant whose seeds develop just one cotyledon (baby leaf). Corn, tulips, lilies, and grasses are monocots.

monoecious (moh-NEE-shus) A plant with both male flowers and female flowers on the same plant.

mulch Organic or inorganic material laid over soil or perennials to keep down evaporation; to reduce weed germination; and to keep the ground cold during the winter or cool during the summer.

mycorrhiza (my-kuh-RY-zuh) A symbiotic (mutually beneficial) association between particular fungi and plant roots.

neutral Having a pH of 7.0.

nitrogen materials In composting, the stuff that is usually green (grass clippings, weeds, table scraps, clover).

nitrogen (N) One of the three basic nutrients provided by organic and chemical fertilizers. Nitrogen provides "greening up" of the leaves and stimulates growth.

organic (1) Derived from or pertaining to living plants or creatures. (2) In chemistry, compounds containing carbon.

organic gardening (1) Growing plants with animal and plant products rather than chemical ones. (2) A natural, holistic gardening philosophy that avoids synthetic chemicals to control pests and diseases and to add nutrients.

ornamental corn A kind of pretty field corn, usually used for Thanksgiving decorations. Ornamental corn nubbins can be ground for homemade cornmeal. You can also strip the seeds off of cobs that have been allowed to dry on the stalks and replant them next year. Some ornamental corns are popping corns.

ovary Part of the flower where the fruit/seed is formed.

overwinter Bringing tender plants like rosemary and bay laurel indoors for the winter so they are not harmed by frost. The plant equivalent of being a "snowbird" vacationing in Florida.

pathogen An organism that causes plant diseases; plant germs.

pelleted seed Seeds that are coated (usually with a very fine clay) to make them easier to plant. Usually small seeds like carrot and petunia are pelleted. Pelleted seeds cost more, of course.

perennial A plant that lives for more than two years (though not necessarily forever).

perlite Volcanic lava that's been "popped" like popcorn to make small white granules, which are frequently used in potting and seed-starting mediums. Perlite is the crunchy stuff that holds water and improves aeration.

pH The abbreviation pH stands for *potential hydrogen*, a datum that only physics and chemistry students care to memorize. The pH refers to how acid or alkaline the soil is. A soil test will reveal the pH of your soil, and give recommendations for correcting this (amount of lime necessary for acid soil). Most plants grow best in a pH of 6.0 to 7.0. Lemon juice is acid (2.0), and baking soda is alkaline (9.0). Blueberries and azaleas prefer a more acidic soil.

phosphorus (P) Another of the three basic nutrients provided by organic and chemical fertilizers. Phosphorus helps root growth, fruit development, and greater resistance to diseases. If your plant's leaves have an unnatural purple tinge to them, they lack phosphorus.

phototropism When the plant grows toward the available light source. Gravitropism is what causes roots to go "down." Thigmotropism is when tendrils coil around a solid object.

pinching (out) To remove a sucker or growing tip by pinching or cutting.

pistil Female part of the flower where the pollen is received.

pole (bean) An indeterminate bean that does best staked or trellised. Pole beans give a longer harvest than bush beans, with more production. Some people think pole beans have better flavor.

popcorn A type of field corn bred to pop. You have to buy popcorn seed; sweet corn doesn't pop. Keep your popcorn and sweet corn 500 feet away from each other if they pollinate (tassel) at the same time to prevent them from cross-pollinating, or stagger the plantings to avoid this problem.

pollen Male cells that begin the seed formation process after they've reached the pistil.

pot-bound A plant that's been in the pot so long its roots take up most of the space.

potassium (K) The third basic nutrient provided by organic and chemical fertilizers. Potassium, also called potash, helps plants resist diseases, protects them from cold, and helps prevent water loss during dry weather. To remember the difference between phosphorus (P) and potassium (K), remember that *phosphorus* comes before *potassium* alphabetically, so it gets the letter P. The fertilizer values are always given in the NPK order.

presprouting Germinating seeds under controlled conditions before planting. Usually done on a paper towel or other damp place. Plant just after the root has come through the seed coat. Also called **chitting.**

pricking out The process of digging up a tiny seedling from a communal flat to transplant it into an individual pot.

quiescence (KWY-ess-ens) (1) A state when the seed will not germinate or the plant will not grow, because the proper conditions for growth are not met. (2) A state when the gardener is absolutely tuckered out and is resting in a chair or bath.

rain gauge Most gardens need an inch of water a week. How do you know it's had enough? Use a rain gauge, a tube with ruled measurements on it to determine rainfall amounts. Most showers provide only 0.1 or 0.2 inches of rain. A whole inch of rain is a real "toad-strangler, gully-washer," unless it's delivered over two days' time.

raised beds A gardening technique where the soil is amended or increased until it's above ground level. Raised beds are often held in with walls, but this is not necessary. Raised beds provide drainage, ground that is not compacted by being walked upon, and early warm-up in the spring. They are easier to maintain weed- and water-wise because of the smaller size. Raised beds should not be more than 4 feet wide, or you can't reach into the middle without squishing the soil.

rhizome An underground stem that grows horizontally, and has nodes to store food (for example, gingerroot).

root-bound *See* **pot-bound.**

run-off Water that runs away from the soil's surface instead of soaking in.

Run-off can distribute fertilizers, insecticides, miticides, fungicides, and so forth to inappropriate places. Flood run-off can distribute your garden downstream.

runner Rooting shoot—in strawberries, mint, and so on—that can start a new plant.

savoy (spinach, cabbage) The crinkly, puckery kind of leaves. Savoy spinach is slightly more difficult to clean, but easier to stab with a fork because it doesn't glue itself to the plate with salad dressing, like flat-leaved spinach does.

scallion An immature onion that has not formed a bulb. Or, a variety of onion (*see* **bunching onion**) that doesn't form a bulb.

seed A plant embryo and its food reserves.

seedling A baby plant that's sprouted.

self-fertile A plant that can pollinate itself.

self-seed, self-sow When a plant releases its own seeds, willy-nilly.

sand; sharp sand ("builders' sand") A soil amendment useful for clayey soils. **Caution:** You must add 30–50 percent sand per volume of tilled soil. Using less will give you something resembling concrete, and will worsen the problem rather than improving the soil condition. Sand particles are between 2.0 and 0.05 millimeters in size (Papa Bear soil grains). (*See* **clay** and **silt.**)

set (onion) Onions grown to baby size and sold in bags for replanting. Bags are often not marked for variety other than the color; you can't always tell if you're looking at a "keeping" onion or not. A single shallot bulb is also called a set, although garlic cloves aren't (don't ask me why; I don't make these things up). A single shallot bulb produces a clump of shallot bulbs (one shallot set produces a set of sets).

set fruit When a flower is fertilized, the ovary swells and begins to grow a fruit. Gardeners call this setting fruit.

shatter When a ripe seed head looses its seed at a touch or wind, or what happens to clay pots left outside in the freezing weather.

side-dressing, top-dressing To fertilize by supplying compost or other nutrients atop the soil around the stem of a plant.

silt Middle-sized soil particles, between 0.05 and 0.002 millimeters (Mama Bear soil grains). (*See* **clay** and **sand**.)

snap bean, snap pea Snap beans and peas are those legumes that don't have a fibrous "string" running from stem to blossom that needs to be removed before eating. Snap beans: The Next Generation are distinguished from the older string beans.

snow pea A kind of Chinese pea that is eaten before the peas swell in the pod.

soil test A laboratory analysis of the pH, nutrient levels, and composition of the soil. Testing is available from your state university (the extension office) for only a few dollars. You don't know how much nutrients or lime to add to your garden without one.

soil amendments Stuff added to soil to improve drainage, nutrient-accessing ability by the plant roots, and water retention. Sphagnum peat, compost, manure, large amounts of sharp sand, and lime or other minerals are common additions.

solanaceous Members of the *Solanaceae* family, which includes eggplants, tomatoes, peppers, potatoes, ground cherries, and others. Leaves of these plants contain solanine, a poison.

species Plants that are closely related enough to interbreed (without shame or even your permission).

spit (1) An old-fashioned term meaning the depth of a spade blade, about 11 inches. Double-digging is done "two spits deep." (2) To expectorate.

spore Reproductive body of ferns and fungi (non-flowering plants).

sport In the seed world, a mutation.

squash Members of the cucurbit family (also including cucumbers and melons), which include the perishable summer squash (zucchini, etc.) and storable winter squash (acorn, pumpkin, etc.).

stake (1) *noun:* A heavy stick of metal, wood, plastic, or composite materials used to grow climbing or indeterminate plants upward for maximum tidiness, light exposure, ease of harvest, and insect maintenance. (2) *verb:* To support a plant (such as an indeterminate tomato) by tying to a pole.

stamen Male part of the flower that holds the anthers.

sterile (1) A fruit without viable seeds. (2) Free of pathogens.

sterilize To make potting mix free of insects and diseases by heating. Bake moist compost in metal pans in an oven preheated to 275 degrees, and bake for 30 minutes (45 minutes if you're baking a couple gallons of stuff). *Note:* The stuff smells! Or, microwave for 8 minutes. *Note:* The stuff still smells!

stratify To ready some kinds of seedlings (frequently wildflowers) for germination by exposing them to cold for a length of time (usually a month or two).

string bean Old-fashioned beans with a fibrous filament running from stem to flower bud, which "string" needs to be pulled/zipped off before cooking.

sucker (1) A shoot that is usually fast-growing, that comes from the trunk, main branch, or root of a plant. Tomato suckers grow in the axil between the main stem and the side branches. (2) Novice gardener who falls for cheap merchandise in outrageous catalog ads and supplements to the Sunday newspaper.

sugar pea One of the greatest breeding advances of the twentieth century: a pea whose pod is edible (no shelling needed), and that can also be used as a shelling pea. Sugar peas often don't make it to the kitchen because gardeners, family, and friends snack on them raw. Most varieties of sugar peas need trellising.

sweet corn As distinguished from field corn (which is grown for making cornmeal or popping corn), sweet corn is eaten fresh as corn on the cob, or removed from the cob. If you let sweet corn go past maturity, it will soon toughen up into the seed stage. If it's not a hybrid, you can let the plant die and dry, and then twist the seeds from the cob to keep for planting next year.

tap root The main, thick root of carrots and other plants. A severed (broken) taproot usually spells trouble for the plant.

taxa (singular *taxon*) The method of classifying living organisms you promptly forgot after the botany test. The classifications of genus, species, subspecies, variety, and cultivar.

tendril A thin, leaf-type structure that can coil around an object of appropriate diameter. Tendrils aid plants (cucumbers, for example) in climbing.

thin To cut or pull out extra plants to make room for others to grow.

tilth What physical condition the soil is in. If it's in "good tilth," then it's loose, well aerated, and easy to cultivate. Walking over your garden ground is bad for the tilth.

timed planting Waiting until the seasonal affliction of a particular garden pest has passed until planting.

transpiration Natural evaporation of water from a plant's leaves by "exhaling." Transpiration without sufficient watering to replace lost fluids leads to wilting. Some 90 percent of the water taken up by a plant's roots is used to move nutrients around the plant and keep cells plump, and it is then transpirated from the leaves.

trap crop An additional planting designed to draw the insects away from the intended crop (for example, radishes planted to take the blow from flea beetles away from the eggplants).

trellis A structure designed to grow plants upward. One square foot of trellis space usually equals 6 square feet of ground space! Trellising offers maximum sunlight exposure, helps eliminate produce from rotting on the ground, and makes both pest control and harvesting easier.

tropism (*See* **phototropism**.)

tuber The underground stem or root where plant nutrients/food is stored. Roots grow from this to reproduce another plant (for example, potato, begonia).

turgid When the plant has sufficient water to be firm and fleshy; the opposite is wilt.

umbel A flat-topped seed head with seeds arranged on stems like an umbrella's spokes (dill, for example).

university cooperative extension office A resource of valuable, free, up-to-date information produced by state universities to the public. Call to request handouts on vegetables, fruits, lawns, trees, pest control, and many other gardening topics.

vermiculite Mica rock that's been popped like popcorn, to make small tan granules that are frequently used in potting and seed-starting mediums. It's the gold, flaky, squishy stuff that holds water and improves aeration.

viable Seeds that are still alive enough to germinate and grow.

volunteer A plant that is seeded wildly by its parent plant and grows spontaneously.

weed Any plant growing where the gardener doesn't want it to. Even volunteer tomato plants can become weeds in your flowerbeds if they're allowed to take over.

wet feet (1) Potted plants that get too much watering and not enough drainage; the leaves turn yellow and drop. (2) Gardener wearing sneakers instead of rubber boots.

wilt (1) When the transpiration exceeds the intake of water by a plant and it loses its proper stiffness, getting floppy. If the leaves are crispy, they're dead. (2) General term for several plant diseases caused by fungi or bacteria.

Bibliography

The following are the volumes I've used over the years. Some are out of print at the time of writing this book, and are so marked. Often authors will have newer books on the same topics by different titles. Some general topics (composting, for example) are constantly being written about, and you can easily find more current books. Libraries are excellent places to read out-of-print books. If your local library doesn't carry a certain book, ask if your librarian can do an inter-library loan to borrow it from somewhere else.

Aker, Scott, and Ethel Dutky, consultants; and the editors of Time Life Books, *The TIME LIFE Complete Gardener: Pests and Diseases.* Alexandria, VA: Time Life Books, 1995.

Ashworth, Suzanne. *Seed to Seed.* Decorah, IA: Seed Saver Publications, 1991.

Bartholomew, Mel. *Square Foot Gardening.* Emmaus, PA: Rodale Press, 1981.

Bennett, Jennifer. *Harrowsmith Northern Gardener.* Camden East, Ontario: Camden House Publishing, 1988 (revised edition).

Bubel, Nancy. *The Country Journal Book of Vegetable Gardening.* Brattleboro, VT: Country Journal Publishing, 1983.

Bubel, Nancy. *The New Seed-Starters Handbook.* Emmaus, PA: Rodale Press, 1988.

Coleman, Eliot. *Four-Season Harvest: Organic Vegetables from Your Home Garden All Year Long.* Post Mills, VT: Chelsea Green Publishing, 1999 (revised edition).

Coulter, Francis C. *A Manual of Home Vegetable Gardening.* New York: Dover Publications, 1973 edition of original 1942 book (out of print).

Creasy, Rosalind. *Cooking from the Garden: Creative Gardening and Contemporary Cuisine.* San Francisco: Sierra Club Books, 1998 (out of print).

DeWeitt, Dave, and Paul W. Bosland. *The Pepper Garden from the Sweetest Bell to the Hottest Habanero.* Berkeley, CA: Ten Speed Press, 1993.

Ellis, Barbara W., and Fern Marshall Bradley. *The Organic Gardener's Handbook of Natural Insect and Disease Control.* Emmaus, PA: Rodale Press, 1996.

Halpin, Anne. *The Year-Round Vegetable Gardener: The Complete Guide to Growing Vegetables and Herbs Any Time of the Year.* New York: Summit Books, 1992 (out of print).

Harrington, Geri. *Grow Your Own Chinese Vegetables.* Pownal, VT: Garden Way

Publishing/Storey Communications, 1984 (out of print).

Hart, Rhonda Massingham. *Trellising: How to Grow Climbing Vegetables, Fruits, Flowers, Vines and Trees,* Pownal, VT: Garden Way Publishing/Storey Communications, 1992 (out of print).

Jeavons, John. *How to Grow More Vegetables than You Ever Thought Possible on Less Land than You Can Imagine.* Berkeley, CA: Ten Speed Press, 1991 (revised edition).

Jones, Louisa. *The Art of French Vegetable Gardening.* New York: Artisan/Workman Publishing, 1995.

Landau, Lois M. *Too Many Tomatoes, Squash, Beans and Other Good Things: A Cookbook for When Your Garden Explodes.* New York: Harper Perennial/Harper Collins Publishers, 1991.

Langevin, Don. *How to Grow World Class Giant Pumpkins.* Norton, MA: AnneDawn Publishing, 1993; sequel 1998.

Larkcom, Joy. *The Salad Garden.* New York: Penguin Books, reprinted 1996.
———. *Oriental Vegetables: The Complete Guide for Garden and Kitchen.* Tokyo: Kodansha International, 1994.

Lavery, Bernard. *How to Grow Giant Vegetables.* New York: Harper Perennial/Harper Collins Publishers, 1995 (out of print).

Ludlum, David M. *National Audubon Society Field Guide to North American Weather.* Chanticleer Press edition, New York: Alfred A. Knopf, 1997.

Male, Carolyn J. *100 Heirloom Tomatoes for the American Garden* (Smith & Hawken series). New York: Workman Publishing, 1999.

Michalak, Patricia S. *Rodale's Successful Organic Gardening Herbs.* Emmaus, PA: Rodale Press, 1993.

Minnich, Jerry. *The Rodale Guide to Composting.* Emmaus, PA: Rodale Press, 1979 (out of print).

Nancarrow, Loren, and Janet Hogan Taylor. *The Worm Book.* Berkeley, CA: Ten Speed Press, 1998.

Ogden, Shepherd, consultant; and the editors of Time Life Books, *The TIME LIFE Compete Gardener: Organic Vegetable Gardening.* Alexandria, VA: Time Life Books, 1996.

Pavord, Anna. *The New Kitchen Garden: A Complete Practical Guide to Designing, Planting and Cultivating a Decorative and Productive Garden.* London: Dorling Kindersley, 1996.

Poisson, Leandre, and Gretchen Vogel Poisson. *Solar Gardening: Growing Vegetables Year-Round the American Intensive Way.* White River Junction, VT: Chelsea Green Publishing Company, 1994.

Rubin, Louis D. Sr., and Jim Duncan. *The Weather Wizard's Cloud Book: How You Can Forecast the Weather Accurately and Easily by Reading the Clouds.* Chapel Hill, NC: Algonquin Books, reprinted 1989.

Rupp, Rebecca. *Blue Corn & Square Tomatoes: Unusual Facts about Common Garden Vegetables.* Pownal, VT: Garden Way Publishing/Storey Communications, 1987 (out of print).

Shimizu, Holly, consultant; and the editors of Time Life Books, *The TIME LIFE Complete Gardener: Growing Your Own Herbs.* Alexandria, VA: Time Life Books, 1996.

Stout, Ruth, and Richard Clemence. *The Ruth Stout No-Work Garden Book.* Emmaus, PA: Rodale Press, 1981 (out of print).

Thomasson, Joseph R. *Growing Vegetables in the Great Plains.* Lawrence, KS: University Press of Kansas, 1991 (out of print).

Index